The

INNER LIFE

of

CHRIST

JOSEPH PARKER

The
INNER LIFE
of
CHRIST

A Commentary on
the Gospel of Matthew Chapters 1—7

AMG
PUBLISHERS
Chattanooga, TN 37422

THE INNER LIFE OF CHRIST

This edition originally published by
Hazell, Watson, and Viney, Ltd., London, 1889, 1890.

ISBN 0-89957-242-1

Library of Congress Catalog Card Number: 98-70070

Printed in the United States of America
03 02 01 00 99 98 –R– 6 5 4 3 2 1

CONTENTS

FOREWORD

The Inner Life of Christ is a superb collection of twenty-eight classic Joseph Parker sermons that were originally preached in a verse-by-verse series study on the Gospel of Matthew. *The Inner Life of Christ* covers the first seven chapters in Matthew, and is AMG Publishers' first installment of Parker's three volume study covering the entire Gospel. Though Parker's study is very detailed, you will find no information on the Gospel here that is not relevant or insightful. While this study is a collection of sermons, you may find yourself thinking that you are reading an original commentary—a credit to Dr. Parker's writing style.

In our continuing effort to introduce modern readers to the classics of Christian literature, and to preserve their original clarity, we sometimes find it necessary to update spelling and some archaic terms in accordance with how our language has changed over the years. In some cases, unusual forms of punctuation are simplified in order to eliminate confusion. Brackets are also inserted where we have added scripture references. However, we at AMG Publishers feel that it is our responsibility to restore and preserve these classics for generations to follow by making as few changes to the original works as possible; therefore, readers should also note that points of current history cited by Parker are from the latter-half of the nineteenth century.

It is our hope that these compelling, yet colorful sermons by Joseph Parker, will inspire in readers an ever-growing love and appreciation for the Word of God.

r.a.s.

PREFACE

This life of Christ is not like any other with which I am acquainted—
a fact which encourages the hope that it may form a humble companion
to the truly great biographies which have distinguished the Christian
literature of the current century. In this book the Evangelist is allowed
to tell his own story in his own way, and I follow him in a strenuous endeavor to interpret that story so as to reveal the very heart of Christ
to the men of today. Others have with competent learning and most noble
eloquence traced the outer history of the Man Christ Jesus, and have
thrown around that history the superb coloring of a high and reverent
imagination; by their almost superhuman labors they have laid their age
under obligations which can be but imperfectly discharged; and, therefore, if I venture to give another view of the sacred Life, I cannot but
hope that the authors who have preceded me will see in my labor not
so much a proof of my audacity as an illustration of the infinite fertility of the subject. I might indeed almost dispute the claim of precedence
in some degree, inasmuch as my book entitled *Ecce Deus* is older by
several years than the immortal work of Canon Farrar.

I have paid next to no attention to points of purely historical interest,
as my one purpose has been to acquaint myself with "the mind of Christ"
and with "the travail of his soul." Nineteen centuries do not separate between me and the Son of God; if they did, in any divisive and time-
worn sense, he would not be the Son of God to me. He is the same forever.
Today he walks with me; in many a sacred interview he makes my heart
burn within me; and in all bread-breaking he reveals himself in new light
and tenderness. I know not Christ after the flesh. Judea and Galilee,
and the whole theater of action, have all practically disappeared; the

sunset glow, the blue wave, the light wind sighing in the grove, all these have gone, and the poet can but recall a dramatic image of their effect; the Visible Teacher, too, has gone, and is no longer to be known after the flesh. But the Life is here; the Thought is immortal; the Love still holds out its redeeming offer; and the Cross gathers into itself the whole tragedy of life. Within this spiritual sphere my studies have been conducted in the hope of showing to some extent what Christ has to say to the present age. This purpose will account for the style of the book. Most of the book was spoken—spoken to men of business, world-weary, and sick at heart because of grief and loss and pain. Such men wanted to see Christ without delay; nor did they care for pomp of speech, or cunning art in literary structure; they were sick, and asked for healing only; or they reeled under strong temptation, and besought the Son of God to give them rest and hope. In comforting them I have comforted myself; and the comfort has not been a sentiment only, but a deep and complete conviction.

My supreme desire has been to reveal Christ to this age, and to show how he takes upon himself all the varying forms of civilization, and addresses every man in the tongue wherein he was born. I have not hesitated to repeat as one of the central truths of my religious creed that Jesus Christ is not only a historical character, but at once the forerunner and the contemporary of all ages. This is the sovereignty of the Son of God! The moldiness of time gathers upon every other name, and every other name is preserved simply in deference to the instinct of historical veneration, but the Name of Christ—the Jesus of Bethlehem, the Carpenter of Nazareth, the Emmanuel of the world—reigns by right of present power to break the dominion of sin, and bring the contrite heart into immediate forgiveness and ultimate sanctity. He is with us always, even unto the end of the world. For myself, his companionship today is as real as his historical identity is undisputed. Out of this glowing and thankful consciousness I have spoken much of this book, and so the heart will be seen in some workings which are not always so frankly disclosed. But why this dumb secrecy about our chief joy? If I have said much, I have left more unsaid, but have so left it for want of choice words and tones, rather than for want of thankfulness and courage. The "shout," the "loud voice," the "cry," have all been stifled, and every vibration has perished out of the temple walls. Is not Christ still worthy? Is he not worshiped with thunders of hallelujahs in the upper world? Do not the blessed ones cry day and night in the heavens praising him with infinite rapture, and with voices storm-like in their sacred energy? Jesus never discouraged the enthusiasm which was awakened by his own name. Never did he decline the smallest oblation offered by the hand of love; he took the box of ointment, the two mites, the cup of cold water, and I now offer him this attempt to reveal his character and to preach his gospel. Son of God, Lamb of God, Savior of the world, receive this morsel of bread, and break it for the satisfaction of the heart's hunger.

The Apostle Matthew

The following results in reference to the authorship of the first Gospel have been established by modern criticism—

(1) Matthew was the son of Alpheus, and probably the brother of James the less.

(2) Matthew is called Levi by Mark and Luke (Mark 2:14; Luke 5:27, 29).

(3) Some scholars think there is ground for believing that Matthew and Thomas were twin brothers.

(4) The old name Levi referred to his legal attachment and dependence; the new name Matthew may be interpreted as meaning "God's free man."

(5) According to a very ancient tradition, Matthew remained in Jerusalem for fifteen years after the Ascension of the Lord.

(6) Matthew does not observe the chronological order of events.

(7) "The very depth of St. Matthew's patriotism impels him to glory in the universality of the Messianic reign. The kingdom of God must overpass the limits of the Chosen race. Hence it is no matter of surprise that the Hebrew historian should alone commemorate the coming of the Magi and the refuge in Egypt, and that he and not St. Luke should tell the story of the Canaanitish woman."

(8) "We possess in the Gospel of Matthew, a delineation of the life of Jesus, which presents it in all the distinctness and fullness of a peculiar view. This Evangelist makes our Lord known to us in all the certainty and depth of his relation to history. Nowhere else is that golden thread which connects all history, the ever-advancing though secret progress of mankind, so clearly displayed; and nowhere does the Eternal appear so pure and bright in history, so free from all contamination of the corrupt and perishable, nay, in sharpest and most sublime contrast to all the pretensions of mere dead statutes."—Lange

(9) "From Papias, almost if not quite contemporary with the apostles, downwards, we have a stream of unimpeachable witness to the fact that Matthew was the author of a Gospel; while the quotations which abound in the works of the Fathers prove that at least as early as Ireneus the gospel received by the Church under his name was the same as that which has reached us."—*Kitto's Cyclopaedia*

one

CHRIST'S RELATION TO THE PAST

Matthew 1:1–17

THIS IS a genealogical tree. One sometimes wonders why such lists of names are in a book which is specifically known as a revelation of the will and love of God. Who cares to read a genealogical table? Most of the names are unknown, many of them are difficult to pronounce, and once read, who can remember a solitary verse of the whole catalogue? Yet the names are here, and if here, there must be some purpose in the record. God is a severe economist of space as of everything else: he does not throw anything away, though there may be wastefulness here and there, according to our present incomplete notions of things. Fasten your attention upon this genealogical tree for the purpose of studying it with a view of finding out whether the matter ends within this formal tree, or whether it does not become a tree that fills the whole earth and heaven, yea, and spreads itself over all the spaces and liberties of the universe.

The great mistake which you have to overcome in your Christian studies is, that Jesus Christ lived within a few days only, and then ceased to live upon the earth. In only a very narrow sense is that true. I am interested for the time being in learning the peculiar circumstances under which my Lord's ministry was conducted. I am not unwilling to listen to pictorial descriptions of the scenery through which he passed: it gives me but momentary delight to know whether he spoke in the sunrise or in the sunset, yet I like to hear the rhetoricians' beautiful way of setting forth the surrounding circumstances of his ministry. But Jesus Christ was *not a figure on a landscape*: he was and is the life of all living things. Paint the landscape when you are going to give some hint of mighty discoverers or warriors or men of local and perishable renown; the landscape

1

may be more important than such men themselves were within the immediate lines of their earthly history, but in the case of Jesus Christ. I want nothing but Christ: I want the landscape to fade away into an invisible fleck, and nothing to be seen but the CHRIST filling all things and making all things look small under his infinite presence.

We speak of Jesus Christ as a historical character. In no such sense can I be constrained to speak of him except for momentary convenience. Jesus Christ is the contemporary of all ages. He is living as certainly upon the earth as he ever lived in Nazareth. He is the Man of today, and there is no man beside. All good things flow from him, all beauty takes the hue of its tenderest color from his countenance, and all strength is but a flash and throb of his almightiness. It is in this way that I study Christ, and it is so that we come to live upon most intimate terms, so that everyday he baptizes me with his blood, and I sprinkle him with my tears. Do not go to the grave to find Christ, you will only find an angel there who says, "He is not here, he is risen" [Matt. 28:6]. That is the daily speech which may be made about Christ: he is risen, so as to claim a still higher place in the attention and confidence of men, so as to fill a wider place, so as to claim a higher, stronger throne—always rising. The resurrection is not a miracle, measurable within five seconds, or within the twinkling of an eye—it is the perpetual miracle of truth and purity and divine life.

Realize the *nearness* of Christ. Do not vex your souls by thinking that he lived centuries since. The centuries have nothing to do with his life except to continue it, and to open up some new unfolding of its infinite compass and resource. I will say to my soul—Thy Savior is looking upon thee: he is watching all thy growth, he is sending his daily blessings upon thee, he is always dying, always rising, always interceding—a contradiction it may be in literal words, but the soul that has passed through the mystery of that agony which is birth, will understand that amid all this contradiction of letters there is a solid and melodious reconciliation and unity of meaning.

Every name is more or less historical. Even *your* obscure name has around it a little circle of associations peculiarly and incommunicably its own. What we call obscurity is only a relative term. God knows all the insects that are in the air: all the ephemera that are born in the sunbeam and that die in the moment of their birth, he registers in his great record. Do not say it does not matter what you, so little, obscure, unknown and socially contemptible, do. Every atom has its own shadow, every life has its own charge, and because you are obscure and uninfluential now, it does not follow that you need be so in the lapse of time. Besides that, consider your son. Sometimes a great figure stands upon a common and rough pedestal: who can tell on the spur of the moment the name of the father and mother of Moses? Yet Moses stands up in the gallery of history, the most towering and indestructible figure. Do not let us therefore look at our own personal standing alone: we cannot tell what lives we may be, under God, creating, guiding, stimulating, blessing. We may bless others by sympathy, we may help the great by prayer—many an obscure suppliant gladdened the great heart of Paul by nothing but simple, loving intercession for him, that he might set his feet upon the neck of his enemies and be crowned with the glory of Christ's honor.

Some of these names were in the *direct* line of the royal succession, and some come into the genealogical table, as it were *indirectly*, so that commentators have to pause in their annotations and wonder how such and such names came into the genealogical table at all. We are soon puzzled by divine providence—things do not always fall into easy straight lines; life is a complication, a problem, a difficulty. Now and again we catch a clue, and think we can unwind the whole, and presently we come to a knot which we cannot disentangle, and which it would be impious to attempt to cut. You know not what your incidental and indirect relations to the great lines of history are. You may be startled someday to find how much you have been and how much you have done. And when you ask how it is that this sudden renown has brought upon you the flame of immortality, the answer may be this: "Inasmuch as ye did it unto one of the least of these my brethren ye did it unto me" [Matt. 25:40]. Do not say that you are not upon the great lines of history, that you are not tributaries to the great river that seems to fray for itself an infinite channel through the earth, and pours its noble waters into a great sea. All streams trickle into the rivers. There is a royalty of mind as well as a royalty of blood. There is a royalty of behavior as well as a royalty of descent. The question for each of us to consider is, whether we are acting up to the measure of our endowment and responsibility, and having answered that question in the affirmative, all the rest will be settled by the Supreme Power.

These words are spoken that I may break the spell of delusion and self-despair under which some men may be suffering. Do we not all suffer from that unhappy spell sometimes? Now and again we say, "Let the gourd wither, and let me cease to live, for all my efforts are but beatings of the air, and I seem to have no relation to the great currents and swift deep movements of divine providence—and why I am here at all I cannot tell: I wish to God the sleeping hour would come, when I might fall off into an everlasting self-oblivion!" [see Jon. 4:6–11]. It is foolish talk. The very least of us has a mission to fulfill, a function to discharge, a reward to secure. Let me then, as an apostle of Christ, call upon myself, upon every other soul, to seize the privilege and magnify the office to which we are called by the all-wise and all-good Creator.

All generations travail in birth with one greater than themselves. The great man is not yet come, he is always coming. The Son of Man has come? Yes, but not in his glory. Christ has come? Yes, but in his everyday clothes, to begin his work, to give the earnest of his blood—but he is always coming. That was the explanation of apostolic fire and unquenchable enthusiasm, and it must be the explanation of the inspiring force under which our own life is stirred and whirled in its daily course. I am always looking for and anticipating the coming of Jesus Christ. He will never come as a man. He will come with a new coming, wider and more beautiful and satisfying than as a visible figure. Let those explain the meaning of such terms, who have felt what it is to have the heart move to apprehensions and seizures of realities for which there are no words. "Thy kingdom come." Do I thus pray for some great square figure to fall out of the blue heavens and establish itself upon wheels to roll around the earth? I pray, rather, for the infinite domination of ideas, purposes and intentions of the most elevated and sacred kind. When Christianity comes, Christ will come: when the spirit of self-sacrifice has established itself upon the earth, then tell the heavens that the arrival has been completed, and that earth is just outside heaven, sunned with all its light, and made tuneful with all its music.

I find from these genealogical records that the most illustrious lines often dip into strange places and seem to become lost in great moral swamps, so much so that it appears to be impossible they can ever be found again and reunited. There is many a bad man in this list. There are men here who have broken every commandment of God. There are women here who have done the same. And yet the grand purpose moves on: it is not in the power of men's hands to break the threads of the divine purpose and scheme. The Savior comes, notwithstanding at times the whole history seems to be depraved and utterly lost. I remark upon this fact the more pathetically because it is even so in the individual life. Sometimes we find ourselves where it seems to be impossible that God can ever find us more. Yet the life is redeemed with great cost to God, for he pays blood for blood, but his redeemed ones are not given over to the power of the destroyer. Cast down, but not destroyed; smitten on the cheekbone, but not forsaken; cursing, swearing, denying Christ with oaths and blasphemy, flat, black—and then saying, "Lord thou knowest all things, thou knowest that I love thee" [John 21:17]. As the predicted man came through all the troubled lines, now illustrious with moral purity, now shamed with infinite disgrace, so through my life, and thine, with all their slips and falls, their mighty prayers and horrible blasphemies, our better self shall come, the saint that is in us shall be delivered, nourished, and perfected, and through our ungainly life, most depraved and occasionally most loathsome, there shall come that glorious body, that shining self, which is like Christ.

As I read this genealogy, I feel how true it is that grace is *not hereditary*. The good man, so good as to be almost an angel, has a son that shames the very genius of decency and insults with violence the very spirit of righteousness. This is a great mystery, that a mother, whose voice the angels might well mistake for a voice of their own, gives birth to a son that breaks her heart with his great wickedness. And a more astounding wonder still that a man whose name is a disgrace to humanity shall have a daughter beautiful as an angel, a son both philosopher and saint. Despise no man, blame no man, for circumstances over which he had no control, and praise no man for advantages which were thrust upon him without any spontaneity on his own part. Remember what your children may be; though oftentimes your minds become shocked and confounded because it seems as if the divine purpose were broken off, know that God is at the head, and through all the process of the suns, his grand purpose is developing and widening itself. Judge not by the accident: do not come to broad generalizations upon the circumstance of the passing moment, remember that all history, all time, all influences are under divine molding and direction, and when God says, "It is finished," he and the universe may hold quiet and solemn Sabbath together.

In reading further these genealogical records I find that *Jesus Christ came through all sorts of people*. If I were minded to challenge him I could upbraid him with some names that are here, and with cruel taunting I could add bitterness to his cup. He tells me that he came through all sorts to all sorts. It must be so with your life, if you are to be a great minister of God. You must not belong to any one class. You must have been depraved in your ancestors, however holy you are in yourself. O thou Son of Man, I have found thee, ancestrally, in the very pit of shame. What a history lay behind him: how he brought it all up into one focus and lived it over again in his tender sympathy, his universal understanding of human want and his infinite beneficence while ministering to all classes of human kind. O you are my preacher who comes up to every mood of my soul, so that when I am less than beast, you know how to speak to me, and nearly angel, you can accost me in the better tongue.

This is the Christ that we preach, the Christ who came through all sorts of people, that he might teach and bless all sorts of people, so that you, wise sage, can go to him and find that your ingenuity is a blunder and your profundity the shallowest of surfaces—so that you, poor sinner, can go to him, and find him girded with a towel, ready to wash with water or with blood the stain that no other but himself can ever reach. And you too little child, dear sweet little girl or boy, you can go to him, for he himself was the Child Jesus, and he knows everything that swells the child's breast and makes the child's eyes glisten and the child's soul laugh with glee. Behold, this is no class-man, no local deity, no special missionary, no man who can speak in one language only. His tabernacle is in the sun, and his speech as impartial and universal as the wind.

In looking still further into this genealogical table, I find that Jesus Christ did not always come through the eldest sons. Some of these names are the names of the eldest sons of their families and some are younger sons. God will not be bound in his movements by our little laws of primogeniture and precedency. Today he says, "I will go through the eldest son," next time he says, "Younger son, come, I will elect thee." And thus he moves, not by our ceremonial arrangements, but by a grandeur and a sweep of movement which takes in all elements and all arrangements of human life, and gives a tender sanctity to the things that we often foolishly despise.

The question has arisen again and again as I have been perusing this genealogical table, Why did not Jesus Christ come *earlier?* Thus I come upon a mystery in divine providence. Jesus Christ came before he came in the flesh. I want you, therefore, to recall the very first lesson of the morning, that as he comes now, since his flesh was buried, so he came before his incarnation in Bethlehem. Said he, "Abraham rejoiced to see my day." As a Guest, a nameless Presence, a wrestling Angel, a Cloud by day, a Fire by night, an Eye in the wheels of the chariots of Israel, in a thousand ways he came to the olden church, in a thousand ways he comes to the baptized church of today. Have all your doors and windows open, for you cannot tell by what means he will find access to your individual life or to your organized existence as churches. Be ready for him. What I say unto one I say unto all—Watch!

Let me say that there is a record in which even *our* names may all be found. Rejoice not that the spirits are subject unto you, but rather rejoice because your names are written in heaven. Let every soul remember that his name may be written in the Lamb's book of life. When the Savior was told that his mother and other relatives stood nearby, desiring to see him, he said, "Who is my mother? and who are my brethren? . . . whosoever shall do the will of my Father which is in heaven, the same is my brother, and sister, and mother" [Matt. 12:48, 50]. So we may all be in the genealogical tree of which he is the root: we may all be in the great sky, as little stars indeed, of which he is the central and inextinguishable glory.

two

THE NEW DEPARTURE OF HUMAN HISTORY

Matthew 1:18-25

FROM THIS time human history takes a new departure. How otherwise would you have Christ come? You suggest a difficulty or two as to the acceptance of the story we have read: will you be good enough to suggest *another* story by which we shall escape all difficulty, the object being to bring into the human race a man different from all other men, and yet a Savior and Redeemer of all mankind? How will you escape difficulty in carrying out that grand design? It is not enough for us to criticize the method by which Jesus Christ was declared to have come into the world; we ought to go one step further if we can, and that is to suggest a method which would have been clear of every difficulty and which yet would have obviously covered the whole ground and accomplished the one supreme design. We are awaiting suggestions: as soon as the right ones come we shall know them: we cannot mistake true music, we shall know whether the wind comes along the earth and brings the earth's dust with it, or whether it comes resoundingly from the heavens and brings with it voices and utterances of the upper and better world. Observe what had to be done: a Redeemer like ourselves in all points had to be introduced into the race, and yet so unlike us as to be wholly separate from sinners. Put that problem distinctly before your mind, and answer how it could have been accomplished as a grand historical success, except on the basis which is laid down in the Evangelic narrative.

Wherever Christ is born it is a miracle. When he is born in us it is by a miraculous conception. You do not suppose that a man becomes a Christian by some simple and obvious method which anybody can suggest and which any mind can fathom and understand? When Christ is

8

born in your heart and mine, precisely the same operation is gone through as is indicated in this opening chapter of the Gospel. It is an unexpected event, it is an event brought about by the overshadowing and ministry of the Holy Spirit. It is associated with ineffable joy, it enlists the cooperation of the angels in lifting up our gladness to its true pitch of utterance. The language of the Gospel is only romantic and intellectually distressing to those who bring to bear upon it nothing but the effort of an unassisted mind. Regarded sympathetically, seized emotionally, read in the light of our own individual experience, no other language can so adequately and correctly set forth the infinite wonder and the ineffable emotion as that which we find in the Gospel story. Moreover it is in the line of the divine development, it is in harmony with the creation of the first Adam: out of the dust was brought the man, out of the man was brought the woman, out of the woman was brought the Son, out of the Son is brought the Church, which is his body, the glory of his ministry, the conquest of his almighty arm. It is all one line, beginning in the dust, ending where God ends, a development historical, gradual, sequential, complete. In very deed, great is the mystery of godliness.

Human history then, I repeat, breaks away into a new line at this point, namely, the 18th verse of the first chapter of the Gospel by Matthew. The great exception takes place here. From this moment human history has an upward direction, and focalizes itself in a Personality hitherto but dimly indicated by the voice of often enigmatic prophecy. There are such distinct points of departure in your life and mine. The point of departure, therefore, given by the Evangelist, ought not to startle us as though it had no analogy or confirmation in human experience. I object to the law which says that it can receive nothing that has not a counterpart in human consciousness and experience, because human consciousness and experience may yet have themselves to enlarge: they have not reached the highest and last point of their own development. On the other hand, I would call attention to the fact that there are a great many things within human consciousness and experience which are not distinctly recognized as being there. Why recoil from the first chapter of the book of Genesis or the first chapter of the Gospel by Matthew? If I regard these chapters in a merely literal and verbal way, I am filled with distress. If I regard them sympathetically, and in the light of what takes place in the dime sanctuary of my own consciousness, I understand them every whit. That subtle old serpent, the devil, has talked to me. I do not ask the naturalist to tell me whether, by the confirmation of the serpent's mouth, it was possible for the serpent to practice the utterance of articulate language: that is the question of a charlatan. The serpent has spoken with fatal eloquence to every man amongst us. Object to the *figure*, if you like, but the grim, stern, damning *fact* remains. And as to the tree in the midst of the garden, and the fiery, flaming sword and guarding cherubim, I know them. It is impossible to get back to the lost chance, it is impossible to sponge out one spot of crime, it is impossible to find the way to the tree we have once despoiled. To try it is to fight with fire, and the fire roots itself in the inextinguishable furnaces of the divine anger.

And in very deed, if I go further back still, and think of man being shaped out of the dust, I know it: I feel the dust, I feel the DEITY too. I know it must have been out of the deepest dust of the earth some parts of my nature were made, and I also know that there burns within me a fire which only God could have lighted. Observe, therefore, that I do not go back with the grammarian and the pedantic etymologist and ask those teachers to be kind enough to explain to me the opening chapters of Genesis or the opening chapters of human life in any of its grand beginnings and developings. I go down there alone, all silent, all wondering, and MYSELF is the best annotation. So it is with this opening chapter of the Gospel of Matthew. Jesus Christ is born in me, and a new departure is taken in my life by processes which can never be explained in words. In your development from infancy to spiritual manhood there comes in the story this all-separating—"NOW." When did it enter? You cannot tell. The chronometer has not yet been made that indicates these millionths of seconds in which great divine ministrations accomplish themselves in births that have no deaths. Have we passed from death unto life? Has Christ been born in us the hope of glory?

Read the chapter still further until you see the wonderful union in Christ of the human and the divine—the human on the mother's side, the divine as indicated by the mysterious operation of the Holy Spirit. This was no imaginary Mary. This literal history was required in order to vindicate her memory from the charge of her being a merely dramatic woman. She was real, like ourselves, one of us; she lived the common human life, wept the common human tears, enjoyed the same enjoyments that fall to our lot: there is enough said about her in the Gospels to prove the pure human nature of the woman, and little enough said about her not to magnify her into a feminine god. She is here long enough to be seen, understood, spoken about, attested, initialed by every witness that knows human nature, and behold she is *gone!* The mother of Emmanuel must not remain *too long*: she must be before my eye long enough for me to know that she is Mary, and none other: not a theatrical woman or a paper minister, conceived by the wild imagination of a delirious theology, but a WOMAN, a sister, a friend, a sufferer, a loving one — and then she must go, and I cannot tell how. Buried without a funeral, buried without a grave, buried without an epitaph — gone, and the eye cannot follow the swift movement of her translation.

As for the operation of the Holy Ghost, it begins and ends in the word *miracle*. Yet it, too, is a miracle which has its correspondence in our own nature. I cannot tell the source of my prayers. When I pray with you, it is not I praying, it is a voice I never heard before in that same tone. When I close my eyes to lead you upward, is it by some utterance I have committed to memory, some paragraphs I have formulated in the library, some sentences I have caught and detained as friends? God forbid. *It is a birth of the Holy Spirit.* The poor words, half dumb, and trembling through and through with a throb of conscious weakness, may be partly mine, but the thing they labor to say I know not. Can you tell me the genesis, and give me the roots and starting fibers of all the purposes that have distinguished your life and made it as a flame of sacred fire, burning upward unto the heavens? You can rehearse to me the history of your commerce, and even that you can give in some instances only in part, for you know not whence the brightest suggestions came. You can tell me somewhat of the outward history of your life and body during the day — as to where you have been and partly what you have seen, but even then the story is remarkable mainly for its incompleteness. Behind, and around, and above there are forces and ministries which have entered as living factors in all you have done, for which you have no name — forces that have broken your thigh in the night's wrestling, but left you in the morning with a nobler name [see Gen. 32:24–32].

Such is the work of the Holy Spirit. It is not to be settled in language. "The wind bloweth where it listeth, and thou hearest the sound thereof, but canst not tell whence it cometh, and whither it goeth: so is every one that is born of the Spirit" [John 3:8]. We *prove* our birth, we do not explain it. I cannot tell you how I came to be; the Lord help everyone of us to vindicate his being by temper pure as fire, by love noble as sacrifice!

There was one man who looked on with great wonder. All the ages have crowded around that man, and, so to speak, have thronged him into an infinite multitude, all looking on with the same amazement, all distracted by the same perplexity. Joseph knew not what angel was coming to him along the crooked lines of his mental distraction. We seem to be born to misunderstand everything that is at all great and noble: we cannot understand ourselves, we can give but foolish answers to all the great questions which relate to our own being and our own destiny. No man yet ever satisfied his friend fully and left him in the position in which he could ask no question or suggest no doubt regarding any movement in life which was really tragical, involving suffering when that suffering might have been escaped. You are looking at your life as a great perplexity. God delights in our embarrassments—you cannot see how this knot can be untied, and you feel that it would be impious to attempt to cut it. Be in no haste. I have had a thousand knots like that in my life. When I touched them my fingers were too soft to get hold of the lines that bound them together in hardness. When I have called for steel, I have been guilty consciously of a coward's trick, and the angel has said, "Do not cut it; let it alone: the answer of all things is not yet; in due time that knot shall prove itself to be part of the strange but ever beneficent ministry of the divine and Holy Father."

A most remarkable reason is given why the name should be called *Jesus*. Referring to the 21st verse, you will find that the reason is "for he shall save his people from their sins." Christ is the only man known in history who was born with specific and exclusive reference to the sins of the human family. He does not come into the race with a small program. The world had sickened at its heart of programs an inch long; in its intolerable soreness of soul it could not have endured another. Make way: here is a man who is going to remove the dust from our house windows. We are glad to see him. Make way again: here is a man who is going to remove the dust from our doorstep. Welcome to him also. Again and again make way for a thousand men, each of whom has a short purpose and a superficial program. So far as they go we bid each a cordial welcome. But when all the thousand have done their little work, and have gone away from our door, we feel that ANOTHER must come with some fuller purpose, with some grander ministry. I thank all men who have done anything for me, but there is a fire in me that is burning up my life— who is to put that out? For all temporary mitigations of suffering I am thankful, but there is an asp biting my soul, and I am dying of its injected poison. Who can touch a mind diseased? This Son of Mary, Son of God, comes with the avowed purpose of *doing this very thing I want to have done.* By so much, therefore, as he even *seems* to rise to the dignity of the occasion, I hail him, for he has caught the genius of my malady—perhaps he may bring with him the one remedy. If he had made light of my disease, I should have run away from him, for he had not then understood me. If he had come with light and jaunty words upon his lips, I should have called him liar, and found the evidence in his tone. But when he meets me he says the case is grave, the case is fatal, the disease is sin, the malady is in the soul, the blood is tainted, the life is rotten, the burden is grievous. I say to him, as a mere man, "Sir, thou understandest me: what is the answer to all this suffering?" And when he says *"Blood,"* I feel that we are grappling with a Man that has at all events the right words. Let him prove them—then will he be the crowned Savior of the race, and his name shall be worn by no thief, but by himself only, every other Jesus forgotten in him whose surname is Christ.

All that we have now read was done in fulfillment of *prophecy.* God does not work extemporaneously, the suddenness of his movements is only apparent; every word he says comes up from eternity around the birthplace of Jesus Christ. There, assembled the prophets and the minstrels of ancient time. "All this was done that it might be fulfilled which was spoken by the prophet." The prophets were misunderstood men; they seemed to sing a song which found an entrance into no heart. Their forecasts were met with derisive laughter, their predictions were thought to be nothing but the lamentations of a disordered and unbalanced mind, and many a time, wrapping their mantles around them, travel-stained, they lay down, saying, "I sometimes wish to God the prophetic inspiration had never moved me to speech." Prophets always suffer. It is a crucifixion to be born before your time. Happy he who speaks the language of the day; popular as a god is he. The man who projects himself by divine energy through centuries ahead, dies a thousand deaths. The prophets suffered for us: Isaiah, Ezekiel, and Daniel, and the mighty tribe of men who never spake to their own day, but shot their thunder voices across the ages, died for us. They have their reward. I cannot think of them as dead dust, scattered upon the winds and going to make up some other man's grave and there an end of them. I must, following the instinct of justice and nobleness of compensation, think of them as seeing the triumphs they predicted, and turning into songs all the tears and woes that afflicted them during their misunderstood ministry.

Joseph was put to sleep by God, and was talked to through the medium of a dream. It is God's old plan: he puts us into a deep sleep, and behold when we come out of it, there is the beautiful companionship of our life standing before us, or there is the great answer to a small difficulty that turned our life into a sharp pain, or there is the way out of an entanglement difficult as a labyrinth, puzzling as a thicket, devised by all the cunning cruelty of our worst enemies. Sometimes I have done, as you have; many a time fallen off into sleep quite unable to do the work that was pressing upon me. A refreshing slumber has blessed the brain, has wound it up in every energy and force, and the awakening has been as a resurrection, and we have gone to the work that defied us, and lo, in the hands recovered by sleep there has been cunning enough to lift the burden, or to dispel the difficulty, and we who had fainted in weariness, rejoiced in a renewed and apparently inexhaustible strength.

We are most *alone* when we are asleep. God loves to speak to us in our loneliness. We are more spiritual when we are asleep than when we are awake. When I am awake I have to do with all this world: I am lost and dazed amid countless eyes that are watching: I am struck by a million wonders that challenge my attention; my ears are filled with countless noises that fall upon one another and make rough tumult in my soul. God says to me, "Come into the darkness, and I will close thine eyelids and speak to thee alone." If you ask me if I believe in dreams, taking the word dream in its wholeness, I say no; if you ask me if I believe in particular dreams, I say yes. Who would give up his dream-life? In the dream-life we are larger than in our waking hours. In dreams I float through the air by easy and pleasant levitation; I move across difficulties I dare not encounter when I awake. In dreams I step from star to star and cross the horizon at a bound. I know that these things appear to me in a light almost laughable when I awake, yet in my better thinking I get out of them hints, hints that startle me, make me think of possibilities which never come within the dull routine of life, and which have no place in the reckoning of the book-makers.

Thank God for sleep, thank God for dreams, thank God for every ministry that gets you out of your littleness. If any minister of God in any church can charm you away from your counter and your desk, and make you feel, even for one moment, that the universe is larger than you had supposed it to be, go and hear that man: he is your soul's true friend. If by tone of the voice, if by vehemence of appeal, if by tenderness of prayer, he can turn you to an upward look, he is God's minister to your soul. Love him, honor him. You may disagree with him in many of his words, some of his propositions you may be quite unable to accept from an intellectual point of view; again and again he may provoke you into controversy by statements that appear to you either rash or irreconcilable, but by as much as he has the power to make you look up and see God's wonders in the heavens, and to excite in you a desire to be broader and nobler than you are, he is the anointed minister of God to you, and should be received as such. I read the books that make me larger; I follow the authors that tell me of bigger things than I have yet seen. I love the souls that lure me into sleep that is enriched with dreaming, that extends the horizon, and doubles the stars, and heightens the sky in which they shine. From such companionship I return saying, "I have seen heaven's gate open today, and there are lines in this universe that were never dreamed of before in my philosophy."

Thus, then, Jesus Christ comes into the world. We have now, from time to time, to follow him in his wondrous ministry. I will not attempt to prove the miracle of the incarnation by any verbal argument, but I will ask him to meet us here morning by morning, and to vindicate, by the eloquence of his own speech and the marvelousness of his own action, the claim that is set up for him in this chapter—that he is at once the Son of Mary and the begotten of the Holy Ghost.

REVIEW OF THE WHOLE CHAPTER

You will find it a delightful and profitable study to look at the first chapter of Genesis and the first chapter of Matthew together. I have found it useful to read the one chapter immediately after the other. The contrast between Genesis and Matthew is most vivid, and in some points most startling. In both cases you have what is termed the *Beginning*— a term that cannot be defined. There are compasses, one point of which we can lay upon these terms, but the other point cannot be stretched to the full extent of their meaning. Both chapters, with a most startling audacity, give us a point to begin at: they create history, they draw a line and say, "History begins here." How far the beginning is right, has to be ascertained by long-continued investigation. No answer can be immediately given to the bold assumption: it must be found in the course of persistent and enlightened inquiry. Let us, having read both the chapters, look at some of the points of contrast and some of the points of union, and learn as the result of our study how with completeness the Bible confirms itself and challenges attention to points which lie below the surface and are likely to elude the most watchful criticism that is not inspired by the purest desires of the heart.

In the first chapter of Genesis, we see how order and beauty were brought out of confusion, and in the other how spiritual harmony was brought out of infinite discord. In Genesis you have chaos turned into cosmos, in Matthew you have a tumultuous, fierce, rebellious humanity, shaped into dignity and worship, and blessed with the completeness of rest. If these chapters were mere poetry, I should be struck with the manner in which both the conceptions are expressed. The manner is, in this case, nothing less than an argument. This to my mind is one of the most beautiful of the incidental illustrations of the truth of the Bible. In the first instance we have to deal with *matter*. What is the tone in which matter is dealt with? It is a tone of command, it is a fiat. Put into words, the words would be—Let it be done. There is no consultation, there is no entreaty, there is no persuasion, there is no remonstrance. The fiat is omnific. As a mere question of poetic conception this manner is equal to the occasion. When we go into the region of matter, we do not say "If you please"; we stand above it, we command it. This is a fact of our own consciousness and experience. When you want to shape that long stretch of iron into an arch, what do you say? You say precisely what is said in the first chapter of Genesis. You cannot get away from this biblical tether, you say "Let it be done." Is your tone one of beseeching entreaty—do you ask the iron to be kind enough to allow itself to be molded into an arch? When you want the quarry to yield you stones wherewith to build a temple, what do you say? You copy the first chapter of the book of Genesis: you are biblical without the Bible, the tone cannot be changed, you say, "Let it be done," and therein you echo the fiat that rounded the heavens and populated the seas.

This then is true to our own consciousness and experience. I say, "Let my house be built, let it be decorated, let it be richly furnished, let it be thus and so." Why is my tone so dogmatic and positive? Because I am within a region where the human will is supreme. You may remind me of incidental circumstances, and I am not oblivious of them, but their being in the case as details does not for one moment alter the principle which I am endeavoring to elucidate, namely, that wherever mere matter is concerned, our *will* determines its uses. There shall be a bridge across that river, there shall stand a temple on that site, there shall be a picture on that wall. So far as the matter is one purely materialistic, the will is supreme, the word creates, the word determines.

In the second case, it is not matter that is dealt with, but *manhood*. How different is the process, how long the delay, how intricate the method, how innumerable and subtle the perils. Instead of commanding, we have persuasion, entreaty, nurture, encouragement, even the whole ministry of long-suffering patience and all-hoping love. Looking at this also as a mere conception of manner, how true it is to our own consciousness and experience and method. You can order a coat for your child—you cannot order a character. You can command a *dress* to be fashioned, you cannot command an *education* to be received, except in the only sense, namely, the mechanical, which proves, by a still broader illustration, the very principle on which I am insisting. You can decorate your house with a word, you cannot decorate your child's intellectual nature—nay, you cannot decorate his back without his consent. He tears your jeweled rags from his shoulders, throws them on the ground, steps on them and defies you.

Look, therefore, at both the chapters as indicating *a wide contrast of manner*, a contrast arising from the fact that in the one case it is *matter* that is being treated, and in the other case it is *manhood* that is being created and trained and completed. Can you amend this method? You give orders for a *building*, you cannot give orders for a *soul*. You will go to your desk tomorrow morning, and with one scratch of your pen you will *order* work for a thousand pounds, or ten thousand, to be done, and you properly say you have given the *order*. If you understood the meaning of your own music, you would be taken back to the first chapter of Genesis and set down there repeating the first words— you have never got beyond that liberty! You will come home after having given your *order*, and you will have, with your children around you, to ask their *consent* to kiss them. It is no kiss upon the child's lip that is given by force—a kiss of the flesh, not a kiss of the soul. Then you will come into the first chapter of Matthew, and find how, by wondrous processes, too subtle to be caught in iron speech, hearts are won, characters are formed, and destinies are determined.

It is by these practical illustrations that I find, again and again, how unexpectedly and wondrously the Bible is confirmed, and how our liberty is restricted by a history thousands of years old. We think we do some things by our own ingenuity and by our own strength, and again and again we are reminded that our originality is stale and our wit a borrowed dart.

If we look at these two chapters side by side from another point of view, we shall find that in both cases the events spread themselves, as to their execution, over vast periods of time. As for the creation, the date is—"in the beginning." Search your calendar for that line, or put a better line in its place. Man likes to know details simply because he is *himself* a detail. But as he grows in the knowledge of God, and in the completeness of his purposed character, viewed in the light of the divine will, he finds that detail is but a momentary convenience. Observe how profoundly true this is also to our own consciousness and experience. Time represents value. We have a saying amongst ourselves to the effect that time is money. Time is more, time represents value: the political economist says that money is nothing, a mere token or symbol, of that which money can purchase—the value is not in the money, it is in the production. And a greater teacher than the political economist tells us that time is nothing; I must look at what time represents: a day is not the same thing to the idle man that it is to the man who is busy.

Lay it down broadly that *time represents value.* "Why," said an artist no sooner born than dead, to a great painter, "do you spend so much time upon your pictures?" The profound and courteous answer was, "Because I paint for immortality." And as a man soweth so shall he also reap [see Gal. 6:7]. "And why," said one who looked upon a great sculptor, "are you spending so much time over that face? I saw it a month ago, and it seemed to be as far advanced in its formation as it is now." "No," said Michaelangelo, "I have been rounding that cheek, and giving a little additional expression to that nostril, and bringing out that under part of the eye more clearly." Said the observer, "These are but trifles." "True," answered the great man of the chisel, "these are trifles, but trifles make perfection, and perfection is no trifle." Thus to the wise time represents value. We say of some buildings that they have been run up in the night time, and when we pass that commentary upon them, we mean it as a sneer, or as an indication of the estimate we place upon the value of the thing done. We call such buildings shells, we say they will need repair in a month or two—no time has been spent upon them, and for no time will they endure.

The expenditure of time, therefore, must have a *moral value* yet to be discovered. What time was spent on building the universe! Men who have made the universe from that point of view a special study, say that the earth must have taken tens of thousands of ages to build. They ridicule the notion of a six-thousand-years-old globe: they take me down as far as they can to the roots of the rocks and show me the stony registers, pile on pile, where the ages are buried under unsculptured stone. When I compare these wondrous things with what I know to be true in my own consciousness and experience, I reason thus—Time represents value: a man spends time upon the outworking of a purpose according to the value he sets upon it: if thousands of ages have been sown upon these barren fields, God's meaning in that scattering of the ages upon a rocky surface, must be profound, and is not now to be understood or explained.

Yet to one test I can put this expenditure of time. It is a common test: it is in use amongst ourselves; we apply it to all things, perhaps even to the most sacred. I can stand on the green surface of the earth and look up into the starry roof, and ask what has come of all this time, what is the *success* which has attended this infinite delay? Then comes to my waiting mind and heart the great answer—"Can you amend anything that is within thy reach, O man? Stoop down and pluck thee a blade of grass from thy feet, look at it and say whether thou couldst sharpen it to a finer point, fill it with more delicate blood, clothe it with a tenderer bloom, make it in any respect more beautiful? Look at the sun: can you sphere him out into a more perfect circle, or add one ray to his effulgence, or suggest a supplement to his infinitude of light?" These questions are put to me with courteousness, yet reading between the lines I feel that they mock me like a defiant thunder. Then I come to the conclusion that time represents value. I cannot paint the lily without painting upon it my own folly. I cannot suggest a single readaptation of any of the functions of my body, I cannot add a healthier color to my blood, I cannot fix my eyes so as to see better than they now see the wonders of this gallery and museum of things infinite and grand. I cannot *amend* God's work. It is to this little test, yet not useless, that I can bring this marvelous fact of the expenditure of what to us is an eternity, in the building up of a globe that holds upon its face all that is beautiful of summer, and hides in its kind heart all that is ghastly in death.

The Lord having thus made me a universe says, "My child, this is a symbol: this is not made for its own sake, this is meant to teach you great lessons; it is my board of illustration; I have inscribed the heavens and the earth with innumerable sermons, and lessons, and poems, and parables—go and find them out, write them in your own speech, and make yourself glad in this deep and gracious study." He is also building a spiritual universe, and it takes him a long time to construct it. He is making Man, and man takes more making than all the stars that throw their light on space. Why, this is true at home: you made your carpet, and your table, and your pictures, and your china in no time; you sent them back and had them altered: but your child, the son that has never stooped yet in filial worship at your knee; that daughter, bad with a fire your love has been unable to quench; that will that seems to hold you at its cruel mercy—there your efforts appear to have been wasted.

I might argue that as it has taken God a long time to build *creation*, so it takes him a long time to build the higher creation of *manhood*. I set up no such contention, nor dare I avail myself of any such illustration. The rocks require a long time, but *they cannot be damned*. What do I care if he pile eternities upon them? They cannot *suffer*. But man dies—and goes to hell! To me, therefore, some tenderer and deeper argument must be addressed than the argument of analogy from the long periods required for physical formations, and the spaces and periods of time required for the development of moral harmony and beauty. I find the necessity for the expenditure of long time, in myself, in my moral nature. I will *not let* God complete his work. I find the reason of the delay in me, *not in him*.

Nor need this be considered as a piece of theological metaphysics. It is a piece of matter-of-fact life. Everyone now hearing me I could summon as a witness to bear testimony to the fact that to do right is not pleasant to any of us. If the religion of Jesus Christ is to be discounted or set aside simply because it takes a long time to make itself universally felt in the world, then with it, by parity of reasoning, must go down everything that is beautiful and noble in human education, morals and progress. Do not suppose that your blow terminates upon the faith of Jesus Christ when you say that if that faith were divine it would make more rapid progress in the world. That blow, if it have any effect at all, shatters the entire temple of beauty, morals, and all that goes to make up completeness of human character. We all agree, for example, that honesty is right and good. Not one dissenting voice is raised to that proposition. But, according to the reasoning by which you wish to upset the divinity of Christ's religion, honesty cannot be good, otherwise every man would be honest. We are all further agreed that temperance is excellent, self-control, personal moderation, having all our faculties, passions, fires of our nature under our entire dominion and sway. To that proposition not one single dissenting voice is raised. But, according to the reasoning referred to, *temperance cannot be a good thing,* otherwise every man would practice it. The very fact that it is rejected, would, according to the reasoning now in question, upset the claim of temperance to be a virtue at all. We are all agreed that cleanliness is beneficial to health: we say properly that without cleanliness there can be no permanent health. That proposition is unanimously carried in every intelligent assembly, but if I am to avail myself of the reasoning which is now leveled against the divinity of Christ's religion, then I reply, cleanliness cannot be beneficial, otherwise every man, woman, and child would instantly be cleanly. Every man, woman, and child is not cleanly, therefore cleanliness cannot be the excellent thing you try to prove it to be.

So with the pleas of God, the expostulations of the Most High, and the offers of the gospel—they all fall into the ruck of these common reasonings, and I, who have been convicted on every point of the former indictment, am convicted with a ten thousandfold conviction upon the supreme point of all, namely, that God waits to be gracious, and I keep him waiting.

But as in the former case of the creation, so in this latter case of the completeness of the human character, the result will be worthy of him who has been conducting the process. I cannot amend his heavens, add a deeper tint of blue to his sky, increase the richness of the green which he has spread over the earth, suggest an improvement to a single spore of moss or blade of grass, or feather on bird's wing. In all these things, I have to say, "It is very good." If amendment might be possible, not on my side has the possibility been realized. So he will build this other creation, the great house of Manhood, the infinite temple of redeemed and sanctified humanity, and when it is done he will say, "It is very good, a glorious church, not having spot or wrinkle or any such thing, complete, rhythmic, restful, majestic, immortal." I must, therefore, make right use of the material symbol, and translate it into its highest spiritual meanings. I look for new heavens and a new earth and a new Jerusalem, a church beautiful as the Lamb that redeemed it.

This brings me to the last point of contrast which I can now notice, namely, that in the first chapter of Genesis the endeavor, the process rather, is to *make* man, in Matthew the object is to REDEEM man. In the first instance, we had no part or lot. If you will search into this matter, you will find how at all points you are restricted and humbled, so far as your birth is concerned. For a moment look at this matter. You are *born* without your own will, configured without your own consent: whether you were to be dark or fair, tall or short, strong or weak—not a word had you in that solemn covenant. You were *nationalized* without your own consent, you were not asked, "Will you be born in the temperate zone, or in the torrid zone? Will you be born in a little island or in a broad continent? Will you prefer to be an Englishman or a Turk—an Indian or an African?" In that destiny you had neither part nor lot. Why, your consent was not asked even to the *name* you bear! You were born, nationalized, named, and over these things you had no control whatsoever. How wondrously we are limited on that side of our nature, yet on the other what marvelous freedom we have! We who can curse God to his face, cannot add one cubit to our stature. We who can say "No" to all the eloquence of the divine love, cannot make one hair white or black. Calvinism is true, and Arminianism is true, and they are both in the Bible, and they are both in your life. Limit and liberty, law and freedom, you find everywhere. You are pinned down and cannot break the pin. Yet you have tether enough to give you the notion of infinite freedom.

We were no parties to our being *made*, we are asked to be parties to our being *redeemed*. "Come unto me all yet that labor and are heavy laden and I will give you rest" [Matt. 11:28]. "Whosoever believeth shall not perish but have everlasting life" [John 3:16]. "Ye will not come unto me that ye might have life" [John 5:40]. "How often would I have gathered thy children together and ye would not" [Matt. 23:37; cf. Luke 13:34].

I have spoken of two beginnings, yet the two are but one. Jesus Christ is not a point in history, he is the point which antedates all history. "In the beginning was the Word, and the Word was with God, and the Word was God" [John 1:1]. "And the Word was made flesh and dwelt among us" [John 1:14]. He is the Lamb slain from before the foundation of the world. He created all things, and he is before all things, and by him all things consist [see John 1:3]. When, therefore, we speak of the beginning of the gospel as subsequent to the beginning of creation, we only use a phrase for human convenience. The divine meaning is that all things begin in God, and that God never began!

three

THE RISING OF THE SUN

Matthew 2:1-10

HERE WOULD seem to begin the *inquiry* about Jesus Christ which has never since ceased to be the supreme question of the religious mind. That inquiry, I take it, is more eager and widespread today than ever it was in any period of human history. Still the great subject is—*where* is Christ, *who* is Christ, *what* is Christ? The books that reveal him most profoundly and lovingly to the human mind and heart are books which hold their own today amid the fiercest possible literary competition. All this means something. There is in it a deep and all but tragical mystery; an agony of the heart speaks in this inquiry of the lips. The life of man wants something more than it has yet secured; it tries to evade answers that bring with them severe moral obligations, and yet it recurs to those answers as if they were the only profound and vital replies. It is a great mystery, it is even a sharp pain, it is a dense cloud, and out of it there comes, in strange and terrible gleaming, lightning that might affright and destroy the mind that inquires and wonders.

The great inquiry related to that which was *essential* rather than to that which was *accidental*. Of course that which was accidental had to come into the inquiry. Certain things had been prophetically written, certain places and times had been specifically indicated, and therefore attention must be directed into those quarters. Still the grave and ever-lasting inquiry relates to that which is essential and immutable. The word upon which I would lay the strongest emphasis is the word *born*. Not upon the word *young*, not upon the word *child*. "Young" is a term that lives on for a few days, and then melts out of our sight and becomes age while yet we admire its tender bloom. "Child" is a beautiful bud that bursts into a full flower while we are looking at it. But *born* is a historical word, it is the same always, it indicates the revelation of life, the setting up of new ministries and forces in the universe. To be young is to be a child, is to pass through very transitory stages and attractions, but to be *born* sets up a fact, immortal as God. We have been born. Our youth has gone like the mist of the morning, our childhood is a hardly remembered sun-spot in our recollection, but our birth hastens to shape itself into a permanent destiny.

This interest in childhood should teach us a great deal. Childhood in itself is little, but it is a quantity that is always growing. Let Pharaoh of old teach us what to do with the children. He said, "These Israelites will be too many for us one day" [see Ex. 1:8–12]. What, then, did he propose in the view of their over-multiplication? To kill off all the men, or all the women? His was a more profound policy. I wish to God the Church could seize it and apply it to the current questions of our own economy. He said, "Kill the boys, drown them." Am I appalled by the idiot's philosophy? No, but I am struck by the wisdom that sees in *childhood*, boyhood, a growing power, and that directs its attention to the early life of nations, for they who begin with the adults begin at the wrong end, and they who begin with the little ones begin at the right point, and may achieve profound and permanent success. Do not sneer at the boys. Do not count them for nothing. They will be your successors, they may now be your scholars. For a time they may grieve you and annoy you, and, by an impertinence that is only for the passing day, they may again and again bring momentary annoyance or distress upon you, but it is a grand thing to be involved with them. Let your gentleness make them great. Show yourself so deeply interested in them, by many an inquiry, as to start in their minds the question whether they be not something greater and grander than they appear to be merely for the passing moment.

Pharaoh and Herod directed their attention to young life. If they could have gotten hold of the young life and turned it in their direction they might have built up very bad sovereignties, but it was one of two things with them, either the boys would overcome them or they must overcome the boys. Let me speak words of strong encouragement and genuine comfort to those of you who are young. You cannot tell what you may be yet. Work with a high aim, be moved to noble and pure ambitions. You will have your broad chance in the world. O may every finger you have, and every faculty, be made keen enough and strong enough to seize the chance and turn it as it were into fine gold.

In reading this text one is struck with the power of *one life* to arouse a world. Observe who they are that gather around this young child. Wise men from the East, kings, chief priests and scribes of the people, and elsewhere we hear of the interest of shepherds who were keeping their flocks by night. A strange thing for these old Persian astrologers to come four months from their homes to see one who was born—not king of the *Persians*, then their journey would have admitted an easy explication—but king of the *Jews*—why should those Oriental star-gazers be interested in Jewish history to this extent? There is more in the question than appears on the surface. This king of the Jews is not king of the Jews only, but he is the King who springs out of the Jews to be the King of all men. He will choose his own name presently. Our fathers called us what they pleased without consulting us: not a man was asked what name he would bear: his name is the finger-mark of a power he can neither understand nor resist, but there comes a time when every man may make himself a name, may by his spirit and his actions build up an appellation which will endure through all eternity. When Jesus Christ comes to speak of himself he will explain this Persian eagerness. He will call himself the Son of Man. He will broaden away from his birthpoint until he covers the whole area of human nature, answering every throbbing pain, anticipating every distressful prayer, and giving answers greater than any questions that ever could be framed.

Herein is the explanation of all kinds of people wanting to know about Jesus Christ. Philosophy calls in to see what he is. Kings pause a moment on their royal processions to ask questions about him, chief priests and scribes of the people engage themselves to literary research and religious investigation that they may be able to answer popular inquiries concerning this unnamable Man. And all kinds of poor people want to know where he is, that they may speak to him a prayer that has come back from every door, a bruised bird that could find no space for its flying. We have read in the seventy-second psalm written by Solomon, a type of a greater, who shall have dominion from sea to sea and from the river to the ends of the earth—why? Have you heard the sweet answer? *For he shall deliver the poor and the needy and him that hath no helper.* This is not a painted majesty, a gilded dominion, a great comet-like blaze of transient splendor: it is a monarchy built on *beneficence.*

He who makes it his supreme business in life to help the poor and the needy, the Woman and the Child, the far off and the destitute, the misunderstood and the friendless—nothing can hinder him putting on his head crown upon crown until other kings look petty beside his majesty.

It is thus that Jesus Christ will reign. Not by force of chariots and multitudinousness of horses, not by the grandeur of his earth-state, but by that loving sympathy which understands everybody, by that infinite beneficence that stops not at donations of the hand but gives all the blood of its heart. Hereon you may build the Christian argument, and nothing will be able to overthrow it. They will be able to ask you difficult questions about miracles and mysteries of every kind, they will be able to puzzle you with grammatical inquiries, they may lose you altogether in historical and archaeological investigations and references: your heads may become bewildered there—you stand to this grand sovereign fact, let *him* be king who can do most for men. Here you have the key which explains the inrushing upon Christ of all the nations and climates of the world.

Yet one cannot but be struck with the different purposes of the inquiry. The Magi said, "We have come to worship him,"—literally meaning to do homage to him. Trust the men who can do homage to anything, out of and greater than themselves. Always set a high price upon reverence. Veneration is the basis of all noble and tender and beneficent character. I would distrust the man who has proved himself destitute of veneration. It does us good to bend the knee to an object which we suppose to be greater than we are ourselves. We have all seen the poor superstitious creatures, as we deem them, on the continent of Europe, coming into the churches for a moment and bowing and getting down on their knees in a manner which we could not understand. I never could mock that service. I have thought I have seen upon the peasant's face a tenderer expression, a more glowing solemnity because of that little service in the house of God. There are men who are greater in blasphemy than in reverence, who never have anything good to say of anybody, and they never do anything for mankind worthy of a moment's remembrance. Why have we come into Christ's house this morning? If we have come to worship him, we shall retire from the house larger and better men: the small critical function with which we might have distressed ourselves in passing through the service will be suspended, and in our hearts there will glow a fire of new love. By so much as we have bent the knee lovingly and loyally to the Son of Man have we thrown off the worst part of ourselves, and taken upon us part of that which constitutes his beauty and strength.

Herod's purpose was not to worship him—he said it was to worship, but he lied. Can men lie about religious things? Yes. Can men say *worship* when they mean *destroy?* They say it everyday. Can men be found who will put up a church for Christ and yet not know what they are building? Oh, it is not only possible, it is the saddest fact of our business, that we build temples, and curse the stones as we put them together. We set up minsters, not with songs but sometimes with oaths. There is a possibility of destroying Christ, under the guise of worshiping him, and there is a further possibility of destroying Christ more or less unconsciously, by giving false notions of him, by making him a class-Redeemer, by setting him apart for sectarian uses, by attaching to him badges and labels, scarves, and memorials, that make him belong to one corner only, by narrowing his words down into denominational slogans—by a thousand such ways we destroy Christ's influence in the world. Know ye that Christ is a Sun which cannot be touched, and also a light which plays with loving familiarity upon the one-paned cottage of the poor man and upon the stately palaces of royalty and wealth? He is a Sun not to be clipped by your instruments or rearranged by your eager fingers, and he is a light that will bless you, but must never be trifled with.

Then there are other men who do not come to worship Christ, and who certainly do not come to destroy him—who simply come to *speculate* upon him. They make him an intellectual puzzle. He is the mystery of the day to them, they must say something about him, he is an enigma they cannot afford wholly to ignore, and it is heart-breaking to hear the chaff they pour forth without one grain of wheat in the innumerable bushels. And it is sadder still to hear the *patronage* they offer the Son of God. Have you heard how they speak about him? They speak with measured approbation, with a fine critical discrimination as to his properties, and qualities, and place in human history. It makes me sad to hear how they damn him with faint praise. They say he had upon him the inspiration of genius, they allow that he was an excellent character, perhaps a little too amiable now and then. He had wondrous prevision, he saw a great deal more than many of his contemporaries saw. He was a very excellent man in all his purposes; his motives were unquestionably good. If he is not more than that, he is the crowning hypocrisy of history. What I dread amongst you most is not that you will destroy Christ, but that you will patronize him. You who laid the hand upon the fat bullock and said "Good," will put the same paw upon the Son of God and say "Not bad." He will resist such patronage, and denounce it, and decline it, and return it to rest upon those who gave it. It will be a curse that they can never survive.

Jesus Christ is nothing to me if he is not the Savior of the world. I never heard persons in moments of great agony or distress speak about the inspiration of genius being upon Christ. I have heard them say so when they were doing well: I have heard them speak thus about Christ when they were parenthetically interposing, "No more, thank you," about their fat dinner. But when I have seen them doubled up with great distress, and thrust into dark corners, and carrying burdens that break the back, and shuddering under clouds that may be laden with death darts, I have heard a whimper that would have disgraced a dog. You will know what Jesus Christ is most and best when you are in greatest need of such service as he can render.

You will also find very different results flowing from these inquiries. Herod was troubled, but the wise men rejoiced with exceeding great joy. This is a summary of today's experience. Christ is one of two things in your life. He is either the source of your keenest troubles, or he is the beginning and the end of your most supreme joys. The good always troubles the bad. The honest clerk troubles you who are not honest. You hate that young man: he is good to look upon, he is pleasant to speak to, he is most companionate, many an attraction attaches to his method and ways amongst men, but his honesty is a continual judgment upon your dishonesty. If you were to hear that he had dropped down dead, it would only be a hypocrite's sigh that would answer the announcement. It is a law of the universe, if we may judge by its being a law of society, that the bad are always troubled by the good, the generous giver is a daily trouble to the penurious man: he finds motives for his generosity, he attributes his liberality to false inspirations, he wonders if he could not be more prudent, careful, and thoughtful: all the while in his heart he hates the man who by contrast throws him into very cold and distant shadow.

On the other hand, no man has given such joy to the world as Jesus Christ has given. He carries all his disciples up to the point of rapture. Such have been the feelings of Christian men that a new language has had to be invented for the expression of their lofty and sacred emotions.

Religion, you say, has a dialect of its own: it is only a dialect to those who have not been fired to the same intensity of zeal, and brought to the same nobility of sacrificial temper. When the Christian man shouts, "Praise the Lord," "Amen," or "Hallelujah," he utters a fool's language to those who have never been in his temper. It is a foreign tongue to them, which they can only answer by foolish mocking. But there are times in the religious experience when only such a word as Hallelujah—a word not to be explained in smaller terms—expresses the dominant feeling of the excited and grateful soul.

Have you seen Christ's star in the East? That is a sight which we may never behold, but we may see a greater sight than that. We may see himself. It is only the accidental that drops off—such words as "young," "child," "Bethlehem," "star"—fall away into their proper insignificance, but such words as "born," "King," "Christ," "Redeemer," "sin," "salvation"— abide with a most indestructible permanence in human recollection. It will be a happy day when we are more eager to see Christ than we are to see any symbol of him that could be found, either in the heavens or on the earth. I do not want you, as my fellow-students of his Word, to care about baptism and the Lord's supper, and the Sabbath-day, and the church built with hands—except as these may lead you further into the inner sanctuary where Christ himself is enthroned. If I found men now earnestly searching the heavens with the most scientifically constructed telescopes, that they might find a star resembling what the Persian sages saw, that they, too, might follow its guiding light to some distant Bethlehem, I would say to them:

> Christ is not here nor there: he is not to be found in sign or symbol now, except in some low and momentarily convenient sense. He *himself* is with us; he is to be found in our consciousness, he is to be the answer to our sin, he is to be the satisfaction of our hunger, he is to be the light of our intellectual firmament, he is to be the glory of our spiritual hope.

What, then, is our supreme anxiety today? Is it to see the star or to see the Savior? Is it to make a prophetic calculation of years and months, or to go out of the heart searching for One who is the answer to sin and the balm for its cruel wounding? If you say, "Sirs, I would see Jesus" [see John 12:21], you will find him in the Holy Scriptures; you will find him in every Christian's experience, in proportion as it is enlarged and true; yes, you will find him in the very question itself, for no man ever asked that question with the sincerity and earnestness of fire, without the answer beginning the moment the question ended.

four

THE WISE MEN'S WORSHIP

Matthew 2:11-15

"THEY FOUND the young child with Mary, his mother." Surely this is an inversion of the right method of stating the case; judged by our little rules, pedantic and inadequate. A critic might here interpose and say, You have adopted the wrong order of sequence, you have inverted the proper method of statement. Instead of saying, Mary, the mother, and the young child, you have actually put the young child first, and thus you have inverted the order of time. Nor is this a slip, for I find the angel of the Lord adopting the same sequence, in the 13th verse, saying to Joseph, in a dream, "Take the young child with his mother," and afterwards in the 20th verse, the angel again says, "Arise, and take the young child and his mother," and, in the 21st verse, "Arise, and take the young child and his mother." The frequency of the repetition shows us that to indicate the young child first and the mother afterwards was not a literary slip.

When will we learn that life is larger than logic? When will we keep our little technical rules away from great providences and mysteries? We are ruined herein by our own exactness. The literalist can never be right in anything that challenges the highest efforts of the mind. He who is right in the mere order of words, after a pedantic law of rightness and accuracy, often misses the genius, the poetry, the overflowing and ineffable life of things. He boasts of his exactitude, he is very clever in defending himself against etymological and critical assaults, but he is vitally wrong. Within the limits which he has assigned for the movement of his powers he is right, but those *limits* themselves are wrong, and, therefore, it is possible to be partially right and yet to be substantially and vitally in error. He, for example, who says the earth stands still, is in a popular sense right, and yet his statement is absolutely wrong.

If we could apply this great thought of the largeness of life to the interpretation of Scripture, we should not be fretted by many of those petty and distracting criticisms which bring down heaven to the scale of earth, and vex us with unworthy controversies. The rule is Christ *first*—the young child mentioned at the top of every list. "He was before all things, and by him all things consist." If he is Alpha, he is Omega; if he is the young child, he is the Ancient of Days. He takes precedence of the whole universe, for he was before it—he laid its foundations, and arched its canopies. Refrain, therefore, from little and dwarfing criticisms as to chronological sequence, and abandon those neat exactitudes which, by their very superficial claim to being considered right, may prevent the entrance into the mind of the larger light and the broader revelation.

When the wise men came into the house they fell down and *worshiped* the young child. They did not fall down and worship Mary—they hardly saw the mother. Who can see anything but Christ when he is there? To see anything in God's house but God is to waste the opportunity. The wise men worshiped the young child, they did him homage, they bent before him, they became oblivious of themselves in his presence; not a word might they say, for worship when deepest is often silent. Words are to blame for the thousand controversies that afflict and distress the Church. I would to God we could do without words, for who can understand even his friend? Who can catch the subtle emphasis, who has eyes quickened to see the coloring of the word, and sagacity to set it in its right place, so as to lose nothing of its rhythm, and harmony, and sweet intent? Whatever the word worship may mean here, religiously—for that word is used ambiguously both in the classics and in Scripture—it is evident that the wise men offered homage to the young child. The right attitude of wisdom is to bend before Christ, to be silent in his presence, to wait for him to lead the conversation. If wisdom venture to utter its voice first, it ought to be in inquiry or in praise. Wisdom is always reticent of speech; it is the fool who chatters, the wise man thinks. When Socrates was told that he was the wisest man in the world, he ran away, and yet returned to accept the compliment, for, said he, "I knew that I knew nothing, and I have met with no other man so wise."

If we come into the house where Jesus Christ is, our business is to imitate the wise men who came from the Far East, namely to bend the knee, to put our hand over our eyes, lest we be blinded by the great light, to be silent, to wait. It would be well, if in our brief time of worship we could set aside a few minutes for absolute silence. No minister to speak, no organ to utter its voice, no hymn to trouble the air. If we could, with shut eyes and bent head, spend five minutes in absolute speechlessness, that would be prayer, that would be worship. The fool would misunderstand it, and think nothing was being done, but as the last expression of velocity is rest, so the last expression of eloquence is silence, and sometimes the highest liturgy is to be dumb. We have banished the angel of silence, the angel of quietude is a nuisance to our fussy civilization; we have set noise in the front, and silence has been exiled from the Church.

Not only did the wise men worship Christ, they presented unto him *gifts*, "gold and frankincense and myrrh." This is the method of love. Worship is *giving*, it is not receiving. We are never to see Christ without giving him *ourselves*. Jesus Christ does not seek the homage of a courteous recognition, he seeks the loyalty of absolute *sacrifice*. The wise men gave him all they had, and Jesus Christ never says, "Hold, you have given enough." Never, till the heart's last fiber is given to him, and the last red blood-drop falls upon his hand—then, having received us in the totality of our being, his soul is satisfied.

"And being warned of God in a dream that they should not return to Herod, they departed into their own country another way." God is in continual communication with the right-minded. He speaks to them by starry eloquence. He speaks to them in words and visions and dreams. He is a God nigh at hand, and not afar off to all those who are rightly disposed towards him and whose hearts rise up in vehement desire to know his will. He will be as near us as our desire is pure: the fire of our earnestness will be, as it were, the measure of his readiness to come and give us guidance and defense. He spake to the wise men in a dream. We have debased the word dream, and then we ask one another with a hilarious skepticism if we believe in *dreams?* What word have we not fouled and despoiled, and then, having brought it to its smallest significances, we have turned around and asked if we believe that such terms can be measured by divine revelations? By overfeeding, we have brought upon ourselves all the distresses of dyspeptic nightmare, and having come out of the nightly struggle, we say, "Now do you suppose that there is any truth in dreams?" See how the argument is put upon a false center, see how, first, we *waste* the inheritance, and then demand its value!

What does the word dream signify? Not a nightmare, not the incoherences and ravings of a disordered brain, resulting from overfeeding. It means the outgoing of the soul towards the invisible, distant, spiritual, incomprehensible, eternal. We have lost the dream out of the Church. We have lost *everything*—prophecy, tongues, miracles, songs, gifts of healing, helps, governments, enthusiasms, heroisms—we have lost them all! It is just like us—fools, we ought never to have been trusted with anything! What have we left now? Nothing. Miracles gone, prophecy gone, the devil gone, God—GOING. As for dreams, we have long survived their foolish means of communicating with the invisible. As for dreams, we despise them, and laugh mockingly over our hot coffee, and ask one another if we believe in dreams! Reclaim the original signification of the term, rebuild the shattered inheritance, and then ask the great question, and you shall have a great reply.

The dream stands for that grandest of all powers, the religious imagination. That, again, is a word which must be used with great guardedness, because the word imagination has itself been stripped, wounded, and left half-dead. Who can now define imagination with the original fire and with the original grandeur? We abuse and misapply the terms. We now say, speaking of a man who makes false suppositions, "He *imagines* things." When we so use the word, we use it with improper limitations, and in short we give a wrong turn to the term. No wonder, therefore, that we are afraid to use the grand word Imagination in any religious sense. It is only a man in a century or two who is really gifted with imagination. Imagination is a *creative* faculty, imagination *images* the unimaged, gives visibility and palpableness to the immaterial, the unmeasured and the unnamed.

When we charge certain persons with having no imagination they start and say, "If we have one faculty more than another, it is imagination." When we ask them to provide the proof, what do they reply? They mistake description for imagination: thus they will describe an object as blue on one side and yellow on the other and surmounted by a coronal of red, and then they will claim for their speech the sublime epithet of imagination! It is a house painter's imagination. It is the imagination of a man who paints rustic signs for rustic inns. Imagination!—it is God's supreme gift to the human mind. When a thought presents itself to the intelligence, imagination *bodies* it, gives it form, configuration, color, and enters into high dialogue with the strange and most wondrous guest. Most of us have no imagination; the next best gift we can have is to listen with patience rising into delight, to the man to whom God has given this great gift, of making the dumb speak, and calling into visibility the unseen and impalpable.

The wise men "departed into their country another way." God knows the way into your countries and kingdoms, however distant they may be. You have made a high road out of your Persia into the distant Judea, how will you get back again? Why, by the same road—there is no other, say you, in conscious wisdom concerning the whole topographical arrangement. The angel of the Lord says, "I will show you the way home: not one step of the old road shall you take, I will make a way for you." Do not say there is no way out of your difficulty. It is a family difficulty, or a difficulty imperial or ecclesiastical, or a difficulty upon which you can take no human counsel. Do not, therefore, say that your way is passed over from your God, that you have been brought into a *cul de sac*, and must bruise your heads against the resisting and defiant walls. Stand still, and say, "Lord, show me thy salvation: take me home by another way: I thought this was the right road, I find that my thinking has been misinformed, or that circumstances have arisen which throw my calculations into perplexity and environ my life with strange and mighty opposition. Lord, I will not move one inch until thou dost lead the way." Say you so— is that your heart's sweet litany? No weapon that is formed against thee shall prosper. "Commit thy way unto the Lord: trust also in him and he shall bring it to pass. Oh, rest in the Lord and wait patiently for him, and he shall give thee thy heart's desire" [see Ps. 37:4–7].

This incident shows us in how many ways God interposes in human affairs. The angel of the Lord *warned* the wise men, and he also warned Joseph. There is a ministry of warning in our life. Why that sudden start? You cannot explain it. It was a frightening angel that looked upon your life for a moment, and by his look said, "Not this way—straight on." Why tear up the program on which you have spent months? You cannot explain why, but a voice said to you, "That program is all wrong, tear it to pieces and throw it into the fire: there is danger there. Beware, take care. Not this road. Trust not your own understanding. That program is a witness to your folly and shallowness: throw it away from you as you would throw away poison, and stand empty-handed before God, and ask him to write the way." "In all thy ways acknowledge him, and he shall direct thy paths. Lean not to thine own understanding" [see Prov. 3:5].

Sometimes God sends warnings to us in extraordinary ways by extraordinary people and under improbable circumstances. I am conscious of the presence of this warning ministry in my life, though I have no words subtle and keen enough wherewith to express all that I feel on that solemn subject. Shall I shake hands with yonder man? I think I will, he looks healthy, he looks kind, and yet in the midst of all these hopeful observations, my hand takes sudden palsy and I will not shake hands with him, and cannot. How so? There is a warning angel in my life. I, poor unsuspecting fool, would shake hands with every man who smiles upon me, for I have no eye for the detection of the villain's cheek, but the warning angel says, "Take care, go aside, he is an attractive apple—but rotten at the core."

Not only is there a warning ministry in this incident, there is also a *watching* ministry. The angel of the Lord watched Herod, watched the young child and his mother, watched the wise men. O those watchers that fill the air—your mother, your child, your friend, your guardian angel—everyone of us has a guardian angel, to be seen only with the eyes of the soul's inspired imagination. They watch us night and day. "Are they not all ministering spirits, sent forth to minister for them who shall be heirs of salvation?" [Heb. 1:14]. I am alone, yet I am not alone, for God's angel is with me. Do not live a little fleshly life, do not shut yourselves up within the limits of your constabulary arrangements and imagine that no eye is upon you but the eye of detective and suspicious law. Love watches, redemption, embodied in Jesus Christ, watches, we are beset behind and before, and there is a hand upon us, and a kind eye is behind the cloud, looking now and again upon our life, and flashing a tender morning ray upon our long-bound and darkness-wearied souls.

Learn from the next passage in the incident, that man's simple business in perplexity is to *obey*. "Joseph arose and took the young child and his mother by night, and departed into Egypt." Obedience sometimes requires *activity*. The angel said, "Arise and flee." That is the easiest part of obedience. There is no difficulty about fleeing, about exerting oneself; the blood heats, and activity is delight. God puts these calls to activity into our life at the right times and with the right measure of appointment. Why, you say, you would have died on the dear friend's coffin, but that you were obliged to arouse yourself to attend to his last rites. Kind is the way of God even in these matters. When death darkens your window and turns your day into night it always says to you, "Arise and flee, work, arrange, settle," and one of the first things you have to do in the midst of your intolerable agony is to stir yourself. In that stirring there is sometimes salvation.

After activity comes *patience*. The angel said, "And be thou there until I bring thee word." That is the *hard* part of life. While I am climbing the mountains, passing through the wildernesses, daring dangers, I feel comparatively quiet, or even glad. But to sit down when the angel tells me to sit, and not to stir till he comes back again—who can do it? I inquire of the first man who comes near me, whether I cannot get away out of Egypt? He says he thinks I can if I try the next turn, and I, disobedient soul, move towards the next turn, and if a wolf sent of God did not show its gleaming teeth at me there, I would be off, so fond am I of activity and self-direction, and so impossible is it to me to sit still and see the outworking of the divine will.

The true interpretation of human purposes is from God. Herod said, "I will worship him, when you bring me word." The angel said, "Herod will seek the young child to destroy him." Herod said *worship*—Herod meant *destroy*. The angel knows our meaning: God does not take our words always in the sense in which we offer them. He reads between the lines, he peruses the small print of the motive and of the inward and half-revealed or even half-formed desire. He shows us to ourselves. Sometimes when we say *worship*, he shows us by an analysis of our own acceptance of the term, that *destroy* is the proper meaning of our language. Lord, interpret my speech to me: I use words of false meaning, I think sometimes I mean to be religious—show me that some religions are lies, and that some prayers are offenses. Save me from being my own lexicographer: when I write a word, do Thou, gentle Father, ever wise, write after it its true and proper meaning.

The young child, Mary and Joseph, are now, at this point of the incident, away in Egypt. There are times of *retreat* in every great life, times when Christ must be driven into Egypt, when the prophet must be banished into solitude, when John the Baptist must be in the desert eating locusts and wild honey, when Saul of Tarsus must be driven off into Arabia—times when we are not to be found. An asylum need not be a tomb, retreat need not be extinction. For a time you are driven away—make the best of your leisure. You want to be at the front, instead of that you have been banished to the rear: it is for a wise purpose. Gather strength, let the brain sleep, yield yourself to the spirit of the quietness of God, and after what appears to be wasted time or unprofitable waiting, there shall come an inspiration into thy soul that shall make thee strong and fearless, and the banished one shall become the center of nations.

five

LESSONS FROM CHILD-LIFE

Matthew 2:16–23

"THEN HEROD, when he saw that he was mocked of the wise men" —
yet the wise men did not mock him at all! When will people get away
from the region of secondary causes, and understand that life has a divine center and that all things are governed from the throne of heaven?
It is not only a philosophical mistake to drop into second causes for the
purpose of finding the origin of our miseries, it sometimes, yea often,
becomes a practical mischief, a sore and terrible disaster of a personal
and social kind. Therefore with great urgency would I drive men away
from secondary lines and intermediate causes, to the great cause of all —
God, and King, and Lord, and Christ. Herod was mocked, vexed from
heaven, troubled from the center of things. The fog that fell upon his
eyes came downwards, not upwards; it was a blinding mist from him who
sends upon men delusions as well as revelations.

We have ourselves been mocked of God, and we have taken vengeance
upon human instrumentalities. If we insist upon having our own way,
there is a point at which God says, "Take it, and with it take the consequences." If we resolutely and impatiently say, "We will find success along this line and no other," God may say to us, "Proceed, and find
what you can." And at the end of that line, what have we found? A great
rock, a thousand feet thick, and God has said, "You may find success
if you will thrust your hand through that granite." So we have been
mocked. We have determined to proceed along a certain course, notwithstanding the expostulations of heaven, and having gone mile after
mile, what have we found at the end of the course? A great furnace, and
God has said to us with mocking laughter, that has shaken the skies, "Your

success is in the middle of that furnace: put your hand right into the center and take it,"—knowing that he who puts his hand in there, takes it out no more.

In proportion, therefore, as we are mocked and vexed, as we come back from the wilderness, bringing with us nothing but the wind, as we return from the mountains bringing with us nothing but a sense of perplexity, it becomes us to ask serious questions about our failure. *Who* mocked us? Not men, not women—we were laughed at from heaven. There is no passage of Scripture which has upon me so weird an effect as that which says that God will mock at our calamity, and laugh when our fear cometh. We have seen his tears—they baptized Jerusalem, they have fallen in gracious showers upon the graves that hold our heart's treasure, but we have never heard his *laugh*. There is a human laughter that turns us cold—God forbid we should ever hear our Divine Father's laughter, when the great fire-waves swell around us and all heaven seems to be pleased with the discomfort of our souls.

When Herod saw that he was mocked of the wise men, what did he do? Let us suppose that the passage is interrupted at that point and that we are required to continue the story in our own way. Now let us set our wits to work to complete the sentence which begins with "When Herod saw that he was mocked of the wise men." Let me suggest this continuation—He saw a *religious mystery* in this matter, and said, "This is not the doing of the wise men, there is a secret above and behind and around this, which I have not yet penetrated: I am troubled, but it is with religious perplexity. I will fall down upon my knees, I will outstretch mine arms in prayer, and will cry mightily to God to visit me in this crisis of my intellectual distress and moral consternation." Let me now turn and see how far my conjecture is right. "Then Herod, when he saw that he was mocked of the wise men, was exceeding wroth, and sent forth and slew." The power of wickedness is *physical*, the power of goodness is *moral*. Wickedness says, "A sword"; goodness says, "A pen."

We know that this narrative is true in the case of Herod, because it is made true everyday *in our own experience*. When we are vexed and mocked and disappointed, we do exactly what Herod did—we grow very angry, and slay. You need not consult the ancient historians to know whether Herod really did this work or not, when we ourselves are doing it everyday of our vexation and disappointment. We all play the fool under such visitations. Not unless we are regenerated by God the Holy Ghost and cleansed through and through by the atoning blood do we rise to the high dignity and grandeur of moral dominion and spiritual conquest.

There are two victories possible to us, the one is physical, the other is moral. I want this child to attend public worship. I say to the child, "You *must*: if you refuse I will *scourge* you until you go to church. I am older, I am stronger than you are, and you shall feel the supremacy of my age and the oppressiveness of my strength. To church I will *make* you go." I have succeeded, the child is in the church today. The child is here, but NOT here! By a perverse will the child is turning this church into a desecrated place. The child's *will* is not here, nor is the child's *love* present with us: our prayers have been burdensome, and God's own word has lost its music, because of the constraint under which that attendance has been enforced.

Let me take the case of the child from another point. I have been dwelling upon the advantages of going to church; I have been speaking about God and God's love, Christ and Christ's cross, about the tender music and the beautiful word and the loving gospel, and I have said to the child, "I should like you to go: it would make my heart glad if you did go—I only *ask* you, I do not *force* you." And the child has said, "Certainly I will go; show me the way, I should be *glad* to go." The child is here, every blood-drop in his heart is here, his eyes are rounding into a great wonder, and his breast heaving with an unusual but most glad emotion. Which is the conquest? The conquests of force exhaust themselves and perish in ignominious failure, the conquests of love grow and increase with the processes of time.

When Herod saw that he was mocked of the wise men, he was very angry, and ordered to kill all the children that were in Bethlehem. The power of evil is *destructive*, the power of goodness is *preservative*. We need direction in the qualities and uses of strength. It is easy to destroy: even a beast can crush a flower, but no angel in all the heavens can reset the broken joint. We mistake destructiveness as a sign of power. What power there is in the act of destructiveness is of the lowest and coarsest quality. You cannot drive evil out of men by any merely negative and destructive process. If you call out "Repent," you must immediately follow the word with "For the kingdom of heaven is at hand" [Matt. 3:2; 4:17]. The call to repentance is in a sense a negative call, the announcement that the kingdom of heaven is at hand is the positive and affirmative call, which tends to the upfilling of the emptied heart with the better dominion, the sanctuary from heaven. You may cut down all the weeds in your garden, but if you do not attend to that garden, putting in the place of that which was noxious that which is useful, the old roots will reassert themselves and your garden will become a scene of confusion. Jesus does not destroy without creating. If we suppress anything we do not believe in, we ought to set up in its place influences of a higher and nobler kind. It is no use for you, my friends, to empty the saloon unless you open some other place that shall attract within its better limits those whom you have expelled. It is of no use you driving the devil out of a man unless you have something to put into the man. That devil will wander about and will return and bring with him seven worse than himself, and the end of the man will be worse than the beginning.

"Then was fulfilled that which was spoken by Jeremiah the prophet, saying, In Rama was there a voice heard, lamentation, and weeping, and great mourning," distress night and day, the cry of pain and the moan of agony. The result of selfishness is human distress, the result of goodness is good-will towards men. See then what the world would come to under a selfish rulership. Selfish rulership says, "If I cannot have my own way easily, I will have it at all costs and hazards." Selfish rulership will purchase its own ends at any costs of mourning, lamentation, and weeping. Thus the bad man seems to succeed more than the good man; his way is rougher, his manners are ruder, he destroys, he does not create, and it is always easier to pull down than to build up. Jesus Christ proceeds slowly because of the depth and vitality and permanence of his work. It is easier to curse than to pray. Under Herod the world would become a scene of selfish triumph; under Christ it would become a family united by tenderest bonds, made holy by mutual and sympathetic love, and sacred by the exercise of those obligations which elevate and ennoble human nature. I ask you, therefore, today, as the end of this part of the exposition—who is to be King, Herod or Christ, violence or persuasion, force or love, selfishness or beneficence? The choice is sharp, the division is distinct: he who would seek to muddle and confuse these distinctions, is not the friend of progress, he is the victim of a mischievous pedantry. The world can only be under one of two kings, God—mammon, Christ—Herod, beneficence—selfishness. Choose ye; put high his banner over your life and let it float so that men can see it from afar.

In the next paragraph of our text we find the appearance of an angel of the Lord in a dream. The angels are ever mindful of the good. "Are they not all ministering spirits, sent forth to minister for them who shall be heirs of salvation?" [Heb. 1:14]. You say you have had no experience of angel ministry: be careful what you say, lest you narrow yourselves unduly by the mere letter, and miss the poetry and grandeur of your life. You say you are bound by things visible and palpable, and beyond those things do not venture to go. I am not asking you to venture to go any distance beyond those limitations, but I am asking you to allow God the power to come to you by any one of a series of innumerable ministries. You must not "limit the Holy One of Israel." The question is not, What can *I* do? It is, What can *God* do?

I could imagine a little boy with his arithmetic saying that all things that could be reckoned up, in space and in quantity, were reckonable upon the basis of his book of figures. He begins and ends with the multiplication table; he says the multiplication table ends at twelve times twelve, and beyond that he will never go. He is not going to be wise above what is written: if any man should venture to ask him how many are thirteen times thirteen, he would shudder with arithmetical aversion, and reply that thirteen times thirteen was not to be found in the multiplication table. Would he be *right?* He would be as far *wrong* as possible! Thirteen times thirteen is as much in the multiplication table as two times one or five times five. He will find that out by-and-by. He thinks he is keeping himself within due limits and must not transgress certain boundaries, when he says the table ends at twelve times twelve. He is going to be arithmetically orthodox: other people may dream about thirteen times thirteen if they please, he thinks that inquiry involves a very grave responsibility; he shrinks from their society, and he concentrates himself with renewed ardor to the four corners of the table that begins at one times one and ends at twelve times twelve. Is he arithmetically pious and arithmetically orthodox? He is arithmetically narrow and arithmetically bigoted and arithmetically foolish!

By-and-by he will advance further. I will say to him, "What is the square root of twenty-five?" And he will say, "Anybody knows that the square root of twenty-five is five." "What is the square root of *negative a?*" "Ah, I do not go into that sort of thing at all." "But there is a science which tackles questions of *that* kind." The boy replies, "I know nothing about it; I do not want to be wise above that which is written. I can give you the square root of one hundred in a moment, but the square root of *minus a*—he must be a very presumptuous and arrogant person to discuss such a question! If it be not presumptuous, which it appears to me to be, it is exceedingly foolish." He lives within his arithmetic, he does not know that there is another science just over it, which undertakes to find out sums by signs, and to discuss deep problems by letters and symbols that appear to be foolish to those who have never entered their higher education.

When I come to these angel ministries, they baffle me. I say "They are not in my arithmetic, they are not in the multiplication table." Let me never forget that algebra continues and perfects common arithmetic, and let me never forget that even beyond algebra itself are methods of calculation unknown to those who are in the lower ranges of human thought. I must not set *myself* up as the measure of all things. If the Bible comes to me with angel ministries, with assurances of what has been done by angels and through the medium of dreams, by high efforts of the religious imagination, I must not play the boy-fool by saying that reckoning ends with twelve times twelve; I must remember that the universe is larger than I have yet imagined it to be, and that there are men who are older and wiser, and it is not for me to say God's ministry begins here and ends there. I love to live in an enlarging universe, I love the horizon which tempts me to touch it, and then vanishes to an infinite distance.

The angel of the Lord said, "They are dead which sought the young child's life." The good have everything to hope from *time*, the bad have everything to fear from it.

The bad man is in haste, the good man rests in the Lord and waits patiently for him. The bad man says, "It must be done now; my motto is '*ad rem*,'—now or never, strike the iron while it is hot, let passion have its way instantaneously." They that believe do not make haste, they are calm with the peace of God; they trust time; they say, "All things will be fulfilled in the order of duration and the process of the suns." Innocence can wait. Innocence can go into any land and tarry there until sent for by the angel; innocence can go into any prison and wait not till helped by a butler, but until sent for by the king. If thou art innocent, be quiet; if thou art really good at the core, through and through, simple-minded, honest in motive, pure in purpose, high and sacred in ambition, wait; thy funeral will not be first.

Yet another fear fell upon the mind of Joseph. When he heard that Archelaus reigned in Judea, under the inferior title of Ethnarch, in the room of his father Herod, he was "afraid to go thither." There are some families of which we are afraid: there are whole generations that seem to be blighted with a common taint. There are some chains whose links are all bad. Joseph thought that Archelaus might inherit the prejudices and hostilities of his father. There was no need for him to do so. Thank God, a man may break away from his own family, a child may be a stranger to his own father. Thank God for these possibilities of beginning again. I see what is called *fate* in the order and destiny of men: I have taken hold of the chain and find it to be thick and strong—yet I see also the wonderful *liberties* of men, so that they can detach themselves from a melancholy and shameful past on the part of others, and begin again, by themselves, under God's blessing and direction, for themselves. Was your *father* a bad man? You may be a good *son*. Fear not, do not droop under the blighting cloud. If it be in your heart to be better and you mention this purpose in prayer to God, your father's name shall rot, and yours shall be a memorial of goodness and hope, as long as the sun endures.

They are DEAD which sought the young child's life. That is always the ending of wickedness: that is the history of all the assaults that ever have been made upon Jesus Christ and his kingdom. I have seen great armies of men come up against the young child, and behold they have perished in a night, and in the morning the angels have said to one another, "They are DEAD which sought the young child's life." I have seen armies of infidel books come up to put down Christianity, to expose it, and refute it and cut it to pieces, and destroy it as Herod's sword the children of Bethlehem, and lo, in twelve months not one of them could be found, and the angels have said to one another, "They are DEAD which sought the young child's life." I have seen critics come up with keen eye and sharp knife, and a new apparatus adapted to carry out its processes and purposes of extermination, and behold the critics have cut their own bones and died of their own wounds, and the angels have said, "They are DEAD that sought the young child's life." I have seen whole towns of new institutions, created for the purpose of putting down the Christian Church. All kinds of competitive buildings have been put up at a lavish expenditure, the preacher was to be put down, the Bible was to be shut up, the old hymn-singing was to be done away with, a new era was to dawn upon the wilderness of time, and lo, the bankruptcy court had to be enlarged to take in groups of new mendicants, for they DIED that sought the young child's life!

No man ever died who sought the young child's saving ministry: no man ever died who went to the young child and said, "My Savior, thy grace is greater than my sin, pity me and lift me out of this deep pit by the hand of thy love." The angels never said about such a one, "He is dead who offered that prayer."

No dead man is found at the foot of the cross, they live who touch that tree, they are immortal who open their hearts to receive that baptism of blood, they are a triumphant host that take hold of hands around the young child.

He is always young; he is always in bloom. Time cannot wither him: as for custom it cannot "stale the infinite variety" of his ministry and his worship. God delights in youth: there is no wearying in the duration of goodness—wickedness runs down into exhaustion, goodness runs up into renewal of efflorescence and beauty, and eternal spring.

NOTES

1. "December 25th was not kept as a festival in the East till the time of Chrysostom, and was then received as resting on the authority of the Roman church."—*Ellicott's Test.*

2. "Herod the Great—Son of Antipater. An Idumean by an Arabian Aristobulus. Died in the 70th year of his age, the 38th of his reign, and the 750th year of Rome."

3. ARCHELAUS—"Mother was Malthaké, a Samaritan. After a cruel and disturbed reign (under the title of Ethnarch) of about eight years he was banished to Vienna, in Gaul—the modern Vienne. His dominions, including Samaria, Judea, and Idumea, then passed into the direct government of Rome."

Verse 22. "He turned aside."—"The English 'Anchorite' is derived from the Greek word in the original."

Verse 23. "He shall be called a Nazarene."—"The passage gains fresh interest from the fact that the early Christians were called Nazarenes in Rome (Acts 24:5). For them it would be a point of triumph that their enemies thus unconsciously connected them with a prophetic title of their Master."

4. "THE CHILDREN OR DESCENDANTS OF HEROD THE GREAT mentioned in the New Testament are—(1) Archelaus, (2) Herod Antipas, Tetrarch of Galilee [Matt. 14:1; Mark 6:14; Luke 3:1; 13:31; 23:7], (3) Philip Tetrarch of Iturea; [Luke 3:1], (4) Herod Philip, husband of Herodias, [Matt. 14:3; Mark 6:17], (5) Herod Agrippa, grandson of Herod [son of Aristobulus, one of the sons Herod put to death {Acts 12}], (6) Agrippa II, son of No. 5; [Acts 25:13], (7) Herodias, sister of No. 5; [Matt. 14:3], (8) Salome, daughter of No. 7 [not *by name* {Matt. 14:6; Mark 6:22}], (9) Bernice and (10) Drusilla, daughters of No. 5 [Acts 25:23; 24:24]."

six

A REVIEW OF MATTHEW 2

Matthew 2

THE SECOND chapter of Matthew is a record of *trials*. Everybody engaged in the tragedy seems to have been pierced through and through with the same sharp sword. This is the more wonderful, seeing that the object of the chapter is to set up *the kingdom of heaven* amongst men. One would have supposed that with a purpose so lofty and so beneficent, the career would have been one perfectly clear of all difficulty, broadening like a dawning day, and offering to everyone engaged a right hearty welcome, and crowning each toiler with a gentle and loving benediction. If the people engaged in this exciting narrative had been about to do something very *bad*, we would have followed their punishment with keen interest, and after each infliction of the deserved blow we would have said, "This is merited; no man can do wrong and yet enjoy prosperity." But nothing of the kind is here. With one exception everybody wants to do what is *good* so far as the kingdom of heaven is concerned, and yet everyone engaged in this marvelous development of human history is smitten, pierced, thrown down, banished, or otherwise visited with some heavy and inexplicable penalty. This chapter is a record of trials, and these trials acquire a keener accent and a more painful significance from the fact that they all occur in connection with the establishment of a beneficent kingdom, whose avowed object is the salvation and holiness and infinite blessedness of all who accept its dominion.

There are trials purely *personal*, for example those of Joseph and Mary. Mary comes into the story by the pressure of an infinite destiny. She does not ask to be an actress in this scene—she is modest; violet-like she seeks the shade, she craves for no renown, she does not ask to be put in the forefront of any battle or contest. Yet to a variety of pains is added the agony of misunderstanding and banishment, suspicion of the foulest kind, and abandonment by those who should have loved her most. This, in connection with setting up the Christly kingdom on the earth! Our narrow, short-sighted sympathy says she might have been *spared* this; an angel might have rolled a white cloud for her to sit upon as upon a throne. Instead of this, behold the severity of her lot, behold what unmerited punishment darkens her little patch of sky and makes her earth barren and desolate, without green thing or root of promise.

And Joseph, a negative character, a man who is in, and yet hardly knows why he is in, the story, sustaining an incidental and relative position to it, wholly secondary, almost yet not altogether needless — even he is afflicted with great visions and great distresses, startled by unexpected ghosts, aroused from his sleep that he may be told to flee away as if he were an offender against human law and social decency. He must needs be up and flee like a thief in the night-time. And all this, in connection with introducing to the world the only Friend it ever had! These historical recollections would always be interesting to minds who study the unity of the human race, but they are more than interesting, they are religiously suggestive and comforting to those who remember that all these trials are repeated in the life of every honest man and woman today.

Then there were trials, *imperial* as well as personal. *Herod* was troubled. Not Herod the individual man, but Herod the *king*. His throne, which had been steady as a rock, began to quake under him, and he said, "What ghost is shaking this firm seat?" He was distracted, his mind was split in two, he was in perplexity, in intellectual vexation — he could not bring the pieces together and shape them into coherence and meaning. He was a shrewd man, a man to whom councilors appealed in the time of their perplexity, a man high in authority, to whom was committed the giving of great decisions; and yet something occurred in his history which brought a great blinding mist over his eyes. He mistook distance, proportion, color, he could see nothing as it really was; he rubbed his eyes to cleanse them of the mist, but it grew as he rubbed, and he was more blind at the end than at the beginning. And this, let us constantly remember, in connection with setting up a kingdom of light and peace, righteousness and love.

Instead of the king having the first revelation, and receiving that revelation as the earth receives the bright morning, he seems to have been left out of the count altogether. He stumbles into it, he does not walk lovingly and loyally into this inheritance. The revelation is a ghost, a flash of light, a rattle of thunder, a shaking of the throne, a darkening of the window, an overturning of the hot brain. Herod cannot speak coherently; all other questions have dwindled into commonplace or into trifles since this great inquiry thrust itself on his reluctant but startled mind. Hitherto he has sat on his throne or presided over his court, he has been attentive to everyone, and has meted out justice with an even hand, with a balance that could not be tampered with. He has acted in a manner that claimed and secured the confidence of those who were around him, but a question has arisen in his intellectual thinking which makes all other questions ordinary, and covers them with infinite contempt. Since that question arose and gave direction and color to his thinking, all the questions that he had hitherto thought to be great have fallen away from their eminence, and he can hardly command patience to consider and balance and decide the trifling inquiries. This again would be an interesting historical fact, if it were only confined to Herod himself, but it broadens into something greater, brightens into something more fascinating, when we remember that this trouble, vexation, or pain is repeated in the case of every king and every country receiving or inquiring about the Son of God.

Surely the trials end here? We must now have come to the end of the black catalogue. The light will come now. As a faithful expositor of the Word, I must say, not yet can the light come. There were trials personal, as in the case of Joseph and Mary; there were trials imperial, as in the case of Herod the king: I have to add, in pathetic and distressing culmination, that there were trials *domestic,* as in the massacre of the innocents. "Herod was exceeding wroth, and sent forth and slew all the children that were in Bethlehem and all the coasts thereof, from two years old and under." It was truly called the massacre of the innocents, it was making the many suffer for the one; it was a picture of the indiscriminate vengeance of excited and uncontrollable human nature. It was the thrust of a blind man who said, "I will strike who comes first, if haply I may strike the offender." Who can calculate the number of little ones slain by that fierce and cruel sword? Who can hear the mourning, lamentation, great weeping and distress? We stand more than a thousand years away from those desolated homes; we can take with some comfort a tragedy two thousand years old, but that is to our shame and not to our honor. It is possible to set ourselves back along the historical line, far enough to sympathize with those whose children were given up to that unsparing sword. All this, let me say again, was in connection with the setting up of the kingdom of Jesus Christ upon the earth! A sword through his mother's heart, a shadow across the path of his reputed father, a king smitten by invisible lightning, troubled as with a cloud terrible with the presence of innumerable ghosts, homes made black because of the death of little children. All this was not in our reckoning. This never came into our dream. No poet dare have dreamt this poem; it would have damned his reputation. Truth is stranger than fiction, reality is hardly reached by poetry; when it is the highest poetry of all it is the most real, it touches heights which men call insanity.

What then have we, as Christian readers, to say about these trials in their relation to the kingdom of heaven? I have three things to say about them, and the first is that the kingdom of heaven, as represented by Jesus Christ, was *not responsible* for them. It is a fine matter, is this allotment of responsibility. We are sometimes occasions without being causes. Who is responsible for the pain suffered by that poor man whose limb is being amputated at this moment? Do we say, "Cruel surgeon, why do you inflict such pain on a fellow creature"? We do not hold the surgeon responsible for the agony of the sufferer: he may be the occasion of it, but he inflicts agony that he may save from some greater distress. You must look into causes preceding the ministry of the surgeon; the limb was beginning to putrefy — it was momentary agony or death, and the surgeon beneficently advised the infliction of transient pain. When he said, "Cut off the limb," he did not say it loudly or unfeelingly, he spoke the language of sympathy and beneficence. Let us know that in all our education and uplifting pain is unavoidable, because of the moral condition into which we have brought ourselves. When the father uses the rod upon the criminal child, does he inflict the pain cruelly? He inflicts it beneficently. If he loved less he would strike less, if he were less loving he would be less severe. His very severity is an expression of his pity and yearning love.

It is hard to understand this, it cannot be defended as a mere theory; it is not open to any discussion that could be conducted in words, but it comes up as a great fact in the swelling human heart, that sometimes we are obliged to prove our love by our severity. When the Son of God came into the world there was no room for him: he had to make room for himself, and sometimes when a tree makes room for itself it overthrows old walls and strong buildings—those silent, ever swelling roots thrust out the masonry of man.

This leads me to say, in the second place, that these trials were part of *a happy necessity*. All education is but another word for pain, trial, trouble, discipline. The education that comes otherwise may disappear as it came. We learn by pain, we advance by strange and often intolerable agonies, we cannot understand why our ignorance should be driven away only by processes that tear and wear the finest sensibilities of the soul. Look back upon your education: oh the headaches, the smartings, the disappointments, the troubles, the evasions; and yet the result of the whole is wisdom. Your will was curbed at every point, your little plans were turned upside down, you were made to know that you must begin at this hour and work till that appointed time, or if not you must suffer the penalty. The tasks we had, the lines to commit to memory, the sharp visitations of the rod, the chidings and reproachings and scoldings and buffetings, the shamings with the uplifted finger of the mocking master, and yet now, somehow, it seems as if all these things worked together, being duly and lovingly controlled, to the formation of a massive and broad character not easy of destruction.

As civilization widens, trials multiply. You did not introduce the locomotive engine into civilization without a great massacre of innocents. When the locomotive engine took his breath and gave his first utterance into the startled air, what a slaughter there was all over the country of innocent speculators, innocent investors, innocent people of all kinds! What vested interests went down, what arrangements of stabling and hostelry and hospitality of every kind were knocked on the head! Every grand improvement in civilization means death as well as life, in proportion as a man or an improvement is great. No introduction can be effected into old habits or established upon old lines without great rending and tearing of things long-existent. No preacher could arise with any dominating power of light and wisdom without having to make room for himself and inflict pain upon many innocent people. He would not be otherwise admitted. He must come by fighting, battling, blood, fury, vehemence, for seven years be suspected and misunderstood and reproached, and only as the divinity is within him would he create his own space and liberty. His friends would be troubled, driven off into Egypt: all Herods would shake on their thrones, and innocent people of all kinds would be caught in a shower of stones. It is the mystery of civilization; it belongs to the widening course of things; it is true of all departments of life.

The third thing I have to say about these trials is that they imperfectly, yet definitely, represent the *greater trials of God* in the education and maintenance of his universe. He can do nothing without pain. He is tried everyday. He builds a wall around his vineyard and sets up a tower in it; and he comes at the appointed time to gather the grapes that he may crush them into wine for his heart's drinking, and behold the vineyard bringeth forth wild grapes. He nourishes and brings up children; the ox knoweth his owner, and the ass his master's crib, but his children do not know, do not consider; take their bread as if it had come from the earth, and not fallen from heaven; drink their unblest water, and sleep an irreligious slumber. He looks on from the heavens with a great face of trouble, more marred than the face of any man [see Is. 52:14]. He cannot rule his children without being insulted everyday. He cannot propose to add one beam of light to the glory which falls upon them without criticism that amounts to impiety, or without reproaches that add up to the sum total of blasphemy.

Let us not, then, suppose that these are merely historical trials, and that they have no counterpart in the current experience of the day or in the mysteries of the divine government of man. The glory of the New Testament is that it is new. I would not charge myself with boldness if I undertook to show that every line in this New Testament was printed only yesterday, so true is it to human life, so photographic of everything that is immediately around us, so ardent with the warmth of our own life, so throbbing with all that is quick in our own pulsations. Have you read the New Testament as an old book, say sixteen or eighteen hundred years old? I do not wonder that you have stumbled in many places and been caught in many a thicket, and in trying to disentangle yourself have come to great difficulty and distress. I read the New Testament as just written, just put into my hands, printed afresh with the ink of heaven every morning, and sent down for the day's guidance. It is the part of the Christian preacher to freshen old histories, to throw upon them the dew of the morning, and make them sparkle with immediate light.

What is true of these trials, so far as the establishment of the kingdom of Christ upon the broad earth is concerned, is painfully and often insufferably true of the setting up of the kingdom of heaven in the *individual heart*. It is not easy to go over from Baal to Jehovah. Some of us are now only on the road, with the journey merely begun, though we have been endeavoring for twenty-five years to take a step or two. Could I address some dear young heart looking upon these statements as great mysteries, that heart would say to me, "Oh, you must be such a happy man, you are free from all these trials and bitternesses, and are already in Beulah's fair land, blest with the spirit of peace, lighted with the glories of heaven, far above the cold winds and darkening fogs. You have accomplished the journey." To that sweet speech I should make a frank reply. For days, and weeks, and months dear child, I know not what joy is. Sometimes I feel as if I were worse now than I ever was in my whole Christian life before. My wonder is that I am not damned and put out of sight. God has hard work with me: it is difficult for him to build his temple in such a heart as mine: the devil will not let me lay one stone upon the top of another without trying to throw it down, the enemy will not let me get one whole prayer right clear out of me—he stands at my mouth to prevent the word, to twist the prayer. While I am in my highest moods of communion, he whispers to me with hot breath, "What a fool you are: this is mockery, this is emptiness: take your prayer back, you impious idiot, and use your breath for other work." Still the kingdom of heaven is going on in my heart; other voices say:

> Cheer thee; thy way is one of tribulation, but the end is peace. Fear not, they that are for thee are more than all they that can be against thee. God will accomplish his purpose little by little, but he will have the victory. Great are they that are against thee, greater they that are for thee. Hold up they head, fear not, the angel will break the power of the enemy, and out of thy distress shall come thy joy.

These words fall on the breaking heart with infinite healing, and comfort me with a sure hope. By-and-by we shall say to some watcher, fairer than the morning light, "What are these arrayed in white robes, and whence came they?" He will answer, "These are they that came out of great tribulation" [Rev. 7:13, 14]. Tribulation is another word for education if rightly accepted. Let me, then, cheer you and cheer myself. It is a hard fight, the trials are thick on the ground, the air is black with them, but we shall be "more than conquerors through him that loved us" [Rom. 8:37]. Be this your motto: *"The Sword of the Lord—and Forward!"*

seven

THE PREACHING OF JOHN THE BAPTIST

Matthew 3:1-6

IF YOU read the last verse of the second chapter—"And he came and dwelt in a city called Nazareth, that it might be fulfilled which was spoken by the prophets, He shall be called a Nazarene," and then read the first verse of the third chapter—"In those days came John the Baptist"—you might suppose that the two events followed one another within a very brief interval, whereas the fact is that *thirty years* intervened between the last verse of the second chapter and the first verse of the third. The heart is sad at that thought: we do not want the historian to take such wide leaps; we want him to take us down to Nazareth, and give us almost daily glimpses into that obscure but wondrous home. We long to overhear somewhat of the conversation that passes amongst its inmates; especially do we want to look at one with a human face, brightened often with divine flashes, and to listen to a voice like our own, yet much unlike it, so rich, so varied, so tender in pathos, so royal in command. Yet we stand here, at the opening of the third chapter (with one glimpse given by another writer,) with thirty years overleaped in silence that is to the imagination provoking.

"In those days came"—literally "in those days *cometh*," as if all the movement were continuous, without break or gap, as if there were no past tense, as if we lived in a perpetual present, as if history were a continuous breathing, not a succession of shocks, but a perpetual outgoing of the divine purpose and the heavenly will. We have broken up our grammar so that we now have present, past, perfect, pluperfect, and future, but there is another grammar in which there is but one mood and one tense, and it is Christ's purpose to draw us up into his own thinking, until all history and all developments, the whole sweep and current of things, shall

55

be to us a living indicative. You go back to take up the past, you break life up into sections, you cut it up into parentheses, you vex the flowing narrative with footnotes and marginalia, so that I am lost in this wondrous history of the race. He calms me by completing me, withdraws my attention from fractional times and momentary incidents, and fixes it upon the infinite oneness of the divine purpose and way.

In those days came John the *Baptist*. A *transient* name. The Baptist must die, the Congregationalist, the Presbyterian, the Episcopalian must die—his very *name* is indicative of the transientness of his coming and purpose. No man can be known by any one little accent of his case throughout immortality. When a man is so specialized the meaning is that his mission is here and gone, while you are speaking about him— a breath, a shock, a voice, an echo, a vacancy. Do you still follow the Baptist? Poor laggard, what business do you have in this nineteenth century with following the Baptist? He himself said his mission was introductory, symbolical, a plunge, and all was over. Why are you still dogging his steps, as if he had something to give you? He has eaten up the locusts and wild honey, and his raiment and his leather girdle are worn out and are not worth your picking up. O make haste to catch his Master!

Still, John has a mission, and a great one; and it will be our object to measure it in future expositions. John the Baptist came *preaching*—a term but little understood. There are few preachers, and ought to be few. There are too many who bear the name who do not understand the vocation. He is not a preacher who stands in one place year after year, talking to the same people, and overfeeding them with intellectual luxuries. Preaching, in the New Testament, is a term which means *heralding*, going up and down from east to west, crying, shouting, with a ringing voice, "Prepare!" He is the preacher who does so, who breathes through the herald's trumpet, and startles the stagnant air with shattering blast, and says, "The King! The King!" In our days we have degraded preaching into bending the head over a sheet of ill-written paper and mumbling it with very uncertain emphasis. In the New Testament the preacher is the shouting man. Many do not like shouting; many object to exclamation, but the true preacher is one who speaks with a loud voice: "Prepare! Look out! Attention!" After the homiletics or "preacher course" will come the teacher, the pastor, the expositor, the man whose business it is to stand in one place and unfold the infinite riches of the divine wisdom, but the preacher—defining that term in the light of the New Testament—is a herald, a man who has a proclamation in his hands, whose sermon is brief not because it is a speech well-composed and elaborate, but a cry, as of a man who should call *"Fire"* to a sleeping town.

"In those days came John the Baptist, saying, Repent ye, for the kingdom of heaven is at hand." The cry of all widening civilization has been *Repent.* Do not be startled with the word, as if it were a church term and a Bible word only; it is a word you cannot do without in the history of secular civilization. Do not sneer at the preacher when he says "Repent," as if he had picked up a fanatical word and were using it for fanatical purposes. What is the meaning of this word *repent*, as used in this connection? The meaning of it is, Change your purpose, alter your mind, turn around, do an about face, you are on the wrong road, *return!* It is the utterance of men who have a new proposition to make in politics, in commerce, in engineering, in all the ways and processes of advancing life. He who corrects the thinking of his age, having verified his own conclusions in privacy, comes forth and says to his era, "Repent, you are wrong, change your mind, alter your standpoint." When the word is taken up into the religious sphere, and invested with its vital meanings, it still continues the first signification, and enhances that signification with other meanings deeper and grander still. When a man repents of his sin, he knows the bitterness of inward sorrow, his heart weeps blood, his soul is afflicted with grievous distress on account of sin. Then the repentance expresses itself in an outward change of standing, attitude, and relationship, coming up out of an inward conviction wrought through infinite pain, and by ministries for which there are no words.

John's, then, was not a very *cheerful* ministry, or a very popular or comfortable one. It is more pleasant for me to come down to any assembly and say, "I approve all your doings, I confirm your proceedings, I endorse your policies, heaven's blessing shine upon you like a summer day!" He who comes with a speech of that kind to the populace, will, for the time being, be the popular idol. To come into the midst of a city, or to go up and down a land, crying "Repent," is to excite the most desperate prejudice. Who are you? Why this challenging tone? Prove your standing: where did you come from; what is the measure of your responsibility? Then will come insinuations as to sinister motive, and implications of dishonest or selfish purpose. Then the *you also* will be the weapon of the hour. The man whose little sermon is "Repent" sets himself against his age, and will for the time being be battered mercilessly by the age

whose moral tone he challenges. There is but one end for such a man—
"off with his head." You had better not try to preach repentance until
you have pledged your head to heaven.

The negativeness of this ministry accounts for what is popularly
termed the lack of *success*. John's ministry was to clear the ground; he
was a pioneer, he was a herald, he was one whose work was more or less
of a negative kind, or introductory at the best. Such men do not add up
to much in the sum total of vulgar arithmetic. When they are added up
into their total by *God* himself the sum is not inconsiderable. We have
reformers amongst us whose business it is to get men into a state of mind
to hear the gospel. Having heard the gospel and received it, the men who
conducted the introductory ministry are too often forgotten, as though
they had done next to nothing. Your business, it may be, is to go out and
persuade a man to alter his personal habits and his social relationships
so as to bring himself within the sound of the Christian gospel. He comes
to hear the minister; the minister, baptized with fire and clothed with
zeal, arrests the man, and makes him a prisoner of the law. It may be that
your outside and comparatively negative work is forgotten by men, but
God is not unrighteous to forget your work of faith and labor of love. Yours
is a preparational ministry; yours is introductory, and because introductory, more or less transient in its public effects and fame. Nevertheless
it is a ministry without which the Church cannot live. Persevere through
good report and through evil report, and come not to Time's low counter
for your pay, but to the judgment-seat of Christ.

Consider well what it is to preach the gospel of repentance. I would
rather preach the gospel of *comfort*; it would suit me personally better
to say to every man who hears me, "You are altogether right: all you need
is comfort, the kiss and seal of holy peace. Cheer you; it will be well with
you." To stand before any man, and say to him, "If we are to make solid
work we must begin with the fact that you are as bad as you can be" is
to excite prejudice and to create tremendous, if not insuperable, difficulty. Here is the disadvantage of the preacher; he has always to challenge his hearers, charge them with lack of integrity; his indictment is
heavy, every count of it rising above every other count before it in the
gravity of its impeachment. The lecturer comes before you with his kid
gloves and scented arrangements, and tells you how delighted he is to
have the opportunity of speaking to so large, enlightened, and influential
an assemblage. The preacher stands up and says, "Repent"; and who likes

to listen to a man whose voice is a charge, whose sentences are thunderbolts? Yet through this ministry of repentance we must all pass before we can enter into a ministry of reconciliation, and enjoy the infinite calm of God's own peace.

Yet John's ministry was not wholly negative. There is a positive element in it, and that should be carefully noted. He said, indeed, "Repent ye," but his deliverance did not end there. He added a reason, "for, or because the kingdom of heaven is at hand." Do not charge your hearer severely, so as to overwhelm him with intolerable sorrow. Having brought him to his knees in penitence, and broken his heart with contrition, and left him without a rag with which to cover the nakedness of his iniquity, tell him that the kingdom of heaven is at hand, intimating that his repentance is a sorrow that brings joy, that repentance is an introductory necessity, that it endures for a night, and joy cometh, bringing with it its own morning, a day that never dips into the darkness of eventide. So this heroic preacher, so severe, so terrible in aspect, so piercing and rending in voice, has a sweet, sweet tone—"The kingdom of heaven is at hand. The morning cometh, the summer dawns, the rain is over and gone, and the voice of the turtle is heard in the land. Attend, repent, change, turn round—for the kingdom of heaven is at hand." A challenge of moral integrity should always be associated with the presentation of a great opportunity. Tell a man to repent only, and leave him there, and you put a dart into his breast. Tell him to repent, and add that the kingdom of heaven, with all its light and healing and redemption, is at hand, and you preach to him something like a complete gospel. The indictment associated with the word repentance must be followed with the inspiration connected with the term, the kingdom of heaven.

"This is he that was spoken of by the prophet." Every preacher who deeply moves his age is a fulfillment of prophecy. The great man is always *to come*. History is a process of daily fulfillment of prophecy. We are always startled with conformations of the Divine Word, and when the right man comes, there is something about him which indicates his reality. My sheep know my voice. When a man hears the truth, there is something within him which says, "So it is." I may resent what you say to me, may put my imagination to great stress, for the purpose of getting up excuses and pleas in reply to your charges, when you accuse me of being guilty before God, yet all the while, deep down in my self-reproachful heart, I feel that you are right, and that my palliations do but add to my sin.

What was the *result* of this man's preaching, so far as this section of the history will enable us to judge? "There went out to him Jerusalem and all Judea, and all the region round about Jordan." See the power of *one* consecrated and burning heart. John was one—the whole valley of the river was shaken by his voice, and men poured around him from every quarter. Believe in *individuality* of labor, believe that you, solitary thinker, lonely teacher, preacher, reformer—that you in your solitude may have the power given you of God, of moving a whole age and inspiring a whole nation. Take the large view of your mission; do not be behind the very chief of the apostles, not in your own conceit, but in your interpretation of the breadth and grandeur of the divine call. Everywhere do I read of great results attending one man's ministry. One man is sometimes an army, one man is sometimes a congregation. Despise not the two and the three; there is a religion which can condescend to bless meetings of twos and threes: consider what condescension is a proof of the divinity of the doctrine. That which is artificial works for the artificial, that which is real works for the human, the vital, the image of God. Today we call out for thousands to hear us, and if the thousands are not there we think but little of the few who gather in the house of God. If we were in right mood of heart we should see in every little child an opportunity for preaching with all the fire that could burn in the heart of the most consecrated patriot or a twice-anointed minister of God.

Get away from the baptism of John as soon as you can. We are not always to be standing in introductory rites and ceremonial observances. Again and again would I say that the ministry of John was by its very constitution a temporary and not a permanent ministry. Is it possible that there are men and women amongst us today squabbling with one another about the matter of baptism? I am really not concerned by what method of baptism you were baptized—if you have been sprinkled by hands prelatic, or archiepiscopal—or if you have been completely immersed. Either method of baptism is meaningless, if it has not been followed by the true baptism of *blood* and *fire*. Into what baptism, then, have we been baptized? I believe that a sound argument can be set up in favor of the suggestion that in Christian baptism since the apostolic days there is *no water at all*. It does not say that you must have water in order to have baptism, but, my friend, if you want immersion, have it: if a few drops sprinkled on your forehead will suffice you, take it, but they are both nothing but ritualism, ceremonialism and superstition *if you do not seize the inner meaning,* cry for the laver of blood, and mightily implore God to visit you with the baptism of fire.

See that the baptism controversy does not freeze upon you, and encrust you as with ice, and make a bigot of you. The one baptism of which all other baptisms were indications, types and symbols, is the baptism of blood and the balm of fire.

eight

JOHN'S PREACHING (CONTINUED)

Matthew 3:7–12

THIS IS a wonderful, yet not difficult, change of tone in the speech of such a man as John the Baptist. His baptism was the sensation of the day. Everybody seemed to have more or less interest in it. Not to have heard it was to be misinformed or lacking in information, and not to have partaken of it was to have missed a great opportunity. All the valley of the Jordan was moved, people poured in from every center, great and small, in order that they might hear this new prophet, for a prophet had not appeared in Israel for five hundred years. Curiosity was touched, wonder was on the alert, national pride was excited, and a great and hardly expressed hope was moving the ambition of the people.

For a long time John seems to have pursued his baptismal course without interruption, and indeed with some signs of satisfaction. "There went out to him Jerusalem and all Judea, and all the region round about Jordan, and were baptized of him in Jordan, confessing their sins"—not, I imagine, confessing their sins in a minute and detailed manner, but generally acknowledging that they were not as good as they ought to have been, pleading guilty to a certain great, broad, general indictment, which all men probably over the civilized world are not unwilling to do. This was enough, as a starting point, in the case which John the Baptist represented. But when he saw many of the Pharisees and Sadducees coming to his baptism, the great and leading men of the day, pure in their own estimation, not needing any such ministry as he came to conduct, except in an official and ceremonial manner, it changed his tone; he cried aloud with piercing and ringing voice, "O brood of vipers, progeny of serpents, deceitful, cunning, malignant, empoisoned, how do you account for being here? Who hath warned you, called you, who hath entitled you to avail yourselves of this opportunity?" [see v. 7].

John was a man who recognized the possibility of people coming to religious ordinances from wrong motives. The people to whom he spoke did not come for purely religious purposes at all. They thought the baptism was something to be passed through in order to realize a great end. They accepted it as a little ceremonial, preceding some great national endowment or fulfillment of long delayed prophecy. John startled them, therefore, with the tidings that this was a religious ordinance, and that men can only avail themselves satisfactorily of religious ordinances in proportion as they come to them with religious motives.

Are the Pharisees and the Sadducees of the olden time the only people who have come to church through wrong motives? Is it possible that any of us can ever go to a holy place with unholy intent, or with a purpose infinitely below the grandeur of the opportunity? When I ask the questions I kill myself. Do I pierce any of your hearts, or wound, ever so slightly, any of your consciences? Whatever is religious must be touched religiously, or it will yield no true benefit or profit. You are not to touch the Bible as literary men, you are not to come to church as clever men, you are not to sit bolt upright as those who have a claim to judge in God's sanctuary. The true attitude is abasement, the spirit is contrition, the desire is a yearning for a purer and broader life. "To this man will I look—the man that is of a humble and contrite heart, and that trembleth at my word" [see Is. 66:2]. The haughty he will bow down, the wise he will confound and disappoint. He will look to the eager heart, the gentle, simple yearning spirit whose one object is to know God's will and to try to do it.

When men come to religious ordinances, they should be warned of the meaning of the action which they wish to accomplish. They should have a clear and most intelligent conception of the whole purpose of religious worship. It is the business of the heralds of the cross and the ministers of the truth to give this warning, to keep back those who have not the right credentials. This is a kingdom that can only be entered by one right, the right of sin, avowed, confessed, deplored. Blind man, your blindness is your certificate, you need no other. Broken-hearted, wounded man, your contrition or your penitence is your credential; seek for nothing else. Weary, tired soul, altogether overborne and distressed by the burdens and difficulties of life, your weariness is your claim. Do not try to get up your strength. When you lie flat in your weakness, your attitude is most acceptable to heaven. To try to gain your breath that you may appear with some integrity in his presence is to enhance your sin. To come panting, heaving, out of breath, gasping, dying—that is the guarantee of a good hearing in the presence of God.

Why is it that people so little profit by religious ordinances? Because they are too clever, too wise, too conceited, too good, in their own estimation. I never heard Pharisees and Sadducees praise with religious gratitude any service they ever attended. They, mighty men, confer an honor, they add luster to the altar, they lift up the church in which their self-vaunting supplications are uttered. How then can they, who are so full of themselves, who are enriched with the emptiness of their own self-satisfaction, gain any spiritual advantage from any church they ever entered? They do not go to church to get benefit, but to give it. Their purpose is to lay a flattering hand upon the infinite, and to bless it with the paw of their consecration. We should have been richer men today, broader and more massive in all religious instruction, intelligence, and force, if we had come with a true humbleness and bent down before God with an utter, absolute sense of unworthiness in his sight.

Surely he was a wilderness-trained man who spake thus to the high citizens of the day. Look at him, with his camel's hair and the leather girdle about his loins, fed with locusts and wild honey. When he speaks, he will speak honey, but only in his speech to self-satisfied men there will be less honey than locusts. Upon some men you cannot confer any social advantage. They do not want it. The religious man ought never to be one to whom no favor can be shown. A man who can live in the wilderness, read the literature of the everlasting hills, and decipher the poetry of the skies, asks for no favor, can stoop to receive none; his is a marvelous independence of all social patronage and help. "Do not offend the Pharisees and the Sadducees, conciliate them, conceal as much as you can; they have it in their power to do great things for you." Such might have been the speech spoken to this unusual man with the camel's hair and the leather girdle, fed on locusts and wild honey, but he would have hurled it back again in shattering accents of scorn. So the religious teacher has it in his power to lift himself high above the line of patronage and the line of obligation, for religious men should be able to live upon nothing. Every true teacher of God should have bread to eat that the world knoweth not of, so that when men who misunderstand his mission come to him and say, "Let us hear your sermon, and then you shall have the loaf," he should be able to decline the loaf, to preach his discourse, and to vanish into the wilderness.

This gospel of Christ, either in its prophetic outlines, or in this transient dispensation of the Baptist, or in its full revelation in Jesus Christ, has never sought to make itself a popular religion in the sense of bowing down hopefully before thrones on which were seated kings that could confer advantages upon it. Its fierce, all but savage, independence always strikes me with infinite force. When the Pharisees and the Sadducees came to the baptism of John, he said, "You are a brood of vipers." He called them by their right name. We dare not use such names now, because we do not live in the wilderness, we live in a city; we are not clothed with camel's hair and a leather girdle about our loins, we now have gowns and bands and a silken girdle, therefore we must be very complacent with the Pharisees and the Sadducees, and with people who are socially tall. I heard a fine and most prosperous gentleman say that he entered a London church once and only once, because in the course of the service the minister called some person who had been acting vilely—a wretch. "For that reason I have shut up the Bible—I heard a man call the most respectable citizens of his day a brood of vipers, a progeny of serpents, a nest of evil things. And I heard another man call a king a fox, and others he called whited sepulchers, hidden graves, actors, masked men." The age of free, clear, grand speech is dead: we have come into the age of euphemism.[*] He is now the bold man who so utters his sentences that nobody can quote them, who so rounds and oils them that it is impossible to retain them in the grasp. The old grit is lost, the old free piercing speech is gone; we have alighted upon silken times, and hard words would not become the lips that cannot live but on the rich man's viands. We now say, Beware of phrases!

Though the gospel has never endeavored to make itself popular in the sense of conciliating those who might confer patronage upon it, yet it has always welcomed with infinite pathos the hearts that felt their need

---

[*] It seems ironic that Parker is lamenting the end of "free speech" in the nineteenth century, while many today lament the same thing in the modern era of "political correctness." *Ed.*

of its redemption. No broken heart was ever turned away from the cross. No weary and overborne soul was ever discouraged by the Son of God. No poor bent woman, having nothing left but her touch of faith, was ever spurned by God's dear Son. He resents our fullness, not our poverty: it is when we are great he has nothing to say to us, not when we are little in our own esteem.

It is everywhere made clear in these Scriptures, that in coming for divine blessings we must renounce all human satisfaction. Nothing but emptiness can be heard at the divine bar. John gives a hint of this grand condition of entrance into the divine kingdom when he says, "Think not (literally plume not yourselves) by saying, We have Abraham for our father. This is a kingdom that knows nothing of these intermediate and transient relationships, this is not a kingdom of great families, it is a kingdom of humanity" [see v. 9]. Therefore, for John the Baptist, trained in the wilderness, to come up amid all these glittering things, and to lay down this doctrine of the kingdom of heaven being founded upon humanity, was a miracle then—it is a commonplace now, because we have had full instruction upon gospel principles and purposes. But in John the Baptist's day to lay down this grand doctrine—here is a kingdom not for special families and particular kindreds, but for all the wide world—that was a consummation of all the miracles as well as a fulfillment of all the prophecies.

How difficult it is to break a man's prejudice when it rests upon considerations of the kind which John refers to. A man had Abraham to his father, therefore, he wildly reasons, it will be all right with him whatever may happen in the world. Christianity aims a destructive blow at all such pretenses. This is the last fiber of badness. You cannot take out of some men a claim to God's favor, because of something ancestral or official represented by their individual life. Blessed are they who never heard of Abraham as compared with those who turn their Abrahamic ancestry into a prejudice against the divine kingdom or a condition of entering it. Blessed are the poor in spirit, for theirs is the kingdom of heaven. Blessed are they who can say—

> Just as I am—without one plea,
> But that thy blood was shed for me,
> And that thou bidst me come to thee—
> O Lamb of God, I come.

Who can reach this high degree of self-renunciation? Who can deliver himself from the prejudice that he has some claim to God's favor because his father built a church, because his father was a minister, because in his family religion has always had a place of consideration? Everyone of us has to go before God as if his father had never lived, so far as the patronizing of churches and religious sentiments is concerned. All false grounds of hope must be destroyed. God is able of these stones to raise up children unto Abraham—which may be paraphrased thus: Do not suppose that God is dependent upon you for an ancestry, for a progeny, for a religious fame, or the nucleus of a divine kingdom. If you were all swept out of the earth today, he could have a family ten thousand strong tomorrow out of the pebbles that lie in the river's bed or on the face of the wide desert. You cannot lay God under obligation: recognize that great truth, because it involves our proper relation to him as always receivers and never donors of the benefit.

"Who hath warned you to flee from the wrath to come?" This is the first time I have heard you say "wrath"; when you began to preach, you said, "the kingdom of heaven." How do you account for this change in your language and your tone? In reply to this inquiry John tells me that the gospel of Christ is either a kingdom or a wrath. It is a savor of life unto life, or a savor of death unto death. It is a gospel or a judgment, a heaven or a hell, an eye turned towards the zenith of God's heart, bright as morning, or the same eye turned in kindling wrath towards the Egyptians, troubling the camp, and striking off the chariot-wheels though they be made of solid iron. This book cannot occupy a middle place in society. It is either *the* Book or no book, a gospel or a lie, a religion or a blasphemy. No man can entertain an opinion of indifference regarding Jesus Christ. If he has considered the subject at all, he must worship Christ or crucify Him. He cannot be allowed to live as an indifferent person, about whom any opinions may be formed as you please. Where there is earnestness in the inquiry and the criticism, that earnestness ends in homage or in crucifixion.

This sermon by John the Baptist is not the kind of introduction one would have expected to the incoming of the Son of God. No gentle tone seems to escape the lips of this man: it is as if a stormy whirlwind had caught him and borne him on through the wilderness of Judea, and as if a great fire were behind him as he earnestly makes his way. Strange and terrible are these words—Repent, Prepare, Axe, Purge his floor, Burn up the chaff with unquenchable fire. In all these there is not one tone of conciliation, one smile of amiability, one outflow of cordiality. Yet this man comes before the Prince of Peace. Nor does he allude in this report to the gentler aspects of the coming One. He is taken up with the idea of power; hence he says, "He that cometh after me is mightier than I." The preacher in the wilderness deals with the idea of strength; strength as a terror to evil, as a terrible judicial power. A melodious hymn, such as peace would sing in a garden of flowers, might have been expected, trembling, quivering with hopeful joy, but instead, there is a roar as of a sudden storm, and a cry as of unexpected terror. This is not the introduction I looked for, yet it is like the way of God in the making of human history. He is always setting aside human expectations, and building his temples in unlikely places and with unlikely material. God uses the storm. The ages are not all made up of long radiant summer days: night, and storm, and battle, as well as day, and calm, and peace, are God's servants. This age requires voices that can be heard: the world's vast wilderness is open, and the man that is needed now and in every age is the man who, with throat of brass, inspired with iron lungs, can cry, "Repent." The church is now in danger of overfeeding the few and forgetting the hungry many. There is a work to be done in the wilderness; the manner appropriate to the wilderness may not be appropriate to the church: what is needed, therefore, is adaptation, the loud cry or the subdued tone—both are needed, and always will be needed, to meet the world's **great need**.

Yet how incomplete it would be to say that this report of John's ministry given in the Gospel by Matthew fully represents the work done by the energetic Baptist. Supposing we had no other account but the one which is now immediately before us, we should have no conception approaching completeness of the work which John did in his short day. It is so that all preachers suffer. Let us go and inquire of those who have heard John the Baptist preach, and listen what reports they give of this wonderful man. Have you heard this new preacher deliver a discourse— the man whose raiment is of camel's hair, with a leather girdle about his loins? "Yes," is the reply, "we have heard him preach." What do you think of him? "He is a harsh man, his voice grates, he utters austere words." What did you hear him say? "We heard him call the Pharisees and the Sadducees a brood of vipers." He did not call the Pharisees and the Sadducees a brood of vipers to their faces, did he? "Yes." Then we do not care to hear so fierce a preacher.

Ask others. Have you heard John the Baptist preach? "Yes." What do you have to say about him? "Savage, terrible; do not go near him, he will offend, he will frighten you." Why? you say. Can you tell us anything you have heard him say? "Yes, we heard him say, 'The ax is laid unto the root of the tree: therefore every tree which bringeth not forth good fruit is hewn down and cast into the fire'; and after that he said it was an unquenchable fire." Then he is not the kind of preacher that would suit us; we like the gentle and the quiet, the contemplative, the almost silent: above all things we love the pathetic and the soothing—so we shall not go to hear this Jordan-preacher.

But here are others coming from the sermon: have you ever heard him preach? "Yes." What did he say? "He said there was One coming, whose fan was in his hand, and he would thoroughly purge his floor, and gather the wheat into the garner, but burn up the chaff with unquenchable fire."

All these three reports concur: they all represent John the Baptist as a fierce objurgatory preacher. His lips are ironbound, his voice is like a shock of tempest, and there is no gentleness in his heart. By these fierce utterances he disproves his claim to be the herald of the man you expect.

There the report of this great preacher might end. Would you have a true conception of his marvelous power from the report which Matthew gives in this chapter? You must collate the other evangelists and put the story together, piece by piece, until you get its wholeness. This same John the Baptist said the tenderest thing that ever fell from human lips. The man who said, "Vipers—ax—fire—fan—" said the most touching words that ever fell on the bruised and expectant hearts of men. I have noticed that to be the case so frequently—that the men who can denounce the age with so fierce an accent, can bless the age with its softest and sweetest benedictions. I have noticed that the humorist is the master of pathos. I have observed that the man who is most fierce against iniquity, can also be the most sympathetic with weakness and sorrow.

Now having heard the three reports about John, let us wait a few days and then inquire again. Let us suppose those few days to have elapsed, and here is a party coming from listening to the Baptist. Let us inquire—have you heard the Baptist preach? "Yes." What do you think of him? "He has broken our hearts." What, has he said anything about viper, and fire, and ax, and fan? "Nothing." What then did he say? He cannot have spoken any gentle thing: gentle things would not become that fierce mouth. What did he say? Now listen to the reply, and tell me if this does not reveal the character of the Baptist in its roundness. He said, looking upon One who was within sight, and pointing to him, "Behold the Lamb of God, that taketh away the sin of the world." What, did the man who said, "Viper, ax, fire, fan, purge the floor"—did he say, "Behold the Lamb of God"? "Yes." Then he preached the only sermon worth preaching!

NOTES

For a most elaborate and powerful discussion of the ministry of John the Baptist, see the work of Dr. HENRY REYNOLDS.

John the Baptist was about six months older than Jesus Christ.

"Born, according to Rabbinical tradition, at Hebron, but according to modern expositors, at Jutta, in the tribe of Judah."

Repent ye—change your minds, "not *in order* that the kingdom of heaven may come, but *because* it cometh."

John was unwilling to baptize the Pharisees and Sadducees, and he was also unwilling to baptize the Messiah. Easily accounted for. The one *fell below*, the other infinitely *transcended* the standard.

In the East only *fruit* trees are valued. Others are looked upon as cumberers of the ground.

"When men were admitted as proselytes, three rites were performed—*circumcision, baptism,* and *oblation;* when *women,* two—*baptism* and *oblation.* The whole family of proselytes, including infants, were baptized"—*Alford.*

It was supposed that no one who had been circumcised was cast into Gehenna.

nine

THE BAPTISM OF CHRIST

Matthew 3:13–17

THERE IS one point upon which we are all agreed—namely, that the baptism of Jesus Christ could not be a baptism unto *repentance*. "He did no sin, neither was guile found in his mouth." He was without spot or wrinkle, or any such thing, the very Son of God, pure as the bosom on which he rested and out of which he came. We must, therefore, find other reasons than that of repentance for this baptism of the Savior of the world. John must enlarge his own conception of the baptism which he came to administer. He had used the word Repent; now a new word was to be attached to his baptism, and an infinitely older and larger word. What man amongst us is there who knows the exact measure of his work? Yet, for the sake of convenience, every one of us has a name by which he designates his ministry. John, for example, called his service a baptism unto repentance. But there came One unto him who said, "The other word which enlarges your service to its true proportion, and indicates its high intent and purpose, is—Righteousness." John thought his ministry a negative one: Jesus Christ taught him that his baptism was positive as well as negative, a baptism unto righteousness or in accordance with the spirit of righteousness, as well as a baptism unto repentance.

This baptism of Christ was a baptism of *sympathy*. Sympathy means feeling with, having a common pathos or feeling, emotion, or passion, and he, the Savior, was in all points made like unto his brethren, that in all points he might have a fellow-feeling, a kindred passion; that there might be no tone in all the gamut of their life's utterance to which he could not respond, giving it a counterpart, a fulfillment, a higher emphasis, a keener and truer accent. Jesus Christ identified himself with all the dispensations of providence; he was the spirit of the prophets, and now he came into this baptism of John. When he expounded the Scriptures he began at Moses—he could not have begun earlier—and he expounded them to those who listened to him—what was written in Moses, in the prophets, and in the Psalms, and having been present in all these dispensations or varieties of the divine mood in relation to the children of men, was he to be absent only from the baptism of John? So he accepted that baptism, not because the word Repentance was associated with it, but because it also extended itself by subtle processes wholly unknown to the Baptist himself to—*Righteousness.*

It was a baptism of *inauguration* and a baptism of *approval*; John was hereby sealed as a witness and messenger of God. By this act Jesus Christ said, "John is no adventurer, and his baptism is no mere sensation of the passing hour. It goes back to the decree and purpose of God, it looks forward to the infinite gospel which it holds," and thus John himself was sealed, approved, and crowned in this very act of humble service performed by the Son of God. It was, I repeat, a baptism of inauguration. Jesus Christ was not in the priestly line, though in the line royal: he came to be the Priest of the universe, having from eternity been its King, now he was introduced or inaugurated into his high-priestly office.

How little we know what we are doing when we baptize any life. We speak of repentance and cleansing as the meaning and purpose of baptism, and sometimes we are baptizing kings and priests and we know it not. The possibility that we may be thus inaugurating to high office and a noble position some human life should throw over our whole service a tender and hopeful solemnity. You cannot tell who is under your influence: it may be a king, a priest, a deliverer. You thought your work was a preliminary one, you called yourself an elementary teacher, you said, in humble self-deprecation, "I am but a pioneer, I am only a forerunner, my name is a herald and nothing more, and I give introductory lessons, and cannot proceed to the higher learning: I am only a precursor, and nothing more." You limited yourself too much. John thought he was a crying voice, whereas it was appointed of God that he should inaugurate to his priestly office the Savior of the world.

Thus the lesser may be concerned in the service of the greater. "I have need to be baptized of thee." If a man does not feel his own need of baptism, he is unworthy of administering the rite in any of its higher senses to the humblest creature that ever was presented at the altar. "I have need to be baptized of thee, and comest thou to me?" We know the meaning of this in other ranges of thinking. A minister sometimes sees before him persons to whom intellectually he is but slave and minister, and he says, "I have need to be intellectually elevated and illuminated by you, and you come to me?" Yes the coming is perfectly right, for this kingdom of Christ is not merely an intellectual school, it is a school in which intellect has to sit down and humble itself, and patiently wait for the illumining revelation which is shed from heaven. We do not sit here in our cleverness and grandeur and intellectual influence, but in our moral nakedness and necessity, in our spiritual simplicity and childlikeness, waiting not for man, but for God, and for man only insofar as he is the medium on which the infinite silence breaks into momentary speech for the teaching and comforting of the human heart.

Thus, too, God puts himself under his own laws. "The laws of nature" is a mood of God, is but another expression for God himself. Do not speak of laws of nature as if they were somewhat independent of God. They are God, they are God in motion, God made visible, God made audible, God coming down in wondrous condescension so far into our region, and thinking that we can in some degree trace him, and identify him, and judge him. Thus Jesus Christ came unto the baptism of John. It was to him a baptism of sympathy, a baptism of approval, a baptism of inauguration, a stooping of the divine so as to take up its own laws and exemplify its own purposes.

REVIEW OF THE CHAPTER

Now, looking at the third chapter as a whole, having already gone through it in detail, we seem to see in this brief chapter *the history of a whole dispensation,* the dispensation of John the Baptist. It begins and ends in these seventeen short verses. In this chapter I read, "Then cometh JOHN," and I also read, "Then cometh JESUS. God thus condenses much into brief space. Sometimes he takes a long line, and we say he has gone into a far country, and we know not when he will return. Sometimes he seems to work with urgency and suddenness, and in a moment to begin and complete a whole dispensation. He is not to be measured by our lines, or described by our terms: we cannot tell what he will do—he may take ages countless in which to build a rock, he may take a short night-time in which to begin and complete a whole dispensation of his providence. Thus he baffles all our statistical tables. We have no calculus by which we can tell when he will come, or where he will be at a given period; we cannot take him within our circles and lines. He loves to baffle the ingenuity of man. We have reduced everything now to a law of averages, but God stands out of our reckoning, and no man can say whether he will not come tonight to judge the world. Thus are we kept in continual expectations, thus there is ever near us a ghost that alarms or comforts, according to the mood of our heart. Let us learn that our business is to rest in the Lord and to wait patiently for him, so that whether he come tonight or do not come for long ages yet to elapse, we may be found doing our little best, cultivating our tiny corner, watching, waiting, praying, hoping, suffering with a hero's confidence, toiling with a son's delight, and then, come when he may, it will be summer for our souls, release and freedom from all that makes us mean.

Look again at this chapter as a whole, we see that it introduces a new name into human history. May I pause a moment to ask you what that new name is? As we have read the chapter over several times together, did you hear one name that struck you as music strikes an attentive soul? It is a short name, it is—SON. "This is my beloved Son." We have made ourselves so familiar with that word, that we read it as though it did not mark a new epoch in human history, but if we could have read the Bible through at one long sitting, we should have seen that the line of development moves in this form, *Man*—*Servant*—PROPHET—MESSENGER—SON. Last of all he sent his Son also. It is infinitely exciting to see how these new words came into human speech. All the time we felt something was lacking: *Man* was a great name, *Servant* a high office, *Prophet* a marvelous function, *Messenger* a high ministry—but SON takes them up and rounds them into completeness, and lights them with ineffable splendor.

The divine movement is always climacteric, the divine progress is an *ascension*. God does not begin with Son and work down to servant, nor with man and work down to some insignificant molecule: he begins at the other end, and always the better day is to come. Prophecy meant that the day of light was to dawn upon the hills and valleys of time, and that music was to take the place of groaning. That is the thread or line of the Bible, and because it is so I find in that very movement of ascension a confirmatory illustration, not to say an original and complete argument, on behalf of the divinity and authority of the Book which we revere as divinely inspired and final in its moral revelations.

Then, looking again at the chapter as a whole, we see that it completes what other dispensations only began. There are several brilliant proofs upon this point. What is the first word we hear in connection with human history, or with the formation of man? It is *make*. "Let us make man." In connection with Jesus Christ, "This is my only BEGOTTEN Son." A Creator, a Father, an Artist, a God. Still the line heightens itself in the same direction. What is the description of the character of man in the first instance? *Upright*. God made man upright. What is the word used in connection with the Son? *Beloved*. See how God rises, and how his revelation brightens broadly. Upright—an experiment in moral mechanics: upright—an attitude: upright—negative. Beloved—kindred, sympathetic, approved, complete. It is thus that the Bible grows from root to flower; this is development. We claim that word as a Christian term, we cannot do without it in the church; the whole scheme of the divine administration of human affairs is a development, a progress, an upward marching: see it in the blade, the ear, the full corn in the ear: we would have God's Book judged by that law or science of development, and so judged we are brought from *make* to *begotten*, from *upright* to *beloved*, and from *very good* to *well-pleased*. Do you not hear the same old, rich voice? "God saw everything that he had made, and behold it was very good" [Gen. 1:31]. "Lo, a voice from heaven saying, This is my beloved Son, in whom I am well pleased." In both cases he sets himself in a relation of satisfaction to what is before him. Man, standing there, fashioned in his own image, upright, faultless, inexperienced, with a great destiny to work out—on him is written "Very good." The last outcome of this human growth and mystery stands before him on Jordan's banks, and a voice says, "Well pleased," and when God is pleased law is satisfied and grace is triumphant.

Then we come further still, from the *Us* of the creating Trinity to the *My* of the approving Father. Thus, in the creation of man we read, "Let *us* make man" [Gen. 1:26]. In the inauguration of the Son we read, "This is *my* beloved Son." Examine still further, and in other fields and relationships, this suggestion of the continuous, ever-culminating development of the divine purpose, and say if there be not in it a rich fund of spiritual instruction and satisfaction. There has been a divine ideal in the rest towards which God has been slowly moving, through revolution, and war, and distress, and manifold experiences of every human kind, but never did he say "Well pleased" until there stood before him his only begotten Son. Five hundred years before he was not at rest. A century before, his purpose was still a hundred years ahead, but steadily, surely, grandly he moved on, the line now dipping into deep pits, now starting up high hills—still on he moved. You cannot turn God back, though now the ancestral line is lost in a harlot, and now it is put to risk in a wayward king. Still he moves on, and presently he says, "It is finished: this is my beloved SON."

So shall it be in the culmination and upgathering of all things. Jesus Christ must reign till he hath put all enemies under his feet. The last enemy that shall be destroyed is death, and when death lies below his feet, he will deliver up the kingdom to God and his Father, and God shall be all in all. Come quickly, calm morning, a flame with every color of beauty, peaceful with the divine benediction—O, come. The old earth is torn with pain and distressed with intolerable pangs—but that morning will come. Watchman, what of the night? The night will come, and also the morning. We are in sad case just now. Our world was never lower in her moral standards in many public aspects of her history than she is at this moment. She never more foully debased her journalism, or poured out of her history streams more revolting and pestilential. But God is moving on; it is his old movement; he knows every knot in the line, every twist in the road, every difficulty in the path—but if you could see his eye, it never moves from the point he has set before him, and he will bring in all his purposes and decrees, his completed oaths and covenants fulfilled, for his own mouth has spoken it.

Are we now to bid farewell to John the Baptist? Are you still in John's baptism? He was a burning and a shining light, but you ought to have left him long ago. Are you still down by Jordan's banks, wanting to take the plunge? "Verily I say unto you, Among them that are born of women there hath not risen a greater than John the Baptist: notwithstanding he that is least in the kingdom of heaven is greater than he." You ought, therefore, to take the step from the initial baptism into the inner and Christian one. You ought to leave the letter and pass into the spirit. You ought now to be able to enjoy the large, calm, sweet liberty of the gospel, and not be bound by ordinances, and observances, and various ceremonies. We have left these behind us: they were useful in their time, they were elements which God used for the further broadening and illumination of his righteousness, so far as our vision was concerned, but now I know nothing of any ceremony: I have outlived it; if

I do anything, it is merely to remind me, merely as a suggestion; not as a necessity, but as a help to some higher spiritual blessing.

Do you say you have been baptized, and therefore you are all right? All the water in all the seas and firmaments of heaven could not cleanse you. Do you say you sit down regularly to the Lord's supper? All the wine in all the vineyards of creation would not contain one drop of blood to you, if you are not already hidden in the very heart of the Son of God. Do you say you regularly come to church and observe religious fasts and festivals? Away with all these externals, if they do not indicate contrition, self-renunciation, trust in a living Christ, identification with the Son of God. We are not saved by the outward, but by the inward. All the outward is but symbolical—the inward baptism is a shedding abroad in the heart of the Holy Ghost.

The Lord's peace be in our souls, and the Lord help us to see beyond the letter into all the brightness and beauty of the spirit.

ten

THE TEMPTATION
(PART ONE)

Matthew 4:1–11

"THEN." That word indicates a point of time. It will be interesting to fix that point with some definiteness. We like to know under what circumstances great events transpire. Sometimes we want to know not only the fact, but the atmosphere which surrounded it. You do not see any event in its proper altitude, relationship and color, until you take in the circumstances leading up to it or surrounding it. When therefore I read, "*Then* was Jesus led up," my mind anxiously inquires, When? Herod wanted to know what time the star appeared; what wonder if we want to know what time the devil appeared? To find the answer to this inquiry you must go back to the chapter whose exposition we have just completed:

> Jesus, when he was baptized, went up straightway out of the water: and, lo, the heavens were opened unto him, and he saw the Spirit of God descending like a dove, and lighting upon him: And lo a voice from heaven, saying, This is my beloved Son, in whom I am well pleased. *Then* was Jesus led up of the Spirit into the wilderness to be tempted of the devil.

Such are the violent alternations of human experience, baptized and tempted, approved of God and handed over to the devil, standing with a grand inaugural sign upon our heads on the river's bank and then driven as with whips and scourges into the wilderness to fight life's determining battle.

Do not question the validity of your baptism because it was succeeded by a fierce temptation. Do not say you must have been mistaken

78

when you thought the dove descended from heaven and alighted upon you, otherwise you could never have been subjected to this succession of thunderstorms. Read the life of your Lord and Master, and find from that life that our relationships to God seem, in their outward aspects, to change suddenly and even vitally. You are a son of God, standing on the bank of the river, and you are just as much a son of God when tormented and vexed by all the forces of hell in the wilderness. Sonship does not depend upon moods and feelings. You are a child of God, whatever may be your momentary relationship, either to heaven, earth, or hell. God is not variable, his elections are not so many opportunities of recalling his decrees. Be sure of your adoption into the family of God, and then leave yourselves to be operated upon by all the discipline which is of heavenly appointment, for it works only to the maturing and the cleansing of your soul, and the ripening and sanctification of your redeemed powers. Jesus Christ was a Son when the dove alighted upon him, and he was a Son when the devil set his whole force of genius and subtlety to bear upon the citadel of his faith.

Cheer up, then, despondent soul, for God can make the wilderness blossom as the rose!

"Then was Jesus led up." We speak sometimes of temptation as if it were an accident of life: we forget the words "led up." These words indicate that temptation is part of a *plan*, it is a step in the succession to a better life. Sometimes we delude ourselves with the foolish imagination that if we step very softly, we shall get past the serpent's nest without the serpent hearing us, we shall elude the devil, we shall play a trick upon him, and when we are miles off we will laugh at him as an enemy that overslept himself, whose leaden ears were sealed in sleep, so that he did not hear us when we passed him in velvet slippers. Take no such simple and unworthy view of life. Life itself is temptation. To *be*, is to be nearly lost. To be here at all is to be in the devil's hands, in senses which will appear as the exposition advances.

Understand that you *have* to be tempted. The wilderness is not a sphere lying a thousand miles from your course, into which you may go if you are disposed to undertake perilous adventure. Your eye is fixed on heaven, and right across, from sea to sea, lies the wilderness, and you cannot escape it. I do not speak of wildernesses and temptations and devils as if they were parts of a universe over which God had but imperfect control. The Lord sits upon the circle of the earth and upon the very height of heaven, and the devil is his slave, chained with iron and with bits in his cruel mouth, and beyond his chain he cannot go. Do not speak with bated breath about this matter of temptation, as if it were possible to sneak into heaven. I must be assailed, tried, tormented, vexed, thrown down, battered, stamped on, and if I have not passed through experiences of this kind, the whole priesthood of Christ has been lost upon me, and if there be no experiences of this kind to pass through, then the cross of Christ is an exaggeration of remedial measures, and there was no need for the heart of the Son of God to burst in pity or in sacrifice. Count it no strange thing when temptations come upon you; to be finite is to be tempted; to be a fraction instead of a whole number is to have in you the unrest of incompleteness, and the strange restless spirit that says, "Try to complete yourself, for the fraction may become an integer."

From this point of view, then, temptation is part of the divine scheme. The devil is under the control of God. Why there should have been a devil, I cannot tell; I only know that we owe the shadow to the light, and I further console myself in moments of impious intellectual ambition with the thought that I am of yesterday and know nothing, and that there is a time coming for deeper study, and further and more complete investigation. These mysteries are not to be solved here and now; I accept them as mysteries, and I accept them with less hesitation because they tally with my inmost consciousness, with experiences known to the human heart, altogether apart from religious convictions of this or that particular theological kind.

"Then was Jesus led up of the spirit into the wilderness to be tempted of the devil," and when the tempter came to him, he said three things. The tempter has only *three* things to say; the tempter's program is short and shallow; beyond those three things he has never advanced one step. He is not a genius of infinite resource; he is not an assailant that may surprise us with dazzling originality—his temptations are stale—I can weigh them in scales and assign their weight; I can measure them and tell you their circumference, I know where they begin, and how they operate, and how they close. He, the devil, is not the subtle and ever-fertile genius which we have vainly imagined him to be. He has three great clubs with which he endeavors to smite you; I can give you their names, their size, and their whole capability.

Hear what the devil said. "If thou be the Son of God, command that these stones be made bread." This was an appeal to immediate necessity.

The devil comes in a spirit of benevolence; he shrinks into as little devil as possible and says:

> You are hungry; if I could make bread for you I would, but I am only a devil, blamed one, bearing the stigma of the universe; if I could have brought you bread all this distance I would have done so, but if you are the Son of God, you must have power to work miracles—turn these stones into bread.

The devil addresses himself to the appetite of the moment, or the supreme impulse of the passing time. Whatever you want most, he is willing to supply—at what expense will presently appear.

Observe his benevolence, and observe how *seemingly harmless* was the temptation. It was hardly a temptation at all. What harm could there be in making bread in a moment of hunger? The suggestion was marked by the most obvious pertinence and excellent good sense. After forty days and forty nights of abstinence, you must be suffering pangs which none can fully understand; therefore make bread for yourself, and satisfy the importunate and lawful appetite which now maddens you. You know that temptation—you know the voice which softens itself into a tender wheedling and says to you, "There can be at least no harm in this." And there may be no harm in certain words, in themselves considered, but there is always great harm in accepting the suggestion of the devil. If it were possible for him to preach a gospel to us, there might be infinite risk in accepting it at his lips, for they are pledged with a thousand oaths to do another kind of work, and if he has stolen into this service, he has a purpose in it approved of his own soul, and therefore which should excite in us suspicion and alarm.

"If thou be the Son of God, cast thyself down, for it is written, He shall give his angels charge concerning thee." He comes now to develop our faith; he appears with the sacred mission of endeavoring to show us how to become actually more religious than ever. Was there ever such a devil! He shows us how we may be more pious than we ever hoped or expected to be, by entering into daring engagements as pious and all-trusting acrobats. His motto is—Presume upon God, test his strength, bring him the opportunity of showing what he means by his promises. In leveling this temptation at the heart, he takes care to surround himself by circumstances which might substantially aid his malign purpose. He took

Christ to the holy city and set him on a pinnacle of the Temple—surrounded him by *external* religion in order to persuade him to dethrone an *interior* loyalty to God. As if the devil had said, "This is the holy city; within its confines God will permit no lapse of his promise to take place. This is the Temple, and a pinnacle of it, and in connection with his own chosen sanctuary, he will allow no spiritual tragedy to take place. Do not suppose I should tempt you to anything evil in this holy city, and while we are standing on the topmost point of the most sacred house under the sun!"

This was an appeal to the Son of God to be presumptuous, to force meanings into the divine word which the divine Spirit never intended to convey, to force God into situations which he never intended to be occupied. Do you know the subtlety and force of such suggestions? Do you know what it is for men to get themselves almost purposely into trouble, that they may put the divine word to its fullest stress? Do you know what it is to shut the eyes, to lower the head and to run straight against a granite rock, and then to blame God for not softening it into a cloud through which you could thrust your head with ease? Let those answer the pungent inquiries who are best acquainted with their soul's own history.

The third thing the enemy said, and this ends his program, was, "All these things—namely, all the kingdoms of the world and the glory of them—will I give thee, if thou wilt fall down and worship me." It was the temptation of bribery; it was the temptation addressed to every instinct which is in every human heart to turn much into more; it was a short and easy method of becoming rich—the direct shortcut to rulership; it was the simplification of all the intricacies and complexities and difficulties of ordinary life. It was a blade that cut the knot, and made the way short and simple.

Beyond these three things the devil has never moved. I pause now to look at them, with a view of finding in the temptations *the true character of the tempter.* If we are to know a tree by its fruits, so we may know a tempter by his temptations. In very deed the devil has said nothing bad here, taking the mere letter in its littleness. "If thou be the Son of God, command that these stones be made bread. If thou be the Son of God, cast thyself down, and put God to the test. All these things will I give thee if thou wilt fall down and worship me." Given such evidence, we find out by fair induction what the devil is.

Let us now study the temptations in the light of that inquiry. Let us look at both sides of the wedge. Given the thin end of the wedge, to find out the thick end. That can be easily done with these paragraphs before us, thus. As he would have turned stones into bread, *so he would turn bread into stones*; and that is what he means to do. He begins innocently, benevolently: "Turn these stones into bread"; and having obeyed him in that particular, he makes a precedent of that obedience, and by-and-by he will say, "Now turn this bread into stones." That is what he wants to do with everyone of us—wants us to turn our virtues into vices, wants us to turn our prayers into presumptions, wants us to turn our religion into profanity and blasphemy. No worth of character deters him; he would take your dear little child and make an imp of his own that beautiful soul; he would take all the bread of heaven and make a stone of it; he would diabolize the very Deity himself. That is the thick end of the wedge. He believes in processes of transformation, but his is a transformation that operates in both ways—namely, turning stones into bread and turning bread into stones. Beautiful soul, with your high dreams and sacred purposes and noble impulses, the devil would turn all these high excitements and forces of yours into ministries which would serve his own kingdom.

Then with regard to the next temptation. As he would have risked a life on the pretense of trusting God, *so he would risk God on the pretense of saving life*. That is the thick end of the wedge. He is always tempting God to do from his point what he tempted Christ to do from a lower point. He tempted Christ to risk his life to put God's word to the test, he tempts God to save life that he may lose himself. Thus the devil is continually blaming God for the inequalities of human life. He is perpetually sending challenges to heaven, saying, "If you are almighty, why permit these social monstrosities, rebellions, poverty, wars? If you are almighty, why not by a fiat put an end to the lake of fire and the whole region of devildom, and reign over a universe uncut by a single grave—unblasted by a single sin?"

This is precisely the temptation which was leveled against the constancy of Christ. Said he to Christ, "Risk yourself to save a life." The infidel has no weapon that he deems longer, stronger, and sharper than this challenge to God to prove his almightiness by deposing and destroying the devil. If the whole question were to be determined within twenty-four hours, if God's eternity were an affair of one round of the clock, there might be some little force in this temptation, and blasphemy. But God operates by a long circuit; we cannot tell what he is doing in the secret places of the universe; we hear but a very little of his voice, the full thunder of it would break the listening ear. I am creature, not Creator, child of a day, not the Inhabitant of eternity, so I would quietly and lovingly wait till God's processes are brought to their culmination.

Look at the third temptation. As the devil offered kingdoms in return for worship, he knows whoever receives the *worship* actually holds the *kingdoms!* This is the subtlest of all the temptations. Give a sentiment for property; bow the knee for a crown; fall down before me and say, "Thou art my God," and I will give thee kingdoms and dominions, vast and innumerable. Who would hesitate to pay down a sentiment for a nation, who would hesitate to change a god, if by a theological transmutation an empire could be purchased? We are cautioned to beware of sentiment; we are told certain objections are sentimental, we are put on our guard against emotion. Religion has been watered down into a sentiment, and I protest against the infamous dilution. Religion is a conviction, an obligation, a constraint of the soul, an allegiance of the faculties which make me man. It is not an evaporating tear, it is not a transient, dying sigh, it is my life, translated into its highest speech.

Observe how the benevolence of the devil is shown at last to be utter selfishness. "All these things will I give thee, if thou wilt fall down and worship me." To worship is to give; whom I worship I serve. If I worship God and keep anything back from him, my worship is blasphemy. If I love the cross and hold anything back from its outstretched arms, I am a mocker and no saint. We seek not yours, but you—having *you* we have *yours!* We only give where we love. The benevolence of the devil is a fraud, the generosity of the devil is a lie. My young friend, the devil never gives anything good that he promises, you fall down and worship him, and then call upon him for the kingdoms and he will not give them. Show him the writing, recall the oath, and he will mock you, and with leering eye, look, and with a mocking taunting voice, say, "I am not in the mood for your petty demands!" I challenge any man in the world to show me that he ever got anything good at the hands of the devil.

The three temptations, then, are now before us, and the character of the devil, as suggested by these temptations, is also before us in rough outline. The devil has no other temptations. He appeals to your dominant appetite, he asks you to make God your servant, always to be at your beck and bidding, to give you a good harvest, and a fine income, and plenty to eat and drink and abundance of possessions. He says, "Trust him to that extent, force him to the keeping of his word, and ask him, if the harvest is bad, what he means by sending you a bad harvest when you were praying for a good one. Tax him to his face with his promises, and compel him to keep them." And then, last of all, he says, "Give up everything for the world, give up your prayers and your hymn-singing, and all your religion, for riches, and more riches, and more riches—have all the riches you want, and have it for next to nothing, for an inclination of the head, for a mere bending of the knee, for one loyal remark." Satan has no other temptation to level at your hearts. He may vary the form, he may change the manner and expression, but centrally and substantially his program is written in this text, and every man can prove it for himself, and know the measure and the force of every syllable of it.

Thus the devil delivers a threefold knock on the door of the heart. What answers Christ will make when he opens the door we shall see in our next exposition.

eleven

THE TEMPTATION (PART TWO)

Matthew 4:1–11

REFERRING to the remark, that all things were under the control of an independent and Self-existent being, even the devil himself being included in all things, the question has been asked whether, considering there is one Self-existent being, there might not be a possibility of there being two. I think if we look a little attentively into the matter, we shall find that there is only one representative or original of everything. We shall find that there is only one word in human speech: all other words come out of that as the branches and the leaves come out of the root. There is only one verb in all grammar: for the sake of convenience we have, perhaps, a thousand verbs, regular and irregular, but looked at closely we shall find that there is only one verb in all human speech: that is the verb *to be*. All the other verbs come out of it; no other verb can live without it—all the other verbs are phases and moods and aspects of that— "I am that I am." We shall find that there is only one number, and that number is *One*. Two is an invention of yours. The multiplication table is a trick of man's; there is only the number one. Two is a guess, a conjecture, something that has to be granted in order that other reckoning may be made, but all these numbers will run around again and come back to—One. There is only one light; our sun is lighted by some other flame. There is an inner and essential Shekinah in the universe at which all the lesser torches are lighted; planets and constellations catch their tiny blaze from that central and infinite luster. There is but one life, God, and the devil is part of him. So is man, so is every angel. Mystery of mysteries—there is but one mystery in the universe, and that is not how the devil came to be, but how God came to be.

Having looked at the temptations one by one, let us now take the same course with regard to the *answers*. The first answer is, "Man shall not live by bread alone." This is a profound view of life as contrasted with a shallow one. The devil's notion was that life could be sustained only in one way; his short program was, "Eat and live. Take plenty of bread and refuse to die." That is his narrow conception of this wondrous immortality; he thinks it is something that must be spoon-fed, his notion of it is that if a man have enough food, what more can he want? And it is in this way he fools the world, by asking us to put a loaf in every cupboard, by asking us to fill the house from floor to ceiling with food: and then we shall have no difficulty in maintaining and prolonging our life. With what a revealing flash must this answer have fallen upon his stupid mind—Man shall not live by bread alone. There are fifty other ways of living: if God so desire it, there are ten thousand other ways of living. Man need not receive his life from his body at all, if it pleases God to sustain him in some other way. Do not suppose that God is shut up to one way of keeping our human mechanism going: he could feed us with his breath, sustain us by his word, command our life to grow, and we need not resort to any of the contrivances which so vex us by their detail to sustain our bodily life.

We have always been thinking that there was but one way of sustaining our breath: man has been victimized and fooled by the delusion, that if he had no food, he could not live. Jesus Christ comes to enlarge the possibilities of life, to say to you, "Take no care or thought for tomorrow, what shall ye eat or what ye shall drink. Life is not a question of drinking or eating. Seek first the kingdom of God and his righteousness, put your trust in the Lord and he will feed you, he will find bread for you which the soul can eat" [see Matt. 6:25–33]. Thus Jesus Christ strikes at the foundations of our mistakes. He does not say, "Whatever you do, always have plenty of food." He says, "Do not be anxious about food at all. Rest in God, serve God, always desire to do right, always strive to be good, and all these things shall be added to you." The true notion of the text is that God has innumerable ways of sustaining life, and that we live, not because we eat, but because it is God's will that we live. Your food is a secondary cause, or a transient occasion, it explains next to nothing: you live not because you have had an abundance of food, but because God's decree has gone forth, and your days have been appointed and registered in heaven.

Suppose I should make the meaning a little more lucid, by putting it this way. Man can have food by one trade alone. You see the mistake there. Man can have food only in one way of commerce—you laugh at that as a sophism; you say, "There are a thousand trades by which a man may have food." Now make that a spiritual conception and carry it up into the highest regions, and you will understand what Jesus Christ meant when he said, "Man shall not live by bread alone." Bread does not cover the whole possibility of living, it is the divine will that settles everything: if God wants me to live, you may take away from me all bread, and all the fruits of the earth and the juices thereof, all the fish of the sea and the cattle that browse in the meadows, and you will find me, forty years from now, young, strong, without a wrinkle, without one token of infirmity in my body.

That is the true conception of life. We are misled by any other. We say if we do not have food we cannot live. That is true only within very small limits, but the limits themselves may be atheistic. I live, not because I baked a loaf yesterday and ate it today, but because God *wills* that I should live. Your life is not a keeping up of yourself as the result of some cunning contrivance of yours; your breath is in your nostrils, and God himself keeps it there. When I receive that conception, in all its fullness and poetry, into my soul, I know what Jesus Christ meant when he said, "Take no thought for the morrow: sufficient unto the day is the evil thereof. Seek first the kingdom of God and his righteousness." "Trust in the Lord, and do good," said an older speaker still, "so shalt thou dwell in the land, and verily thou shalt be fed" [Ps. 37:3]. We shall have food to eat that the world knows nothing about [see John 4:32 NIV]; our life shall not then be the vulgar result of gluttony, but it shall be a mystery to everybody how we live, and live on so little—that is, so little that is measurable, but he who draws his life from God's heart has more than a little to live on. You fool, your loaf perishes in the handling, God's life seems to grow in the using.

The second answer. "Thou shalt not tempt the Lord thy God." This is a right use of liberty as contrasted with a wrong one. Let us understand the meaning of this word, *tempt*. Let us put it in this broad fashion—you shall not make experiments upon God, you shall not set traps for God, you shall not put yourself into false relations just in order to try God and to put religion to the test. Do not run into danger for the purpose of being delivered from it. That, I take it, is the practical meaning and application of the word *tempt*. Perhaps we shall understand it better by taking a social illustration, for we often see things clearly by means of human analogy.

There are persons who are always tempting our friendship. They do not broadly and lovingly trust it, they do not meet us halfway in joyful and hopeful cooperation, but they continually set little traps by which they may catch us if they can. Have you had acquaintance with such disagreeable persons and their detestable habits? If they are in company, walking with you, they fall a little way behind, just to see if you will look after them. They are always testing you, tempting you, giving you opportunities of showing how much you care for them. They stay away from church just to see whether the minister will miss them. Nice people to have to deal with! They will stay away another Sunday just to see whether the people in the next pew call upon them. That is tempting friendship, putting it to little tests, setting little snares for it to catch it, and then to say, "Now I see just how much you care for me." If you have been around such people, you understand what it is to tempt love, to tempt power, to tempt God.

Jesus Christ says, "Thou shalt not tempt the Lord thy God." Do not put yourself into foolish situations in order to draw him forth from his secret tabernacle and to work some mighty wonder for your deliverance. Do not use him for merely individual ends and purposes, do not fall into a pit, saying, "God will come and deliver me out of this pit, and so reveal his mighty strength in the eyes of all the people." You should try rather to give God as little trouble as possible. Work up to the end of your liberty; say to him, "Father, I would come a longer way to meet thee if I could; I will do all in my little power to carry out thy will, to keep myself, to preserve my life from danger. I will not run risks for the sake of bringing thee out of heaven in order to work some mighty demonstration on my behalf in the eyes of the vulgar and the profane." That is true religion, and that is true friendship also. If I am truly your friend I do not set little traps for you. On the contrary, I take the best view of you, I love you, and if there be anything like mystery about your conduct to me, I say the misunderstanding is mine, there is nothing of purposed trial on the other side; I must be more on the alert, and I must cooperate more heartily and sympathetically with my friend. But if I be only your friend in a superficial and momentary sense, then I am always trying you, setting little snares in your road and watching you, and if I am a member of your congregation, I absent myself to see whether you mark my absence, and if I am your minister, I try your love in this small way and that. Shame on us if such be the way in which we bruise the angel of friendship. Let heart meet heart and man meet God, and work with him, and do not put his almightiness to little strains and stresses, which, being interpreted, mean nothing less than an evil heart of unbelief. Work as if you were God, and trust as though you had no power of your own. Thou shalt not tempt the Lord thy God, but love him and cooperate with him, and be as much to him as you possibly can.

Take the third answer. "Thou shalt worship the Lord thy God, and him only shalt thou serve." This is constancy in worship as contrasted with caprice and fickleness.

"Thou shalt worship." Take that word in opposition to *tempt.* You shall not *tempt* the Lord your God, but you shall *worship* him, give him the heart's adoration, the spirit's whole fire of love, without one spark falling anywhere else. Your religious life should be a concentrated offering, intense as a flame. That is what keeps a man right, religiously and theologically. We are not propped up by little clevernesses, mechanical, ecclesiastical, and theological; we are not shored up by some religious mechanism of man's contrivance; we are only right in proportion as our worship is right. If we live in our ideas and syllogisms, if we secure ourselves behind the covert and defense of our own way of stating theological propositions, the very first thunderstorm that comes will carry us away. I am right only when I rightly pray, I am secure only while I truly worship, I am delivered from fear of death and hell only in proportion as my fellowship with the Father is intimate and sweet. Ask me to define myself in words, and I say words seem to be but temptations of controversy, propositions are only so many opportunities of contradiction, but worship, deep as the life, silent as the springs of being, mighty as the urgency of love, that it is, and that only, that keeps a man right amid all this swirl and hurry, tumult and danger, of a probationary life.

How is it with us in prayer? I do not ask how it is with us in the mere fluency of sentences: that is often a temptation and a mockery, or may easily become such, but how is it with the desire of the heart, with the out-going of the soul, with the supreme and inflexible purpose of the will? Do we love God, wait for him, trust in him, believe every syllable he has spoken, and do we know him, not by some trained act of the intellect, but by an inexplicable and ineffable operation of that sympathetic power of the soul which makes us men? I am afraid lest any of us be living a merely intellectually religious life. There is great danger of hiding ourselves behind verbal statements and trusting to formulated faiths: these are both and all useful in their way, but their way goes but a little distance—the only thing that is invincible is love, the only supreme religion is the sacrifice of the broken heart in complete and affectionate trust in the living God.

Not only must there be this worship, but following it and coming out of it there must be service. Thus the text reads, "Thou shalt worship the Lord thy God, and him only shalt thou serve." Religion is not a contemplation only, religion is a service; religion is not a folding of the hands together and an upturning of the eyes to measurable heavens, and a silent expectation of something that shall fall upon our indolence and act upon our industry—religion is activity, service, sacrifice, devotion, whole-hearted consecration of every power of the life to one object, and if we have not attained that height, let us strive after it with sweet modesty and with burning energy. Let our heart go out in that direction. I should have pity upon a poor wounded traveler whose face was set towards his home, though he could not take one step to it. He says by that action of the face, "I want to be at home, I wish to God I were there. Sickness calls me, want implores me, death beckons me: I cannot go, but I can turn my eyes to the old homestead, and look as if I would be there above all other things on earth." We take the will for the deed. It is so with God: if we really purpose in our hearts to serve him, and if we fail in a great majority of the points which constitute that purpose, yet if our desire be intense and high, it will be set down as an accomplished fact.

These, then, are the three answers which Jesus Christ delivered to the devil's temptations. One point before we look at the answers as a whole.

Jesus Christ said, in answer to the devil's quotation of Scripture, "It is written *again*." What is the meaning of that? It is that the Bible is not made to be of one text; the meaning is that you must compare Scripture with Scripture. It is possible to fasten the mind upon one single line, so as to miss the meaning of the whole revelation of the Bible. We have to compare spiritual things with spiritual—it is written here, and it is written there, and the two writings must be brought together in intelligent, critical, and spiritual comparison. It is written, and it is written again, and the one passage must be read in the light of the other. You must have the whole Bible, and not an isolated text, to rest upon. There is a biblical spirit as well as a biblical letter. Is it not possible that some of us have fixed our minds upon some isolated passage of Scripture that is really torturing us with agony we dare not explain to our chosen minister? Whereas, if it could be pointed out, he might be able to say to us, "It is so written there, but it is also written here . . ."; and thus the light might come and all the joy of liberty. If there is any man here whose soul is afflicted by one special passage of Scripture, and I can be of any service in showing him other writings which illuminate it, it will be the joy of my life to be of that service to any soul bowed down by such distress.

Looking at the answers as a whole, three things strike me. First of all, they were *written* answers. This is no matter of ready repartee; this is not a question of the quickness of Christ's intelligence: this is not an unexpected flash of fire by friction that had not been counted upon—this is quotation; this is rest upon the revealed word; this is an endorsement of all that was written in the Holy Scriptures available to them in that time. Let the word of Christ dwell in you richly. You are not called upon to be geniuses in your conflicts with the devil; you are only called upon to know your Bibles well. Where is the man who knows his Bible well—and yet where is there a man in England who has not some portion of the Bible humming in his head, so much so that he thinks he knows it—who when called upon for quotation, round, complete, direct, can give it? It is no wonder that the devil plays his game successfully with men whose Scripture quotations halt and tremble for very weakness, being uncertain how the words stand, and not knowing whether the point of the sword be the hilt or the hilt the point? Who can fight so, now trying one end and now the other? Let us read the Bible all over again; get it into our hearts as a letter and a spirit—yea, let it dwell in us richly, for as there is but one verb, one number, one light, so there is but one Book—all other books are but broken lights of that. Jesus Christ went directly to the supernatural; he went to revealed truth. It is marvelous that amid all these replies he does not make what we should call an original observation. He quotes, and if you search further into the matter you will find that he quotes— *himself.*

These answers were not only written, but they were simple. There are no deep metaphysics here, which bewilder the heads of poor believers, and makes them giddy with exercises of extraordinary intricacy, and calling for extraordinary intellectual energy. Great answers are always simple, simplicity being understood as the last result of wisdom—not something shallow and superficial, but as the ultimate result of processes which spread over the whole being of God. The whole movement of civilization is towards simplicity: every now and then we startle ourselves by the simplicity of answers which we thought would have been infinitely profound. We had been looking for words six feet long, and behold, all the meaning we wanted was trembling in a word of one syllable, brief and beautiful as a dewdrop when the sun inflames it with tender glory. O, you groper and seeker after deep things in relation to the kingdom of heaven, you who want to climb up to the skies by some clever staircase of your own making, you should know that the way is simple in the sense already defined. It expresses God's eternity, and yet it bows itself down to your littleness and weakness. "It is written"—there is your answer. "It is written again"—that is your further reply. Never go to search for keen retort or flashing repartee within your own genius: the answer is not in you, it is in God! Strike no match of your own wit; pluck your lightning from the heavens—they never fail.

Then the answers were not only written and simple, they were authoritative. They are not quoted as conjectures, they are not submitted as suggestions. When a man goes into war, he must not take with him a sword that has to be tried, but one that has been tested and approved. God knows exactly what temptations every one of us has to endure, and he has written down for us the exact answer. If we try any other reply, we shall get a retort from the enemy, but if we accumulate God's answers, and hurl them at him, he will leave us, and angels will come and minister unto us.

Let us be thankful that in all these answers Jesus Christ has said nothing that we ourselves are not entitled to say. When the devil tells me that I must live by bread alone, I say, "What a liar! I can live in any way God sees fit to appoint. He is not shut up to one way of keeping man's breath in his nostrils. You are a liar!" When the devil says to me, "Do something rash, just for the purpose of testing whether God does love you"; when the devil says to me, as he did to some magazine writer not long ago, "Now let two hospitals be chosen, and in connection with the one there shall be prayer, and let us see in which of the hospitals the patients get better soonest"—I say, "O, what folly, what tempting of God, what trap-setting, what small experimenting, what neat ways of forming ourselves into an innumerable jury for the purpose of putting the Almighty to the test." Thou shalt not tempt the Lord thy God. Providence is not a question of balloting, and snare-setting, and testing and tempting; it is a question of trusting, living in and with God, and knowing that an inch is not a yard, and that a part is not the whole.

I am tempted to tempt God. I want him to bless my wheat fields. I, speaking out of my folly, say to heaven, "God, if thou wouldst give me, a praying man, a great crop, and starve the fields of that profane person over the road, people would begin to think there is a God in heaven — do it." It is a superficial speech, utterly shallow and narrow, and it is a temptation or unworthy trial of God.

When the devil says, "Worship me, and I will give thee the world," then I am entitled to get angry. There is a keener accent in the last answer, "Get thee hence" — the dog was ordered behind. If we could speak with more emphasis we should get a clearer path for our feet, but if we are "if-you-please"-ing the devil, and asking him to be good enough to get out of the way, if we are saying, "By your leave, Satanic majesty, we will go forward," do you suppose he will give us his leave that we may advance? I tell you religion has lost its emphasis, religion has fallen down before conventional moods and standards, and has lost that high accentuation which made its speech heard above the hurtling storm. Hear the Blessed One, see his flushed face, hear that new tone in his voice — we have not heard it before in these readings, "Get thee hence!" Speak with keener emphasis, with broader meaning — open your throat to the fullness of its compass, and let your words shoot out like cannon balls, and God will give you victory.

"Then the devil leaveth him," with bowed limbs and shrunken neck, and eyes fastened on the dust, crestfallen, jaw-broken, his head swimming with a new dizziness, with purpose malignant as hell burning in his heart, but every energy of his being collapsed, made limp, flaccid, his backbone melted like wax in the fire. He left him. Whether he will return, we shall see as the story advances.

twelve

THE TEMPTATION
(PART THREE)

Matthew 4:1–11

OUR PURPOSE will be limited to the setting forth of certain practical lessons suggested by the conflict, which may apply to ourselves in all the weary strife and painful discipline and all but incessant temptations of our own earthly course.

Shall I startle you very much if I say that there is some *comfort* to be derived even from temptation? Shall I for the moment depart from the usual course of preachers and instead of dwelling on the dark side of temptation, show you how light comes in that black hour? There are times enough in the year when I may seek to afflict you with considerations that pain the soul; what if, for the time being, we get lifted in tenderer mood altogether, and speak light to those who sit in darkness? This is of the Lord's doing, and it is as marvelous in our eyes as it is consolatory to our heart.

For example, temptation implies *a measure of goodness* on the part of the man who is tempted. The orchard robber does not go into the orchard in the winter time: he says there is nothing to be gained; why skulk behind the hedge: why watch the doors of the house, why lay plots and schemes for the robbery of this orchard? There is not one particle of fruit to be had upon all these winter-bound branches. The robber of orchards comes in fruit time; it is the fruit that tempts him; it is the fruit that is worth having; he does not want the barren branch, however great and far-reaching it may be, he wants the ripening fruit—for that his fingers itch.

Is it not so, in some degree, with regard to the assault of the enemy? There is some *virtue* he would pluck from us, there is some noble

95

temper he would spoil, there is some high desire he would mar, there is some meditated prayer just taking wing for heaven that he would turn aside. Reflect, then, that your temptations may be, from the diabolical side, but so many indications that you are worth tempting.

Then let us once for all get rid of the delusion that temptation is *sin*. That thought has troubled many an honest heart. A man feels himself strongly drawn in a wrong direction, and he says, "I am a very bad man." Once let a man's hope in himself through God fail, and he will be the very thing that he fears. The temptation doubles itself in its breadth and momentum by suggesting that itself is sin. The best people are the most tempted; we have already seen that in the course of our exposition, when we read these words together, one after the other in sharp succession—"This is my beloved Son. Then was Jesus led up of the spirit to be tempted of the devil." We all remember instances in which the thought that temptation was sin utterly took the sunshine out of our life. You are tempted to take that drink that has ruined you. You say, "I may as well have done it: there is a pull at my heart which wants me to do it, and if I have already drunk it in my heart I may as well drink it with my lips. I have committed my sin spiritually, I may as well perfect it externally." Beware lest you give temptation sharpness, leverage, and the use of all the mechanical powers, by considering that temptation is itself sin. Do not say, "What a bad heart I have, or I could not be tempted so"; on the contrary, reason this way: "What a strong enemy I have, how he plagues me, and does he play his game for nothing? Is he laying all his plots and schemes and plans that he may win a rotten straw?" Through the force and urgency and number of your temptations, see the grandest side of your nature. Who wastes his guns on empty fortresses? Who wastes his fire in burning up that which is itself valueless for all the purposes of cleansing and purification? In proportion as you are great and noble and heavenly-minded will be the force and persistency of the diabolic assault.

There is yet another streak of comfort in this dreary discipline. The struggle *excites interest in two worlds.* In this great battle you find the devil, you find humanity, and you find angels. The last verse reads, "Then the devil leaveth him, and behold angels came and ministered unto him." We are watched. "Seeing then that we are surrounded by so great a cloud of witnesses—what then? Let us run with patience the race that is set before us, looking unto Jesus, the Author and Finisher of our faith" [see

Heb. 12:1, 2]. "Then was Jesus led up of the spirit into the wilderness." Then he will be *alone.* He will be struck at where there is no friend to help him. Not so! Put the first verse and the last together. No man was there, but all God's angels thronged the assaulted Christ. Lord, open our eyes that we may see the reality of things. We think we are alone when all high heaven is around us, and every angel is on guard to defend our life and consummate our purpose. We are blind, we have mistaken the ceiling for the sky, and walls of our own building have we mistaken for thine unmeasured horizon. Give us accuracy and farness of vision.

How differently—let us dream a moment, wildly, almost blasphemously—the verse might have finished, namely thus, "Then the devil leaveth him, and behold his angels, black as himself, pitiless as his own heart, came and dragged him away." O wild dream, nearing the border line of blasphemy, yet not without its wholesome suggestion, for what was impossible in the case of Christ is possible in the case of every one of us, for we are so frail, so short-sighted, so open to seduction and false lure. Shall it be said of me, of you, "Then the devil leaveth him, and sent hounds of hell to drag the wounded soul into the pit. Then the devil, having bruised his heart and thrown him down and cast him to the ground with infinite superiority of strength, left him to be fetched home by some hound of hell"? "I hit my body in the eye, I blacken both my eyes, I push and thrust sharp knuckles into my eye, lest, having preached to others, I myself become a castaway" [see 1 Cor. 9:27, cf. 1 Cor. 9:27 NIV]. What I say unto one I say unto all—Watch. "Resist the devil, and he will flee from you" [James 4:7]. "We fight not with flesh and blood, but against principalities, against powers, against the rulers of the darkness of this world, against forces impalpable and all but irresistible" [see Eph. 6:12].

I cannot look then at the temptation in this light, without seeing somewhat of *the grandeur of* man. Two worlds contend for his possession; the angels want him, and the damned host gnash their teeth upon him and long to devour him. What is he? Some dying insect; some frail, animated dust, some little creature that can be consumed utterly as to his soul as well as to his body, before the moth? It is not so that I read the biblical account of my own nature; the divinity stirs within me, I can utter vast prayers, I can stretch my supplications onward till the stars fall under them, like earth-lamps dimly seen through infinite mists. Do not tell me that I am little and lowly and worthless; I know what I am when the devil would give all he has to get me, and when Christ laid down his life that I may never die. Not the metaphysician, not the psychologist, not the philosopher, can take from me by long and weary-winding reasoning my grandeur. I feel it, I know it; when the long-strained argument has ceased its murky and confusing eloquence, I rise and say, "I feel that I am the bearer of the image of the divine." My consciousness cannot be argued down, my vocabulary may be quite exhausted, my intelligence may be put to shame by the superior knowledge of many a disputant, but when all that can be said on the other side has completed itself in many a weary period, my consciousness rises and says, "You are a King's son; claim your heirship and insist on the possession of your inheritance." Tell me if you have not had moments of consciousness in which you have forgotten your littleness and have stood out in heroic breadth and grandeur, transformed, your very clothes shining with light and your face aflame with a luster not thrown upon it from any external lamp.

Thus would I gather comfort from the temptations of life. Doubt yourself if your temptations are *few*. The man who sleeps in a wooden hut, with not one thing of any value whatever upon his person or within his residence says, "I hear a good deal of burglaries and felonies of one kind and another, but do you know I have no faith in the rumors. *I* am never assaulted, *I* have never seen a burglar, no man ever interferes with me; I fancy, therefore, that all this talk about the criminal invasion of houses is folly." Can you account for that man's never having a visit from a burglar? How would you account for his exemption from that social pest? Instantly you would say, "That man has nothing worth taking; burglars do not waste their time on such, they go where the prey is." So I say to you, my tempted friend, wearying yourself out with much vivisection and cross-examination of your poor tortured heart. If the temptations are many, it may be because the possessions are great. Take this view of the assault and strengthen thyself in God.

Beware of the temptation which comes with an "*if*" in its mouth. *If* thou be the Son of God, command that these stones be made bread. *If* thou be the Son of God, cast thyself down. Suspicion may be the beginning of ruin. Suspect your sonship and you are undone at once. For a moment begin to wonder if you are really a child of God, and the battle is half won by the enemy. The old divines used to preach the grand and savory doctrine of assurance. They used to say, faith is the milk, assurance is the cream. With puritanic zeal, but with a divine enthusiasm, they used to urge us to claim all the enjoyment and security of distinct assurance. Have we escaped from their terms and from their theology? Then we have escaped from a rich banquet, that we might feed ourselves upon the empty wind. Recall the great and noble words of Scripture — "Now are we the sons of God, and it doth not appear what we shall be; if sons [children], then heirs, heirs of God and joint-heirs with Christ" [1 John 3:2; Rom. 8:17]. There is substance in that talk; it is not a colored vapor, it is the substance of the soul's distinct recognition of certain divine securities which God has promised never to withdraw from the faithful and loving soul. Can you cry "Abba, Father"? Can you ever with your soul's tenderest trust say "God is my Father"? Then, never let the devil write his big and hideous *if* upon your faith. Fatherhood like God's does not change with the wind; this divine relationship is not a question of the barometer; this acceptance on the part of the divine Father is not a question of your physical sufferings and moods and indigestions and numerous infirmities. Remember that you built your house upon a rock, and do not suppose any fog can overthrow it. If you had built the edifice of your life upon the shifting fog it would not have been worth one moment's purchase. If your foundation is right, the air will presently be clear. You know what visitations of fog we have had, and suppose anyone had said to you, "All the great buildings of London are now in imminent danger," you would have smiled at the childish suggestion. Why? Because nothing has interfered with the foundations of those buildings. Fogs break no slates, fogs cannot even break the glass; how then should fogs shake the rocks and make the towers totter?

It is even so with our spiritual life. These temptations and times of depression, sad feeling, low-heartedness and lack of courage, are but the fogs that come for a moment. You are founded on a *rock*, then lift up your heads — the fogs will pass and every star will be found to be firm in its place. As for those of you who serve the devil, let me tell you that you are either under the dominion of God or you are under the dominion of God's enemy. Do not suppose that there is a third master. It is God or mammon [see Matt. 6:24; cf. Luke 16:13]. Do not suppose that if you escape religion you escape all service — bondage — you are the slaves of the devil, or you are the slaves of Christ. Let me tell you one or two things about your master the devil. He was formerly my master and I know him. I have studied his plan. I know every move he makes. He has only three moves with obvious variations on the chess-board of life. He has only *one world* to offer, and he offered it to Christ. "All these things," said he, "will I give thee, if thou wilt fall down and worship me." *All*—a little ALL! It appeared great to his eye as it appears great to our eye, but it is a little all, and how infinitely little it must have appeared to him who made all the worlds! If you have devised a little light that will shine ten yards further than the light which somebody else has devised, you will have column after column in the newspaper about it, and it will appear a great light. But if you had made one single sunbeam, you would laugh at the greatness of your supposed illustrious flame. If you could see all the solar system and all the outlying stellar universe, circuit beyond circuit, flame beyond flame, and then be called to look at some little jet of man's contrivance, you would smile at the mighty epithets which he applies to its definition. The devil looks upon the world and says, "All these things will I give thee," to a Man who made the universe, and stands above it, and sets on the proudest sun the imprint of his footstep. Do not be deceived by nearness, and by small proverbs, and by immediate possessions. Have food to eat the world knows nothing about [see John 4:32 NIV]; have the high acquaintanceship of God, and then the petty fellowship of earthly princes will dwindle into its proper insignificance.

I will tell you another thing about your master which will make you ashamed of him. He trades upon my *weakness*; he never comes to me in my strength; for whenever he sees me a little *weary*, then he comes with all his force. When I have fasted forty days and forty nights and become conscious of painful hunger, then he slouches up and tells me his little plan for bread-making out of stones. When I feel tired at night, all my energy gone out of me, he comes to me and says, "You could do a great deal better than this, you know, if you left the pulpit and took up with another line of life that I could put you into—why, there is no telling what you might do." And I say, "I do feel tired, I wish I could escape this weariness." And he says, with pleasant voice, lowered into a soft minor key, so dear to true confidence, "I can show you how." The beast never faced me when I was strong, he was afraid of me when the God shone in my face, but whenever he has caught me weak and depressed and sad, with tears in my eyes, at the graveside, at the bedside of my dying friend, then he has come to me and said, "I can get you out of all this." Be ashamed of such a master, disown him, write a better name on your life-banner—he is a coward, a liar, a murderer from the beginning, a separator of brethren, a deceiver, a usurper. "Resist the devil and he will flee from you" [James 4:7].

And as for you, poor soul, barely living, I want a word with you. You are a misunderstood man, persons come to you and say that you ought not to do this, and ought not to do that, and you know it so well that their exhortation is but so much vitriol poured into an open wound. They call you a bad man and they have no hope of you, and everybody has left you now but your mother, and sometimes you think she is going to leave you too, but if she goes out at one door she will come back through another. When a man's mother leaves him, no angel can come to minister unto him; he is ready then for the hounds that drag him down. Shall I set myself up against you and boast and triumph over you? No! Why? Because you have been sorely tempted, and I may not have been tempted so sorely. It took you a long time to fall, I might have fallen in half the time: who am I then that I should taunt you and mock you? Be it far from me to practice this kind of reproach—it is the meanest use of morality.

And you have lived a poor, poor life and are next to nothing to look at now from a spiritual point of view, and you are almost ready to give up. Do not give up! The friends around you know what temptations you have fallen into, but as Robert Burns says in one of the sweetest of his poems,

> They know not what's *resisted*.

thirteen

WORK AFTER TEMPTATION

Matthew 4:12–17

THE ELEVENTH VERSE reads—"Then the devil leaveth him, and behold angels came and ministered unto him"; and the twelfth verse reads—"Now, when Jesus had heard that John was cast into prison, he departed into Galilee." You must not imagine that the events in the eleventh and twelfth verses followed one another in immediate succession. Jesus had been exercising something like an eight months' ministry in Judea, when he heard that John was cast into prison. Still, I cannot but feel that the temptation prepared the great Worker for his marvelous toil. He was in all points tempted like as we are [see Heb. 4:15]; how otherwise could he have been our priest and Savior in every sense of those immeasurable terms? No angel could have preached to me: he would not have understood me, his language would be unknown, he would have nothing in common with my deepest and most painful experience, he would be altogether above me, too grand and sublime for my spiritual conception; it was needful that he who was to speak the universal language, should pass under the universal experience: he should know the devil, he should have met him as it were face to face, he should have felt the keenness of his subtlest approaches, and the blow of his heaviest assault. Jesus Christ was thus prepared by temptation to preach the gospel to the world, and indeed to do all the work for the world which he had from eternity undertaken to accomplish.

Men are fitted for work in various ways. Some men are fitted for it by the reading of many books hard and difficult to be understood, others are fitted by a wear and tear that seems to have no expression adequate to itself in human words, a continual vexation of the soul and distress of all its best faculties, so that they come up out of great agonies to speak tender words, and they bring themselves out of the night of intolerable despair to utter the word of benediction. But no man can be prepared for any deep and vital work in the world who has not gone through the school of the devil. You cannot be taught to preach by reading many books, however long and eloquent they may be. You overshoot my life; I must hear something in your tone which will enable me to identify you as of my own kindred. Now and again there must break from your heart's voice tones and accents which tell me that you too have been in the pit, have been dragged through the lake of fire, and have understood what it is to be almost—gone. He has wonderful influence over me who can pity me in the distresses of my temptation. He who can only make my intellect wonder, touch my imagination with new and flashing lights, has but momentary fascination for me; I own it, and bid the man farewell, but he who knows the devil in and out, all the temptations in me, and who has come away from the life-battle feeling that the enemy is no small one, but subtle in suggestion and mighty in influence, and who says to me, "The battle is very heavy, do not underrate it; your strength will be tried to its very last fiber and throb, but God will help you; your extremity shall be his opportunity"—then he takes me under his influence, and I yield myself to him and call him, not preacher only, and teacher, wise and true, but friend sympathetic, with whose soul mine has fellowship, and we can go together both in blessed and hopeful union to the common throne of the church, from which is dispensed the blessing which is better than bread, the word which gives the soul immortality.

Have you been fitted for your work? If so, why are you not doing it? To be qualified and yet to be idle, is to incur the most severe displeasure of man and of God. How many more books are you going to read before you begin to speak? How much longer are you going to study the providence of God amongst the children of men before you begin to open your mouth in witness? How many more sermons and prayers are you going to hear and endorse before you begin in the marketplace to say, "My scales are kept in heaven and my standards are set up in the sanctuary of the sky"? It is time that some of us were proving our fitness by our activity; sad is the sight of a man qualified, evidently fitted to do certain work, and yet not doing it. We have all heard of that wonderful stone in the quarry out of which Baalbec was built; it was a great stone, it was cut out of the rock with great labor, the mason squared it, the sculptor chiseled it, nothing more that the tool could do to it remained to be done, and yet there it lay in the quarry, not lifted to its proper eminence, not set amid its designed surroundings, a gigantic miscarriage, a horrible failure; fitted, made beautiful, almost speaking in its perfected sculpture, and yet there it was lying with the rubbish, when it might have been shining like a living presence in some magnificent temple.

What is true of that stone is surely true of some of us. We have been a long time at school, yet we never use our learning for the good of men. We have been much trained in music, yet we do little but mumble in the vocal worship of Almighty God. We have read many books, yet we are silent as the grave. We have passed through many a temptation, but the word of sympathy never falls from our lips. We have proved the vanity of the world and we have never told the young that the world is a gigantic lie and life but an empty wind apart from God and the infinite Savior Jesus Christ. How much longer therefore shall we be qualified to do much and yet be doing so little? How much longer shall we have studied the eloquence which is taught only in the expensive school of experience, and yet shut up our lips in criminal dumbness? Our Savior Jesus Christ having been qualified for his work, went to it. Arise, let us go hence.

When Jesus heard that John was cast into prison—cast into prison by Herod, because the Baptist had reproved the ruler for his evil ways—then the work ceased. Shut up the preacher in prison and you will shut up Christ's Church, would seem to be the short and easy method of persons who take superficial views of divine truth. A man who is plaguing you with his remonstrances: shut him up in jail, and there will be an end of your trouble. That would be a fool's speech to make, if you ever did make one! You can shut up the worker, but can you shut up the work? You can silence the individual minister—what is he but a little creature in the presence and in relation to the power of a reigning monarch? But how can you shut up the divine truth? John was cast into prison, but there came a great light. Now, Herod, rattle your jail-keys, get them all out and shut up the *light* in jail. O the mockery, the satire, the instructive sarcasm of the King that reigns over all! John is incarcerated, and the Lord sends a great light over the lands, and tauntingly bids the kings of the earth shut it up in their dungeons! So it is with the progress of divine truth. A minister dies, but the light increases: the individual speaker comes to the end of his discourse, but there are silent and subtle ministries evermore proceeding with infinite effect to work out the decree and purpose of God. The eloquent thunder ceases, the silent light goes on. This Christian kingdom is a ministry of light; it is a marvelous light, it is a great light, it is impalpable, intangible, immeasurable; it is around us, and we cannot touch it; we put out our hands and dash through it, and still it stands there, an angel that fills the whole horizon. Fear not: your great Baptist is mewed up in prison and the ax is being whetted that shall take off his head: the next thing that ax will have to do will be to strike the beams off the sun. Can it perform that deed, or is the ax not yet made that can shatter one ray from the source out of which it falls?

"When Jesus had heard that John was cast into prison he departed . . . that it might be fulfilled which was spoken by the prophet." Can a man not go from one city or province to another, without fulfilling some old and sacred word of prophecy? The answer to that inquiry is "No." Did you come to church today by the divine decree? The answer to that inquiry is "Yes." You could not help coming. Do not suppose that we are here by accident. We are here that it might be fulfilled which was spoken by the prophet. Do not isolate yourself from the great body of history and the great stream of prophecy, and say that you do just what you like. You think you do: it is your delusion, and it will prove in the long run to be a source of unrest and pain to you. Let me feel my connection with all my kind; let me feel that I am in God's hands, and that the bounds of my habitation are fixed; let me feel that my liberty is itself but part of the divine law. Then there will come into my soul a deep rest, a gentle peace, a profound assurance, and though the mountains be removed and carried into the depths of the sea, yet I shall remain at rest in the very heart of God.

There is nothing trifling in your life. As to whether you shall live on this side of the street or that, will be settled for you if you will put yourself quietly into the hand of God. Why do you undertake anything on your own account? Why do you say you will do this or do that, purely of your own suggestion and to carry out some motion of your own will? I will not go out until the Master sends for me, I will tarry in dark Egypt till the angel says, "The way is clear: arise and go": yes, I will sit down in prison until Pharaoh send for me by God's suggestion [see Gen. 41:14]. Could I talk so I should feel that life were worth living, and as for tomorrow's letters, and difficulties, and fears, and perils, and distresses,

I would meet them all after a long night's deep slumber, and they would vanish before my strength. Oh, fussy little fool, a self-manager and self-controller, sit down and learn that to obey is better than to be clever, and to wait upon God is sometimes the most sublime genius.

Thus wondrously does the Old Testament overlap the New. Men who are critical upon these matters tell us that some two hundred and sixty times there are references in the New Testament to the Old, and thus the Old and the New overlap and intertwine, and the two Testaments are one revelation, as the morning and the evening are one day. Now and again we see a little into the details of life. This is an instance in point—Jesus arises, leaving Nazareth to dwell in Capernaum, that it might be fulfilled which was spoken by Isaiah the prophet. Details vex us; we cannot piece them together and make anything of unity and shape of them; they fall to pieces under our clumsy fingers. Now and again there is a fissure, and I see somewhat of the meaning of detail: I see that there is a hand jointing them, articulating them, and behold it is making order out of confusion. Lord, take up all the details of my life: they are exceedingly incoherent, and they baffle me; they sometimes almost make a non-believer of me; they sometimes arise and fall upon my life altogether as if they would crush it. I bless thee for these little peeps into this inner working of thine, about the hairs of my head, the guiding of my steps, the ordering of my habitation—undertake for me altogether—let me do nothing but in fulfillment of thy providence.

He came and dwelt in Capernaum. Thou art exalted unto heaven, take care lest thou be thrust down into hell. It is an awful and sacred thing to have a good neighbor, to come into contact with a good man, to have amongst us a voice of fire, a teaching of love, a ministry of light. He came and dwelt in Capernaum. He came as the light came into this house this morning, without making any noise, but filling the whole space. He came without noise or cry or tremulous voice, but Capernaum felt that there was a ghost, a spirit, a strange influence within itself, and that Capernaum, if it grow not right up into heaven and be absorbed into Zion, will be thrust down into hell. Our privileges become our judgments.

Zebulon and Naphthali, Jordan, Galilee of the Gentiles—are these a mere cluster of words? What, the Gentiles already? His beginnings are like endings, his first words have somewhat of the ripeness and mellowness of high climaxes. Already is there flashing even in secondary light some gleam of divine luster upon the Gentile places of the earth? Does the word *Gentiles* occur so soon in the sacred narrative? We are Gentiles. Whenever we see that word we should say, "There is something about us; what is it?" It is like seeing our name in a foreign book, like opening a work written in a language we cannot understand, and seeing our name broadly in the middle of the page. We are arrested, and we wonder what it means. God's purpose is one that girdles the whole earth: it takes it little by little, but it takes it all in, and the meadow is not jealous because the mountaintops catch the light first. You have stood on a mountaintop to watch the sun rise—why didn't you stay in the valley? Because you said, "The mountaintop will catch the first light; let us be, therefore, on the highest possible point." And did the valleys below retire from the earth and say they would never grow any more gardens and meadows, and any more harvests of wheat, because the snowy peaks caught the first blessing and warmed to the earliest kiss? You are but a poor reader of history who objects that the Jews caught the first gleam of the new morning. A little more time and that sun will fill the earth, a little more time and this Sun of Righteousness will shoot out his glories until every land shall be bright with the pure luster of divine truth.

When Jesus heard that John was cast into prison he came to the front. It might have been an excellent reason for departing again into the wilderness to avoid danger. It would have been so had the kingdom which they came to reveal and establish been a kingdom of mere sentiment or a conception of merely and purely intellectual energy. This is how the Christian kingdom has advanced from the first ages until now. The front rank of soldiers all shot—Forward next rank, over the dead bodies! That has been done and is being done, and none can hinder the progress of this divine kingdom, connected as that progress is with a heroism that is not of human inspiration, but of divine beginning and strength. Where there is danger there should be a provocation of courage.

We know nothing about courage now. There are some texts I dare not preach from. Dare I preach from this text—"none of these things move me, neither count I my life dear unto myself, so that I might finish my course with joy, and the ministry, which I have received of the Lord Jesus" [Acts 20:24]? You will never hear me preach from that text. It would burn like a conscious lie upon my coward lips. These things do move me. I am annoyed by trifles, discouraged by trumpery circumstances of a temporary nature—dare I preach from a hero's words? There have, however, been times in the Church when Christians have been heroic. We read

in history not more than three hundred years old of Christians who having heard that John was cast into prison went forward to take his place.
I was reading only a few days ago some such occurrence. The Christians
of one town were all driven into one dungeon: they were gathered together and shut up into one prison, and the executioner came to them
and took them out one by one, having first put a blindfold over the eyes
of the doomed victim. He led him out in the presence of the others to
the place of execution, and put a knife through his throat, and leaving
him half dead, he took the blindfold off and went back for the next, the
knife streaming with blood held between his teeth, as he tied the blindfold over the eyes of the next victim. And twenty people were done like
this, and forty and sixty, and seventy and eighty-eight, and that human
butcher failed—not the Christian heroism. It was in this fashion that your
liberties were bought. We were redeemed not with corruptible things,
but with precious blood, and we sit here today, quiet, perhaps indifferent,
as the result of human blood. Are we worthy of our traditions? We dare
not go out if it is raining, we take offense because of trifles, we leave the
work because of some little irritation, not worthy of a moment's consideration. Let us get back into the spirit of those traditions which have
made the country what it is, as far as it is great and noble and influential for good.

What have we done for our Lord? Of the eighty-eight sufferers it
was said that it was well accepted by the elder Christians, but when the
executioner came to the younger ones they were more timorous. Who
wonders? Does the dear young life like to give itself out thus boldly, all
at once, early in the morning? But not a heart fell back. Do not tell me
that a kingdom thus begun and thus continued is going to fall. These
men did not work through some delusion for which they could give no
account; they accepted their fate intelligently, they gave reasons for it,
they were not moved by mere delusions, but by arguments which to them
were as intellectually complete as they were morally influential.

I wish to God we had more heroism in the Church. I ask you younger
men and women to come forward and take the places of the elder, who
are not cast into prison, but who may be disabled by age, who may be
constrained by one uncontrollable circumstance or another to leave the
front. They have had a long and useful day, and now they desire rest,
and it is no coward's prayer they pray when they ask for relief if not release. Will you see the place left vacant? Are you content to see great

gaps in the ranks of the Church? Will you be baptized for the dead? Will you know that it is your turn next? There is a soldier in front of you dying: pluck up your courage in the divine strength, and be ready to take his place. When this spirit returns to the Church, Herod will be troubled upon his throne, and the time is not far off when he will be consumed by the fire of the Lord.

Jesus began to preach, and he repeated John's sermon. The sermon is one. He said, "Repent, for the kingdom of heaven is at hand." Why, who preached that sermon before? John the Baptist, and Jesus Christ, seeing that John was in prison, saw that the sermon should not fail of utterance, and with another voice, that had in it wondrous possibility of intonation and color, he said, "Repent, for the kingdom of heaven is at hand." He *began* to preach. Have we begun to hear? Hearing is an art, listening is not possible except to the attentive soul. Who listens well? Few men do. What happens to him who listens well? He hears the Holy Spirit's music!

NOTES

"Between the 11th and 12th verses there is a great break, and it is well to remember what passed in the interval: (1) the return to the Baptist, and the call of the six disciples [John 1:29–51]; (2) the marriage at Cana and the visit to Capernaum [John 2:1–12]; (3) the cleansing of the Temple; the interview with Nicodemus and the last testimony of the Baptist [John 2:13 to 3:36]. At this stage comes in the imprisonment of John [mentioned here, but not narrated till 14:3–5], and the consequent journey through Samaria to Galilee [John 4:1–42].

Spoken by the prophet—We should say written by the prophet. But to the Jews of our Lord's time books were few, the people heard the words rather than read them; hence the peculiar form "spoken by the prophet."

Verse 17—"Began to preach," i.e., began his Galilean ministry. Before this there had been a Judean ministry extending over several months.

fourteen

THE CALLING OF MEN

Matthew 4:18–25

WE ARE NOT to understand that this event took place immediately after
our Lord's temptation. A very considerable interval passed between
the temptation and this work by the sea of Galilee. Still the incident comes
with infinite beauty and suggestiveness after that great crisis in the history of our Lord. Shall we be too fanciful if we think of the places in connection with the events—the quiet river and the sacred baptism; the solitary
wilderness and the fierce assault of hell's chief; the busy sea and the call
to service? If a painter seeks a background, and if the novelist feels it needful roughly and with the haste of great skill to thrust in a little scenery
and landscape in order to throw up the figures, why should we hesitate
to connect certain great events in our Lord's life and certain special events
in our own life with the peculiar atmosphere in which they were developed—the river and the baptism, the wilderness, silent, solemn,
awful, and its temptations, and the sea, never at rest, and its call to labor,
heroic sacrifice, noble toil?

We are not to understand that these men never saw Jesus Christ
until the day referred to in the text. They knew him perfectly well. Jesus
Christ had been preaching and laboring in many places, and these very
men sustained the relation of a kind of nominal discipleship to him already. There was in them a wonder, nearly equal to faith, there was in
them an expectation which sometimes almost dignified itself into a religion. They knew his person, they knew his voice, they knew somewhat
of his claim, and they had seen somewhat of his power. They were already in a sense followers of Christ just as some of you are, in a distant
way, gropingly, wonderingly, well inclined towards him, with a mind

110

half-set in all the loftiness of the direction which he himself took. They would have been wounded if you had told them they did not care for him, and yet they would have been puzzled if you had asked them why. Why this is just your case; if you could be suddenly and rudely told that you did not care for Christ, you would resent the impeachment. Yet you are not in the circle wholly and forever. The time now came when Jesus Christ called these men with a more definite call to service. This was not a call to piety, to religious devotion, in the sense of mere worship. Understand that this was a call to toil, service, work. "I will make you fishers of men." He was not reasoning with the persons referred to, saying, "Give your hearts to God, be good in the truly religious sense of the word, leave your atheism and worship the true and living God"; it was not an appeal of this kind that was addressed to the fishermen, it was a call to *service*—"Follow me, and I will make you fishers of men."

There is a time in every life when such a call is addressed to it—a ghostly hour in which you heard a voice and could not tell where it came from. You said you were moved, stirred, all but inspired, and you knew not what to make of that strange incident in your life. Did it ever occur to you that it was the voice of *Christ?* Did you ever give a broadly and sublimely religious interpretation to the ghostly ministries which have affected your thinking and toned your ambition? If you have been looking downward for small interpretations that might be written with a fool's finger in the dry dust, let me now ask you to lift up your eyes and see if the meaning be not found in the stars rather than in the cold stones.

You do not deny the call, but how to carry it out is your difficulty. You have nothing to do with that. Hear this voice and tell me if everything be not in it—"Follow me." That may mean a great tax upon my strength. "Follow me." That may mean a rash adventure. "Follow me." I may not be equal to the occasion. But the call does not *end* with "Follow me." He who had spoken these words spoke other words which address themselves immediately to every misgiving of the modest heart. The other words are, "I will make you"—as if he had said, "Rely on me for the power, puzzle not yourselves with vain inquiries as to how this following is to be sustained and completed; he who gives the call gives the power." Herein we are entitled to bind Christ to his own promise. We do not start upon a warfare or a race at our own charges. We have come out at the bidding of God, to do God's work and to do it in God's strength—where, then, is your cleverness, your ingenuity, your self-supplying strength? You have none, you need none: your daily bread is in heaven; go for it every morning, live upon God, make yourself strong with his promises. I know not what I shall do for the next seven years; they will oppress me, they will kill me, they will utterly put an end to me—so would I talk if I were dependent upon my own suggestiveness and fertility of invention. But when Christ says, "I will make you—" he never leaves unfinished any tower that he begins. He has not left any star unrounded, there is no useless rubbish in his universe. I will then even live in him, and wait for his word, and when I am most dumb because of my self-exhaustion, he will be most eloquent if my eyes be lifted up to him in the prayerfulness of a confident expectation.

So many of you are standing back because you think you have to do everything at your own charges. You are afraid you would fail if you went forward to attempt this or that work in the name of Christ. Let me tell you the secret of your fear—you have not read the call right through from beginning to end. You have heard the words "Follow me"—the majority of us only hear parts of sentences; there are very few men that can quote any sentence right through from beginning to end. They hear the leading word, they forget all the other words that give it perspective and tone and color. Men hear according to their moral condition; we often hear only what we want to hear; our attention is not of that round and complete kind that takes in the entire statement and weighs it to the utmost syllable and tone.

How are we to know when a divine call has really been addressed to the heart? There are many calls that may only be voices that we should not listen to—how then are we to know when the call really does come down from heaven, ringing with all its music and filled with all its gentle persuasiveness? The text will tell you—the answer is here. Know that your call to service is likely to be a divine vocation if it involve—sacrifice. You need to know no more. "Leave your ship, leave your father, leave your nets, leave your friends and follow me." A call that summons men to surrender all things in this way is likely to be a healthy and true call.

I never knew God to address any call to any human soul that did not involve loss. Anticipating our natural and eager desire to know whether a call is heavenly or earthly, God has always associated with his calls— *sacrifice.* When Moses was called, he counted it greater honor to follow God than to enjoy the pleasures of sin for a season and to enrich himself with all the riches of Egypt. When Hadad astounded Pharaoh by saying he wanted to go back to Edom, Pharaoh said, "What hast thou lacked?" and the young man said, "Nothing, howbeit in any wise let me go" [1 Kgs. 11:22]. The Lord had stirred up the heart of Hadad, and Hadad went from Egypt to poor Edom, from rest to battle, from assured and continued prosperity to all the perils and adventures of hazardous war.

This man Simon, called Peter, and Andrew his brother, left their nets and followed Christ. Have we ever left anything for the Savior? I have left nothing. He has given me more than I ever gave him—the whole advantage is on my side. If ever he should say to me, "I was sick and in prison, and ye came unto me," I will contradict him to his face. He will have to prove it. There are those of us, perhaps, who think we have given up a good deal for the gospel; I am not of that number—I have given up nothing for the gospel. There have been men who have not counted their lives dear unto them that they might follow and serve Christ. It would be my distress not to follow him. There would be no poorer wretch on all the earth's green surface than I should be were he to dismiss me from his service. I have never been bruised for him. I have had gardens of flowers given to me because I have endeavored to preach him, and all times of comfortableness and honor: if ever he should say to me, "Blessed one, for I was hungry, and ye gave me meat" [see Matt. 25:34, 35], if I have not strength to contradict him, I hope I shall have the honesty to hang my head and deny by silence what I would gladly contradict by speech. Let none of us set up as sacrificing anything for Christ—we have never done it.

We observe further, from this incident, that Christ's calls are always to something higher. "I will make you fishers of men." He gives the broadest interpretation to our daily need. Whatever you are, he spiritually uses as a type of the other service to which he calls you. Are you fishers in the ordinary sense of the term? He comes to you and says, "I will make you fishers of men." Are you builders of stone and wood? He says, "I will make you builders of a living temple." Are you servants of masters who pay you? He says, "I will make you servants of the King of kings." If we have not realized the spiritual side of our earthly vocation, we are still in the outer court, and have much to learn. Oh, you who heal the body, come, and Christ will show you how to heal the soul. Oh, you tradesmen, and merchants, and money-turners, come and he will show you how to make fine gold and imperishable wealth. Accept your present secular position as a type and hint of the call which Christ is addressing to the soul.

So Christ Jesus called men to his ministry, and unless a man is called to his ministry he had better not enter it. I hold that no man is a true minister who is not directly called by Christ. This limits the ministry, but it strengthens it indefinitely. You cannot learn to preach, you cannot learn to expound the spiritual word—all your syllables may be neatly enunciated, you may learn the art of breathing and the art of delivering the voice, but you have not learned on earth, for it is not taught in the schools of men, how to touch the sin-cursed and sin-burdened soul; that art is taught in heaven: there is but one Master, and he never tires.

What is true of the spiritual ministry is true of all the ministries of life. Whatever you are, you will succeed in it only in proportion as Christ has called you to it. Some of you are in wrong positions altogether, you ought never to have begun where you did begin. By providences, over which you had no control, you were turned into wrong lines, and you know it, and your life is a daily pain and a continual sacrifice. After fifty years of age you cannot shift over to the right lines. Make the best of your position. You are like men who are working against the tide, and it is hard work rowing, but inasmuch as you did not enter upon that arduous undertaking of your own conceit or self-will, inasmuch as others are to blame for it more than you are, I now give you good heart, I now cheer you in the name of the merciful One—he knows your distresses and disadvantages, and he will not overlook these when he audits the account of your life.

> And Jesus went about all Galilee, teaching in their synagogues, and preaching the gospel of the kingdom, and healing all manner of sickness and all manner of disease among the people. And his fame went throughout all Syria: and they brought unto him all sick people that were taken with divers diseases and torments, and those which were possessed with devils, and those which were lunatick, and those that had the palsy; and he healed them.

What a world he came into! And he knew it before he entered it. If the world had been less damned he need not have come. In these verses you have a picture of the real state of humanity as Jesus Christ found it. I want to go where the people are all well. Tell me where the lepers are, where various diseases and torments dwell, and where those live who are demon possessed, and those which are epileptic, and those which are paralyzed, and I will run away. What are terrors to me were attractions to the infinite Heart.

This is the real condition of the world in every age — it is a world full of sickness, and disease, and torment, a world in which men live who are possessed with demons, who are struck with seizures, and shivering and trembling with humanly incurable paralysis. Do we want men of culture to go into such a world — nice, dainty-fingered men who faint at the sight of blood, and shudder if they see a paralytic on the streets? Is that the cruel irony we are going to perpetrate in such a world as this? Let us send down a hundred and fifty nice kid-gloved young men, who never speak above their breath, and who are infinitely gifted in the art of saying nothing in many words. They will return, they will sigh for summer days, and nicer surroundings, and fairer sights. You may say, "We are adapted to certain classes of people of a more elevated, dignified, and cultured kind." Shame on you, my friend, if you are cursed with a conceit like that. The world is a sick world, a dying world, a mad world, and your little daintinesses, and prettinesses, and machine-turned sentences will never touch it. The world needs blood; no other price will redeem it. Oh, church of the living God, Zion, Jerusalem, called by a thousand tender names, what are you doing but running away to pick up flowers when you should be laboring with coat off, with both hands earnestly at the deliverance and the healing of souls.

If you do not buy the world with blood you will never buy it. There are those who object to the expression, *the blood of Christ*. We have now refined that very much into the *love of Christ*, the *example of Christ*, or the *sweet influence of Christ*. We are now unwilling to say, *the blood of Christ*. Why? We have never got anything worth having unless we paid *blood* for it. How were the slaves redeemed and emancipated? What was laid down on the counter? *Blood*. You have your *Magna Charta*, or *Bill of Rights* and do you boast of those monumental documents? What was paid for those documents? *Blood!* Show me in all English history a single great treasure you have, and I will show you as the signature of its lawful purchase — red blood, heart blood, human blood. Yet when I come into a church and think of redeemed men, I am told not to mention the word blood, but to substitute for it *example, love, sympathy, kindness*. No, no. The music is one, the anthem is indivisible, redemption is always by blood, and he who has paid less than blood for any redemption has bought it at the wrong counter and paid for it with counterfeit coin.

Imagine a man coming into such a world as is described in the twenty-third and twenty-fourth verses to do anything for it merely by way of *example*. It is by tragedy that we live. Your home-life owes all its beauty and dignity to the tragedy which is at the heart of it. If we are ever to impress this age we must do it by something more than dainty words and accurately regulated ecclesiastical mechanism. When we go nearer the city we must weep over it, and when we go into the city we must die for it. Other programs you may write, but the angels will tear them and scatter them as waste paper upon the mocking winds.

Wondrous is one little word in this twenty-fourth verse. "He healed them," —as easily as the light fills the firmament, without struggle or noise or huge effort. Mark the infinite ease of the expression, "He healed them." Set that expression beside "He created them, he set them in their places, he rolled the stars along—he healed them." It is part of the same music, omnipotence never fluttered on account of weakness, and never despaired because of miscalculation. What is your complaint, O heart of man? He will heal you. Do not go in the detail of complaints, there is but one disease and its short name is—*sin*. All diseases are but details of that awful fact. The blood of Jesus Christ, God's Son, cleanses from all sin [see 1 John 1:7]. There is a fountain opened in the house of David for sin. The details are innumerable, the central and vital disease is one.

Jesus Christ's ministry was thus twofold. It was not a literary ministry, it was a philanthropic ministry in the noblest interpretation of that term, a man-loving ministry, a ministry that loved the body and that loved the soul. What are we doing for the body? I know there are great dangers in doing for the body, lest people should become hypocrites. Better make a few hypocrites than miss the chance of doing good to one really deserving soul. But who am I that I should set up as scrutineer into real deserts? What are my own deserts? None. Shall we pass up to the judgment bar in the official character of scrutineers and say to the great King-Judge, "Lord, I played the part of examiner, I examined the credentials of other people, I plucked the mask from the hypocrite's face, I stood near to see that no undeserving ones got a crumb from the loaf of charity: what am I to have as an examiner?" There are too many examiners. I was the other night accosted, walking with my wife, by a poor creature who said, "I am very faint, sir." I began to play the "judge and jury" by saying to myself, "All due to her evil behavior." How dare I say so? Her evil behavior? If she was faint, it was my business to help her to overcome that faintness. I would rather be taken in, deceived, in response to such a petition, than go home and sit down over a steaming feast and applaud myself as a shrewd examiner.

fifteen

THE SERMON ON THE MOUNT
(PART ONE)

Matthew 5:1–12

"AND SEEING the multitudes, he went up into a mountain." He has already been in the river, and walking by the seaside: today he goes up into a mountain, and presently we shall have to accompany him in his journeys through cities and towns and villages. Thus, little by little, a place at a time, he will claim and sanctify the whole earth. He was baptized in the river, walking by the seaside he called men to service: this morning he walks up the hill as up a stairway his own hands have fashioned; presently he will go further and spread his own gospel typically over all the face of the earth. Thus he will do in symbol what he will tell us to do literally, for what other places are there upon the whole globe besides the river, the sea, the mountain, the city, the town, the village, the house? Thus the kingdom of heaven is like a grain of mustard seed [Matt. 13:31]. In the doing and work of our own Savior he will give us the germ of the missionary idea; we shall see the people of one town getting around him and saying, "Don't leave us," and he will rise above them and say, "I must preach the gospel in other cities also." Thus, when he comes to wind it all up, in the most beneficent climax that ever crowned the eloquence of a lifetime, he will only tell us to expand what he himself began.

He went up into a mountain, into a pulpit not made with hands. He did not go in conventional methods: we wait till the church is built: he said the church was not made with hands: wherever there is a sky there is a roof, wherever there is a floor there is a platform, wherever there is a man there is a congregation, wherever there is a human heart there is an opportunity of preaching the kingdom of heaven.

"And when he was set." Did the carpenter's son do what the Rabbis did? They gathered their robes about them when they sat down in Moses' seat, for the Jewish Rabbi always sat while he talked. It was even so that Jesus did on a larger and grander scale. He begins royally: there is a subtle claim of dominion in this very attitude of his; he does not beg to be heard; he does not say, "If you please, I shall be glad to mention to you a suggestion or two which has been stirring in mine own heart." He sits, and the mountain gives him hospitality. He fills the mountain, it fits him like a king's throne. Close your eyes and open the vision of your hearts, and look at him. We go into small buildings, we ask permission to speak in limited synagogues; why, in the motion of his limbs there is a subtle, strange royalty of mien. When he sits he sits as one who has a right to the mountain, and when he speaks it is as one whose gentle voice fills the spaces like a healing breeze.

"He opened his mouth." The ages had been waiting for the opening of those lips. When some great men amongst us and all over the world open their lips in high places they seem to have the power of making history. Other nations are listening, wondering, hoping, fearing; when this man opened his mouth he uttered words which would fill creation, which would be a gospel set in every language ever spoken by mankind, and easily set in every language. There are tongues into which you cannot teach Milton. Shakespeare must, in many of his utterances, be a stranger forever to those who speak only English, and that not rich in its capacity of utterance. But the words of Jesus Christ go everywhere, and fall into all languages with infinite ease. He speaks of light, love, life, truth, peace, God, home. There cannot be a language without these words having some distinct share in it. He sits down upon every mountain and breathes through every language his most ineffable gospel.

"He taught them." This is a new word, we have not met with this word before in our reading. When we listened to Jesus Christ before, he was preaching, now he is teaching. The preacher was a herald, a crying voice: "Repent," said he. The air was startled by the cry. Now he changes the tone: he sits down and teaches, explains, simplifies, draws the listeners into confidence and sympathy with himself, and makes them co-partners of the infinite secret of the divine truth and love.

Do we run after preachers or teachers? Unquestionably after preachers. The teachers of Christendom today are talking to half-dozens, the preachers are thronged. Who cares to be taught? How many of us bring our Bibles to church and follow the preacher page by page, checking every reference, testing every doctrine, asking for explanations by eager eyes and burning faces? By the trick of an anecdote I will engage to seduce from the wisest teacher in London nine-tenths of his hearers. We are in the anecdotal age: some child's story would tickle us, while the philosopher's doctrine would muddle the heads that are nearly senile because of the coarse and vulgar noises of a coarse and vulgar world.

"Saying, Blessed." That is a new word also. I have not met that word before. What was it that he said when we first heard him? "Repent." And now he says "Blessed"! There is a high logic in this sequence. Preaching first, then teaching. Repentance first, then inspiration—these are the coherences and minute consistencies, the moral unities which you find all through and through this Christian revelation, which make it not a chaos but a living world with a living center.

In this verse I find two classes referred to—multitudes and disciples. Are they not coordinate terms? Far from it. How well it would have read, how noble would have been the music, complete as a sphere, had it said—"When he beheld the multitudes he hailed them as disciples and taught them." Already there begins the division—that terrible distinction which separates man from man, the hearer from the scholar, the onlooker from the inlooker, the particle of a mob from the particle of a family. To which class do we belong? Are we part of the anonymous multitudes, or part of the registered household? We may all be disciples; why should we not be scholars of the one Teacher? Come, let him lure you—give up all other teachers and hear this Teacher sent from God. Lord, open mine ears that I may hear the whole music of thy heaven—unfolding voice.

This discourse was not delivered to the multitudes, it was delivered to the disciples. Some preparation is needed for hearing Christ. Presently he will stand right out in the busy marketplace and speak common words to the common heart, but on this mountain he is speaking to a few chosen ones who have a measure, very inadequate, of understanding and appreciation. Why, it requires a little preparation to go into a picture-gallery; how much more to go into a church? When the uninstructed visitor goes into a picture-gallery, he is seized by subjects, not by art. A pleasing face, a sweet child, a loving home, some little pathetic incident touches him. An idealized tree, a landscape made into poetry, he would not see: he does not look for art, he looks for subjects. You require some little preparation for going into a music-hall; how much more for going into God's sanctuary? What pieces are applauded? Listen. Pieces that are subjects again, that mingle easily with the unthinking—the sparkling, the rattling, or the pathetic: pieces that require to be read with the inner eye are lost upon the uninitiated, and it is certain to me, therefore, and it is no wonder, that some preparation should be needed for listening to Jesus Christ.

His very first sentence is a secret which can have no meaning to the vast majority of hearers. What is that first sentence? "Blessed are the poor in spirit, for theirs is the kingdom of heaven." What did the preacher say last Sunday? Nothing. Quote me one sentence that he uttered. He began by saying, "Blessed are the poor in spirit, for theirs is the kingdom of heaven." Commonplace talk like that; sparkle, brilliance, there was none; he is not worth listening to; he seemed rather weak in his way of speaking, his voice was low, and yet well–heard; I expected another kind of voice altogether, and another type of subject, and he began, after all this weary waiting of the listening ages, by saying, "Blessed are the poor in spirit, for theirs is the kingdom of heaven." He began by healing broken hearts, he began by comforting those that we want to write off the register, for we are sick of pulling and whining and groaning and sighing. He stooped to pick up a broken reed when we thought he would have mounted the stars and passed before us with the wondrous velocity and splendor of the lightning.

The heart needs some preparation to know the meaning of this expression, "the poor in spirit." The expression sounds as if it were simple, and so it is, but it is the simplicity which is a last result. We may have to spend a weary and baffled lifetime before we come into the mystery of this eloquence, "the poor in spirit."

I propose to look at the beatitudes as a whole, and not just now to look at them in detail. The time may come when we shall be able to look at each verse as a single gem; meanwhile my inquiry is, "What was Christ's idea of a blessed life?"

In Christ's idea of a blessed life I find a marvelous union of the divine and the human. Some of the beatitudes look up right away into heaven, others of them look down into all the relations of earth and time. In other words, some of the beatitudes are intensely theological, and others are intensely moral and social. Thus in the beatitudes we have a complete representation of the religion which Jesus Christ came to establish and expound, a religion combining the theological with the moral, the doctrinal with the practical, the God and the neighbor: thou shalt love the Lord thy God with all thy heart, and thy neighbor as thyself [Lev. 19:18; Matt. 19:19].

What is our religion? Theological only, or moral? Have we magnificent doctrine and do we pay our debts? Have we splendid intellectual conceptions of the metaphysical constitution of the universe, and do we forgive our enemies? Are we orthodox in all spiritual conception, and do we feed the hungry and clothe the naked? In Christ's religion earth and heaven go together, and there is not a flower that blooms on the green earth that does not owe its beauty to the sun.

In Christ's conception of the blessed life I find many persons mentioned that I did not expect to find referred to, and I find many persons omitted that I expected would have been first spoken of. Let me take the beatitudes as a picture of heaven. Who is in heaven? Blessed are the mighty, for they are in heaven; blessed are the rich, for theirs is the kingdom of glory; blessed are the famous, for theirs are the trumpets of eternity; blessed are the noble, for the angels are their servants. Why, that is not the text. Who is in heaven? The poor in spirit, they that mourn, the meek, they which do hunger and thirst after righteousness, the merciful, the pure in heart, the peacemakers. Then, then, perhaps we may be there. Not many mighty, not many noble, not many learned, not many brilliant are called. Then perhaps we may be there. Woman, mother, sister, obscure person, unknown life—you may be there. Who cares to seek such flowers as these? Give me the flowers that flame like fires, and I will call these a worthy garland. Who cares to turn their heads to look back to seek such modest beauty? God does. "A broken and a contrite heart, O God, thou wilt not despise" [Ps. 51:17; cf. Ps. 34:18].

In Christ's conception of the blessed life I find that goodness and reward always go together. Goodness is indeed its own reward. The flower brings its own odor, the light brings its own revelations. The goodness *is* the reward, the prayer *is* the answer. There are persons who say, "You have prayed the prayer, have you got the reply?" Certainly, while we are yet speaking. You do not understand this mystery, you thought there would be a telegram or a man with a four-square letter at your door, saying, "Here is the answer." Whatever things you pray for, believe that you have them, and have them you certainly will. This blessedness, therefore, comes with the condition specified. The poor in spirit has the kingdom of heaven already, has it of divine gift and divine right. Sometimes we enter into this high experience right fully, we know what it means without any preacher telling us in so many words. There are times when the heart is just alive with heaven. There are seasons when we could despise thrones rather than give up the high rapture or the sweet tenderness of soul which ennobles us. You have been in those occasional moods, and, therefore, I need not further explain or refer to them. If you have not been caught up into that third heaven, I might speak until the night turns into the morning, and you would not catch a tone of this sacred truth.

In Christ's conception of the blessed life I find that even the *enemy* himself is made a contributor. "Blessed are they which are persecuted for righteousness' sake, for theirs is the kingdom of heaven. Blessed are ye when men shall revile you and persecute you, and say all manner of evil against you falsely for my sake. Rejoice and be exceeding glad, for great is your reward in heaven, for so persecuted they the prophets which were before you." Why, he shows us how flowers grow in the night-time, how the wilderness may rejoice and blossom as the rose, how the black devil with sharp teeth and eyes of fire is the servant of the good man, and waits upon him and minsters to his joy. O that we might enter into this meaning, then all things would be ours, life, death, height, depth — our servants would be a multitude, and in that multitude would be found the angels of God.

Now into which verse can I come? Let each man ask for himself. I am not all these eight — which is my little wicket-gate, through which I pass into God's reward? Let me see what choice of gates there is — the poor in spirit, they that mourn, the meek, they which do hunger and thirst after righteousness, the merciful, the pure in heart, the peacemakers, the persecuted. Let each scholar ask, "Which is my gate?" There is only one gate that I see here that I ever have any hope of getting in at. I think, perhaps, through that gate I might go. "Blessed are they that hunger." If I cannot get through that gate, I fear all the others are shut.

But there is a gate for all of us — which is yours, my brother? Seek and ye shall find, knock and it shall be opened unto you, for he that seeketh findeth, and to everyone that knocketh it shall be opened [Matt. 7:7, 8]. And yet I think that all the gates somehow interfold, and that if we get through one we shall seem to have gone through all. This is a mystery known only to the heart of the elect.

Concerning these beatitudes two things may be said: first, they can be *tested*. These are not metaphysical abstractions that no man can lay his hand upon, these are practical truths that every man can test for himself. And the next thing that can be said about them is that the blessings here promised are *already in possession*. "Blessed are the poor in spirit, for theirs *is* the kingdom of heaven." We do not wait for immortality, we begin it now. We shall not perhaps be the sons of God in ages yet unborn and untold, *we are* the sons of God. We are not to be in heaven a long time after, we are now in heaven—with limitations, but with a deep assurance the world can never shake. Not yet completed, there is infinitely more to come and to shine upon us, but while we pray we enter heaven by prayer. While we love, we enter heaven by love. When we forgive, we are in heaven.

NOTES

Verse 3—"Pauper Dei in animo est, non in Sacculo," or "The poor in spirit are made to grow not in wealth—*Augustine*. "The meek"—"The one staff of Moses breaks in pieces the ten thousand spears of Pharaoh."—*Eastern Proverb*. "Vis possidere terram? Vide ne possidearis a terri," or "Dost thou wish to possess the earth? Beware then lest thou be possessed by it."

Verse 6—"Very beautifully Augustine draws from John 6:26–65 a commentary on this text, making '*righteousness*' here equivalent with 'bread from heaven' there, and urging that in both passages we should understand nothing short of Christ Himself"—*Trench*.

Verse 8—"The pure in heart"—the single heart, the heart without folds. "The purged eye of the soul."

"Augustine contemplating this heptad of beatitudes no longer singly, but as a whole, suggests more than once that perhaps they may stand in some relation to the sevenfold operations of the Holy Spirit whereof Isaiah (ch. 11) speaks"—*Trench*.

sixteen

THE SERMON ON THE MOUNT (PART TWO)

Matthew 5:13–16

THERE ARE two ways of looking at this portion of the Lord's address. He is speaking to the disciples—that may be inferred from the first verse of the chapter, wherein it says, "When he was set, his disciples came unto him, and he opened his mouth and taught them." Are we to suppose that these disciples referred to were the salt of the earth and the light of the world, and a city set upon a high hill? Surely not in their merely personal capacity, and in their present condition. Let us take the first view, therefore; namely, that Jesus Christ is speaking of the Jews, and speaking of them he hesitates not to describe them as the salt of the earth, the light of the world, the city set upon a hill. And yet in a very gentle way, but so broad as to admit of no misapprehension, he intimates that the salt has lost its savor, the light has been put under a bushel, and the conspicuousness of the city has become but its greater shame. The effect of this teaching is to remind men of great calling and election, and of great and appalling declension, and to prepare the way for such remedial and reclaiming measures as were in the purpose and counsel of the Eternal. This was not dust that had become drier, it was not clay that had become harder, it was salt that had lost its savor, light that was in danger of being wholly extinguished. Jesus Christ, therefore, recognizing the greatness and the grandeur of the call in which the Jews stood, proceeded in this most gracious and gentle manner to indicate the declension into which they had fallen. That is one view.

Take the other view. Jesus Christ sees in those disciples what his church is *to be*. Not addressing them in their current intellectual and spiritual condition, but looking into the future as men look from the germ to the full fruition, he regarded them as the beginning of his own divine kingdom, and addressing them as such, he described them as the salt of the earth, the light of the world, and a city set upon a hill.

Both views are, in my opinion, correct. There is enough in each of them to awaken the most solemn reflection, to affect the soul with all the pain of the bitterest humiliation, and to inspire it with all that is most animating in the sacred word. I will take the second view and set it with some breadth before you.

Christ sees the greatest side of our human nature, and he addresses that side, due to the fact that we are more easily and effectually moved by encouragement than by any other influence. Tell a man he is a fool and you cast him into despair. Tell him that he has lost every chance, spoiled every opportunity, neglected all the counsel of heaven and is no longer worthy of being counted a living creature in God's universe, and possibly you may burden him with all the distress of absolute despair. The effect will be according to the nature of the particular man who is addressed. Jesus Christ never gave us a discouraging view of ourselves whenever he saw us set in any relation to himself, of earnest listening or religious expectation or incipient desire to be wiser and better men. When we stood before him in the full erectness of our own purity, and came before him with a certificate of our own integrity, and requested to be heard upon the basis of our righteousness, he turned upon us the fury of the east wind, and banished us from his presence as men to whom he had nothing to say. Whenever we grouped ourselves around him and said we would listen with reverence and with religious expectation to what he had to say, then he opened the kingdom of heaven, and not until our capacity was surcharged did he withdraw his gracious and redeeming revelations of truth.

This is the great law of human teaching. If you want your boy to be a gentleman, do not begin by treating him as an invincible and incurable boor. I wait until that lesson gets right down into your apprehension. If you want to encourage your scholars, begin by treating them as young philosophers. Give them credit for as much as you possibly can—by so doing you will cast them upon themselves in serious reflection, and with some anxiety they will endeavor to respond to the breadth, the sympathy, and the nobleness of your estimation of their capacity and diligence. If you want any man to do his best, trust him with considerable responsibility. Who could do his best if he knew he was watched, suspected, distrusted, and that the object of the vigilant criticism was to entrap him, to find out his defects, and to convince him by multitudinous arguments that he was wholly unfit for his position? Many of us could not work at all under such circumstances; we should simply succumb under their distressing weight if we did not resent them as intolerable humiliations.

Jesus Christ says, "Ye are the salt of the earth"—says to a man who thought himself useless in the world, "Thou art as pungent salt in the midst of a putrid age," or, "Thou art as salt cast upon that which is already good, to preserve it from decay." Jesus Christ adds, "Ye are the light of the world,"—tells a man who never suspected himself of having any light at all, that it is in him to throw a circle of radiance around his family, his neighborhood, or it may be his country. Let us learn to follow this example in some degree. We get from men in many cases just what we tell them we *expect* from them; there is something in human nature that likes to be trusted with *responsibility*, something in us that responds to great occasions. Jesus Christ always supplied a grand occasion to his hearers, and he opened the broad and sunny road of hope. He did not point to the low and dank caverns of despair.

Jesus Christ recognizes the true *influence of good men*. He called them salt which is pungent, light which is lustrous, a city set on a hill which is conspicuous, and may be seen afar by travelers and by those who long for home. Some influences are active—salt and light; some influences passive—a city set on a hill. We must not judge one another's influence by our own, and condemn any man's influence in the Church because it does not take its tone and range from our own method of doing things. Some clocks do not strike. They have to be looked at if from them we would know the time of day. Some clocks do strike, and they strike in the darkness as well as in the light, and it is pleasant to the weary, sleepless one now and again to catch the tone which tells him that the darkness is going and the light is coming. Do not undervalue me because I am a man of but passive influence. Do not charge me with ambition and madness because I am a man of energetic influence. Let each be what the great, loving, wise Father meant him to be. There is room in his heart for all. The brain makes no noise; the tongue no man can tame—is the tongue, therefore, not a divine creation? Sure it is! God taught it its trick of speech and its wizardry of music. Is the brain not of divine formation because it makes no noise? Of course it is! It is as the inmost church of the Lord wherein God shows the fullest of his heavenly and immortal splendor.

George Gilfillan, in his most energetic and inspiring book called "Bards of the Bible," has some observations upon this matter of silence as contrasted with noise. As a boy I used to be very fond of that rhetorical writer, and as a man I do not renounce him. I have not seen the sentence for twenty years, but I think I can quote it even now in substance. He says, "The greatest objects in nature are the stillest: the ocean has a voice, the sun is dumb in his courts of praise. The forests murmur, the constellations speak not. Aaron spoke; Moses' face but shone. Sweetly might the High Priest discourse, but the Urim and the Thummim, the blazing stones upon his breast, flash forth a meaning deeper and diviner far." Young men, store your memory with such words as these, and you will never want to run away from your own society. The chairs may be vacant, but the air will be full of angels.

Yet whatever our influence may be, we may *lose* it. The salt may lose its savor, the light may be put under a bushel, and a city set upon a hill may turn its lights out, or build its walls against the sun and turn its windows elsewhere. The foolish discussion has been sometimes raised as to whether salt could lose its pungency—raised by people who wanted to catch the Savior tripping in his speech. But in proportion to the difficulty is the solemnity. He who made the salt knows more about it than we do, and whatever may become of the salt, taking the mere letter as the limit of our criticism, we all know as the saddest and most tragical fact in life that some of the grandest intellects have lost their glory, and some right hands always lifted in defense of the right have lost their cunning. "Let him that thinketh he standeth take heed lest he fall" [1 Cor. 10:12]. "And what I say unto you I say unto all—Watch!" [Mark 13:37].

Every man sheds a light *peculiar to himself.* No one man has all the light; no one star holds in its little cup all the glory of the universe. One star differs from another star in glory. Suppose one of the least of the stars should say, "I am going to withdraw from the firmament because I see a great flame, compared with whose splendor I am but as a glowworm in the presence of the sun." Better for that little foolish star to say, "The God that made yonder great flame trims my lamp and gives me my little sparkle of light."

There is a right *way* of using influence. Observe how Jesus Christ puts the matter when he says, "Let your light so shine before men"; the word *so* should be emphasized as indicating the manner of the shining. Light may be so held in the hand as to *dazzle* the observer; light may be brought too near the eyes, light may be set at the *wrong angle*, light may be wasted, its beams be displayed so as to be of no use to the man who would read or work. Hence it is not enough to be luminous, but *so* to use our luminousness as to be of *use* to other people. There are men who, from my point of view, are luminous enough to light a whole country, who do not light their own little house. There are men who need to be focalized, all but immeasurable men, with a kind of infinite capacity for anything, and who yet, for lack of right setting and bringing together and focalizing, live as splendid nothings and die as bubbles die upon the troubled wave. It is not enough, therefore, for us to have light and to be luminous; we must study the great economic laws by which even a little light may sometimes go a long, long way, and a great light may throw its timely splendor upon the road of him who is in perplexity and doubt.

Our Savior further teaches us that our light is so to shine that our good works may be seen. He does not say that the worker may be made visible, but that the works may be observed, admired, imitated, may induce men to give glory to the Father which is in heaven. It is thus that his own sun works daily in the heavens: who dares look at the sun when he so shines as to fill the earth with all the beauty of summer? We turn our eyes up to him, and he rebukes us with darts of fire; he says, "Look down, not up; look at the works, not the worker." So we may feast our eyes upon a paradise of flowers, and get much of heaven out of it, but the moment we venture to say, "Who did this—where is he?" "Show me the worker," the sun answers us with a rebuke of intolerable light. So "no man hath seen God at any time" [John 1:18; 1 John 4:12], but we see his Son Jesus Christ. No man hath seen God at any time, yet we count his stars when the great daylight is away; we wonder how they were hung upon nothing, and how they shine without wasting, and what they are— porch lamps of a King's palace, street lamps on a heavenly way—who can tell? None, yet the bare question-asking stirs the mind and the heart with a noble wonder that is almost religious. Little wonder, then, if you cannot look at the sun, that you cannot look at the God that made the sun? If he is invisible in himself, he is not invisible in his ministry. We also are his offspring. In every little child I see his work, in the most common human life I see the infinitude of his wisdom and the beneficence of his purpose. In myself I see the divinity of God.

Thus our lesson stands in the meantime. A kind word of encouragement has been spoken to us: we are not regarded as little, insignificant, contemptible, not worth gathering up: we are spoken of as salt, light, and a city set on a hill. Let us answer the grandeur of the challenge. We have been told that the best influence may decline and die: salt may lose its savor, the light may be extinguished. Let us hear the solemn exhortation, and exercise a spirit of vigilant caution. We have been called to a certain manner of life; let us take heed unto the call, lest having magnificent powers we waste them as rain would be wasted upon the unanswering and barren sand.

NOTES

Verse 13—"They are not thus truly trodden under foot who suffer persecution without shrinking, but they who through fear of persecution become vile, abandoning their faith; for undermost though he may *seem*, yet he is not really so, who, whatever he may be suffering below on earth, has his heart fixed above in heaven."

Lost its savor—The Vulgate reads, "Quod si sal *evanuerit*," etc. Trench prefers *infatuerit*, as singularly happy; *fatuus*, the man saltless, insipid. The French word is *fade*, for which there is no equivalent in English.

Salt—Such as was found in the salt marshes of Palestine; not what we should regard as pure salt.

Verse 16—The word FATHER as applied to God occurs in this verse for the first time in the New Testament.

seventeen

THE SERMON ON THE MOUNT
(PART THREE)

Matthew 5:17–19

"THINK NOT." There is a possibility of having false notions about Christ. Closely observe that the subject may be right, and that our idea concerning it may be wrong. It is not enough to be attached to a good cause, we must worthily represent that cause to those who are looking on or listening. You say, for example, that you believe in Christ, but in having said so you have given me no clear notion of what you really do believe. I must ask you some questions, such as—Who was Christ? What do you believe about him, and why do you believe? The name is excellent, but what is your precise idea about the meaning and influence of that name? So, at the very opening of his ministry, Jesus Christ had to recognize the possibility of mistaken notions concerning himself. We are not at liberty to say that if a thing be true it will so shine upon the mind as to commend its truth to us and to bear down all prejudice and all misconception. Even Jesus Christ himself was not understood by his contemporaries, his disciples, or the friends of his own house. First of all, therefore, he has to do a negative work, he has to call man to the right mental mood and attitude, he has to awaken that latest and fastest of all sleepers—*Attention.* He will not be rushed upon, he will not be seized by the extemporaneous genius of mankind, he will not be treated as a feather that any fingers can catch in the wind. There must be thought, consideration—right thought, close consideration; for only as the result of patient and devout reflection, inspired and directed by the Holy Spirit, do we come to have clear, complete, right conceptions of Jesus Christ.

"Think not." That was a legal phrase, it was used by the lawyers and by the interpreters of the law. Literally it means—"Do not get into the habit of thinking," or, "Do not become accustomed to think that I am come to destroy the law or the prophets." He was warning his disciples, and through them all Christian ages, against a mental habit. What is there so difficult to eradicate as unintelligent prejudice? You think, and think, and think, until, by the very processes of your own mind, you come to the conclusion that what you have thought must be true. Christ warns us against intellectual prejudices; mental habits that start from a wrong base, live and grow up into formidable proportions and strength. Christian attention should always be young, Christian attention should always be impressible, Christian attention should stand a long way from old and hoary prejudice; Christian attention should always be ready to take on the phase of the moment, and to hear the note of the passing tune.

"Think not that I am come to destroy." Gentle One, thou didst not come to destroy, thy name is Savior. And yet he did come to destroy. "For this purpose was I manifested, that I might destroy"—there he takes up the word, takes it up as thunder might take it—"the works of the devil." But no work of God would he destroy; ". . . the Son of Man is come to seek and to save that which was lost." The Son of Man is not come to destroy men's lives but to save them. Think not that I am come to destroy the law—that is, to make a dead letter of it, to treat it as a mistake, to say, "Now we will utterly ignore all the ancient law and take a new point of departure, and begin again upon a new foundation." I am not come to destroy but to fulfill. What does that mean? To fulfill—that is what the noonday does to the dawn. The dawn is cold, gray, struggling, the noon is the culmination of its purpose and interest. The noon is not something different from the dawn, the noon is the dawn completed. When the first gray light fell upon the dewy hills, it said, "I mean to be noon, noon is in me, and I will climb the zenith and stand right above the world and flood it with infinite splendor and beauty." The summer fulfills the spring; there is no schism amongst the seasons: the spring comes and does its little elementary and initial work, plants its little crocuses and does all it can for the outside world, does it quietly, sweetly, fragrantly, with wondrous grace and love, then the summer comes and does in infinite grandeur what the spring could only begin. It fulfills the spring.

Manhood fulfills childhood. You say the child is father of the man. I need no better illustration. The law prefigured and anticipated the gospel; statutes, precepts, and commandments began that marvelous process which culminates in principle, grace, truth, inspiration, the divinely recreated and ruled intuitions, which sees a root by the penetration of vision which the literal schoolmaster could never give.

You are merchantmen and traders—tell me how is a promissory note fulfilled. Show it to me: I will fulfill it thus: I tear it into little pieces and throw it into the dust. Have I fulfilled the note? You instantly tell me that I have not fulfilled, I have destroyed. Then show me another and I will fulfill it thus: by thrusting it into the very midst of the fire and letting it go up in flame. Have I fulfilled it? You tell me instantly that I have done in this case as in the former; I have not fulfilled, I have destroyed. Then pass the promissory note at the date of its maturity into the hands of the man who signed it, and he pays you the money pound by pound to the last demand, and, having got the money into your hand, what has been done with the promissory note? It has been destroyed by fulfillment, and that is the only destruction possible to any law that is right.

The law was our schoolmaster to bring us unto Christ. I prefer another way of stating that. The modern Greek would not understand that expression if he read it in the original tongue. "What is the meaning of that expression?" I have myself said to a modern Greek; and he said, "You have not caught the idea at all in your English." "Then what is the idea?" "Why," said he, "it is this—Not the law was our schoolmaster, but the law was our nurse, or guardian, or caretaker, to bring us to our schoolmaster, Christ." We know what that means by daily illustration in our own life. You send your little child in the care of someone to school. The maid takes the little creature and says, "Come, and I will take you to school," and away they go together to the place of instruction. Now, the law was our care-taker, our companion, to take us to our schoolmaster, Christ; Christ keeps a school, Christ calls those who go to his school his disciples, his scholars; Christ says, "Learn of me." Christ is the teacher of the world. The law took us hand in hand to Christ. The law is one—there is no change in the divine education of the world. We are not to suppose that Christ was an afterthought in the divine mind, or that his coming marked a sudden departure from sacred precedents. All that went before him pointed to him. Every man said, "Not I, but there cometh one after me."

The Bible from the very beginning says, "I am going to be a gospel." If the spire of your church is rightly built it will say to the artistic observer on its very first course of stones, "I am going to be a pinnacle." There will be a set in the very first lines of stones which the artistic eye can see, which, being interpreted, is—Pinnacle, sharp, finger-like, pointing to the sky. It does not begin to be a spire a long way up, but from the very first, if it has been conceived by a true architect; it begins to be a spire when its very first stone is laid in the depth of the earth. So with this Bible-building. I did not know what it was going to be, but I saw that it was going to be something other than it was in itself just at the particular moment of my observation. Now that I go back upon it with more learning and with a keener power of observation, I see that from the very first verse this Book meant to be a benediction, to have set upon its uppermost points these words, "The grace of our Lord Jesus Christ be with you all." So the law is not broken into unrelated parts, it is from the beginning meant to be a complete and final cosmos.

What wonder, then, if Jesus Christ should continue to say, "Till heaven and earth pass, one jot or one tittle shall in no wise pass from the law, till all be fulfilled"? In the seventeenth verse you have the word "fulfill," in the eighteenth verse you have the word "fulfilled," and yet they are not the same word as they were originally written. In the eighteenth verse the word fulfilled means—accomplished, a purpose turned into a reality, a seed fully grown into a great tree, to which nothing could be added in proportion or in beauty.

"One jot or one tittle." Why, then, is there nothing superfluous in the law? There is nothing insignificant in all the works of God. Pluck me a grass-blade, and let me see what I can do with it. How many veins has it which could be done without? How much blood circulates through all this veinous system? How much less might have done? Can you mend it? Can you sharpen its point, can you accelerate its circulation, can you pluck out of it one tiny fiber that the little thing could have done without? Take care how you touch it, for it is God's handiwork.

"One jot." One *yod*, a little thing that is not a letter in itself, so much as the adjunct or the helper of some other letter—a *yot*, a silent thing. The name of the wife of Abraham was turned from Sarai to Sarah, and it was the *yod* that did it: it was that little, silent, insignificant adjunct that turned her into Princess. God is careful of his *yod*, or *yot*, or *jot*—he does not dot his "*i*" for nothing, nor cross his "*t*" merely for decoration: there is blood in the act. Take care; touch not the Lord's anointed, and do his prophets no harm. The destruction of the law by literalists and meddlers, by mere outside observers and worshipers, such as the Scribes and

Pharisees, begins by interfering with the jot and tittle. Who would take a large sharp knife and begin all at once in shocking and impious vulgarity to scratch out the whole law? And yet many a man who would shrink from that coarse blasphemy begins with finer instruments to interfere with the *yod*, the dot, the tittle. He says, "Nobody will miss that." We do things little by little, insidiously, that we never could do by thunder-like assaults.

All character seems to go down by interfering with the *yod*, the dot, the jot, the tittle, the iota, the subscript, the accent, the breathing-point. Who jumps right off the temple top into pits of darkness at one grand leap? A man begins by giving up the morning service, by going to church occasionally, by dropping little customs as he calls them, and comparatively insignificant habits. What is he doing? He has begun a work, the end of which is destruction, ruin, death. It is to me no wonder, therefore, that Jesus Christ should depose and degrade into an inferior position whosoever shall break one of these least commandments and shall teach men so. Observe how these words go, in what perfect and suggestive rhythm they fall upon the ear—break and teach. And in the second member of the sentence observe how the same rhythm is preserved—do and teach. Work begins in the individual relation to the law; when I have broken a commandment I long to get companionship, to bring others into the same condemnation: having broken it, to justify the breach, to show that it was better broken than not, and on the ruins of my own character set up as the seducer of other men.

Then do and teach. Who can teach if he does not first do? If he be a mere hireling the whole words would have been committed to memory and would trip off his reluctant lips without music or force. My teacher must at least *try* to do what he says. If he fail I will not despise him, if his efforts be sincere. I know that human infirmity will mar men, and diabolic temptation will do its utmost to despoil and pervert the purpose of his heart, but his will shall count as his deed.

We learn by doing, we become preachers by being practicers, they that do the will shall know the doctrine. The Lord reveals himself to his industrious servants. It is when we are persevering on the right road, scrubbing and drudging at oftentimes unwelcome duties, that God's angel stands up before us and flings upon our faith a sudden and gracious light. Blessed is that servant who is faithful, he shall have cities in heaven to rule.

Jesus, then, came to fulfill the law. There was a *moral* law, the meaning of which was obedience. He became, obedient, even unto the death of the cross: he had no will but God's—"Not my will but thine be done." There was the fulfillment of the moral law. There was a *sacrificial* law, the slaying of animals and outpouring of blood and offering of gifts. This man was both the Priest and the Victim. He built the altar and slew himself upon it with priestly hands. Thus he fulfilled the sacrificial law. There was a *national* law, a theocracy, a gathering together of the people, a federating of tribes and sections, a grand, nationalistic idea. How did he fulfill that? By founding his Church. Upon this rock I build my Church. Empires mean, when rightly translated, *Churches*; Politics is a word which means, held up to its highest point, *Morality*; Nationality, too often debased into a geographical term, causing many distractions and controversial definitions, really means, when fructified, the Church, the Redeemed Church, the *Theocracy*, the God-Government. The kingdoms of this world become the kingdoms of our God and of his Christ. Then comes the end, when he shall have delivered up the kingdom to God and his Father, having fulfilled the law as a tree fulfills the acorn, and God shall be all in all.

We are in the line of this education, we are helping on this glorious ministry. I wish to God I could arouse every sleeper and inflame with heaven's fire every reluctant heart to take this upward progress. Teach no other notion of advancement, move with Moses, the minstrels, the prophets, the Christ—be in that succession, and if you have not ten cities to rule, you have five, or one, or some share in the final and everlasting dominion.

Behold, I set before you the door, wide open, of a grand opportunity. Seize it, and be thankful and glad with the joy of rapture.

eighteen

THE GREAT CHALLENGE

Matthew 5:20

FOR *righteousness* read *rightness*. Then the text will read, "For I say unto you, that except your rightness, your notion and idea of what is right, shall exceed the notion and idea entertained by the Scribes and Pharisees as to what is right, ye shall in no case enter into the kingdom of heaven." Given, a ministry which begins in this tone, to know how it will end? It is impossible that it can end otherwise than in *crucifixion*. The cross is *here*. If the Scribes and Pharisees get to know that a man has been speaking so of them, they will never rest until they *kill* him. The shadow of the Cross is in everything spoken and done by Jesus Christ. He here assails the religion and the respectability, the learning and the influence of his day. This is more than a speech, it is a *challenge*, it is an impeachment, it is an indictment of high treason—how then can the speaker finish his eloquence but in a discourse of blood? He must die for this, or play the hypocrite further on. A man who talks so, in any age, even including the nineteenth century, must *die*. The reason we do not die now is that we do not speak the truth. The preacher now follows those whom he appears to lead; if he puts himself into a right attitude to his age, its corruption, its infidelities, and its hypocrisies, he would be killed. No preacher is now killed, because no preacher is now faithful.

Consider who these Scribes and Pharisees were. They were the bishops and clergy and ministers of the day. Suppose a reformer should now arise and say concerning the whole ecclesiastical and spiritual machine, "Except your righteousness shall exceed the righteousness that is turned out of that machine ye shall in no case enter into the kingdom of heaven." I do not know that we should nail him to wood with vulgar iron nails, but we would take care to pinch him so in bread and water as to take the life out of him. Christianity is nothing if not an eternal challenge in the direction of honesty, reality, breadth, charity. Has not the whole Church, in all its fragments and communions, become a mere theological grinding machine for turning out certain quantities and colors, of regulation extent and tone?

Religion was polluted at the well-head. It had become a ceremony, a profession, a dead adherence to dear formalities, synagogue-going, word-splitting, hand-washing, and an elaborate system of trifling and refining. Understand who these men were. They *knew* the law: the Scribes spent their time in copying it, in expounding, or rather in confounding and confusing those who listened to their peculiar expositions of its solemn requirements. They were not illiterate, so far as the law was concerned: they knew every letter, they had a thousand traditions concerning it, they formed themselves into synods and consistories for the purpose of extending, defining, and otherwise treating the requirements of the law. They were so familiar with it as to miss its music, as we have become so familiar with the sunlight as not to heed its beauty. A rattle, a splutter in the air, will excite more attention than the great, broad, calm shining of the king of day. The Scribes were the men who professed to have the keys of the kingdom of heaven upon their girdles, and yet Jesus Christ, the reputed son of the carpenter, arises and says to them, "Ye are not in the kingdom of heaven at all; actors, mimics, pretenders, painted ones, ye are not in the spirit and the genius of the heavenly kingdom!" No man dares this day say a word against a bishop or a minister—I speak of all Churches, and not of one in particular—without being publicly and severely reprimanded for his impious audacity. Jesus gathered himself up into one strain of power, and hurled his energy in one blighting condemnation against the whole of the Scribe and Pharisee system of his day. Beware! He was *killed!* He did not talk against disreputable persons, as the world accounts repute; the Scribes and the Pharisees were the most respectable people of their generation, they were looked up to as leaders and guides by those amongst whom they lived. They were the saints, the pillars of the Church, the lights of the synagogue, the very cream of respectable society; yet this Galilean peasant beards them all, lays his soft but sinewy fingers upon their throats, and says, "Stand back, ye defile and pervert the kingdom ye profess to serve." Do not, therefore, let us be too bold and too faithful. The cost of integrity everywhere in a corrupt age is—*death.*

I infer from Christ's treatment of the Scribes and Pharisees that it is possible for men to *deceive themselves* on religious methods—to suppose that they are in the kingdom of God when they are thousands of miles away from it. Is it possible that any of *us* can have fallen under the power of that delusion? I fear it may be so. What is your Christianity? A letter, a written creed, a small placard that can be published, containing a few so-called fundamental points and lines? Is it an affair of words and phrases and sentences following one another in regulated and approved succession? If so, and only so, there is not one drop of Christ's blood in it: it is not Christianity, it is a little intellectual conceit, a small moral prejudice. Christianity is life, love, charity, nobleness—it is *sympathy with God*.

My belief is that if Jesus Christ were to come to us *today* the first thing he would do would be to condemn all places of so-called worship. What he would do with other buildings I cannot tell, but it is plain that he would shut up all churches and chapels. They are too narrow; they worship the letter; they are the idolaters of details; they are given up to the exaggeration of mint, rue, anise, cummin, herbs and weeds of the garden and the field, but charity, nobleness, honor, all-hopefulness, infinite patience with evil—where are they? If judgment begins at the house of God, where shall the ungodly and the sinner appear? In disputing about the letter, the danger is that we neglect and despise the *spirit*; we quarrel about trifles; we are founders of sects and parties, and the champions of our own inventions; we pay tithe of mint and anise, and neglect the weightier matters of the law. The Christianity of this day, so far as I have been enabled to examine it, has no common meeting ground. If Jesus Christ were to come amongst us now he would have to call upon the leaders of the various denominations, and if he did not happen to begin at the right quarter he would have but scant hospitality. If he called upon the Baptists first, the Methodist brethren would decline to see him; and if he called upon the Methodists in the first instance the Baptists would urge the claims of an earlier ancestry. He would find us in pugilistic attitude, separated by cobwebs, or bickering and chaffering with one another over high walls, and pinning sheets of paper over little crevices in those walls lest any of the saintly air should get through to the other side. Is this the Church Christ died to redeem? Is this the blood-bought host? Where is our common meeting ground?

Let me now show you what religion had been brought to by the Scribes and Pharisees in their time. I called attention to some of these points in a discourse not long ago. I cannot do better than ask your attention again to those very points. Take the instance of Sabbath-keeping. To what pass do you suppose the Scribes and Pharisees had brought this matter of the fourth commandment? Recent writers upon the life of Christ have been at great pains in reading the *Talmud* (or doctrine), the *Mishna* (or repetition), and the *Gemara* (or supplement); and it would be amusing, if it were not distressing, to find how these theological carpenters have whittled away the broad, grand, solemn commandments of our Father in heaven. With regard to the Sabbatic observance, recent authorities tell us that the Scribes and their allies laid it down that a knot which could be untied with *one hand* might be untied on the Sabbath day, but not one that required *both* hands. A man might carry a burden upon his shoulder, but if that burden were slung between *two*, or even slung between the shoulders, the carrying of it would be a breach of the sanctity of the Sabbath day. It was unlawful to carry a loaf in the public streets on the Sabbath, but if two people carried the same loaf the act was good. It was so written in the *Mishna* and the *Gemara*. Understand this. If a man carried a loaf in the public streets, it was breaking the Sabbath day, but if he got some other man to take hold of another end, they two could be carrying it without a breach of the commandment! This was the state of things when that carpenter's Son came into the world. The law forbade any visiting upon the Sabbath day—when I say the law, I mean the traditional law—yet the Scribes must visit; how then was this difficulty to be overcome? They fixed a chain at one end of the street, and another chain at the other end of the street, and they called the enclosure one house, and thus the painted hypocrites went backward and forward, dining and drinking, and feasting and reveling, and yet keeping the Sabbath day! Two thousand cubits was a Sabbath day's journey, but two thousand cubits was too short a walk for some of these traditionalists. What did they do? On the Friday they went two thousand cubits and deposited a loaf, and where a man deposited a loaf he was entitled to call the place his home for the time being. So the literalist walked his two thousand cubits to his loaf, and then began his Sabbath day's journey of two thousand cubits further on. Do you wonder that when a man whose soul was aflame with righteousness came into such corruption, he damned the society of his day, and said it was not in the kingdom of heaven? This is the way to try Christ, this will show you what he was—no trimmer, no oscillating theological pendulum, now here, now there—but a fire, a judgment, a stern word, a living critic of the corrupt heart. It is in such instances as these that I see the shining of his real personality, and it is in such denunciations as are in the text that I see the beginning of his crucifixion.

When the Pharisee invited him to dine, he went in and sat down to meat without washing his hands, and the Pharisee marveled that he should eat with hands unwashed. His marveling was audible in all probability, and Jesus Christ answered it with the most severe denunciation. We cannot understand the importance which was attached by the Pharisees and others to the washing of hands before eating. Not to wash the hands before a meal was, we are told by competent annotators, equal to homicide. Dwell upon that fact for one moment. Not to wash the hands before eating was, in the estimation of the Pharisees, an act equal to the killing of a man. Jesus Christ knowing this, went into the house of the Pharisee, and sat down to eat without hand-washing. Did it not take courage to act so upon personal conviction? Was this a weak-minded man, was this an effeminate Redeemer? Does it cost nothing to rise up in daily, manly protest against the most settled and cherished usages of the time? Give him the honor due to his energy, consider the circumstances by which he was surrounded, and then tell me if he was the carpenter's son or the Son of God.

So far was this matter carried by the Pharisees that no man, but themselves probably, could touch the parchment or skin upon which the law was written without being pronounced unclean. So we learn from those who take an interest in such studies that the question was asked of them, "How is it that a man can touch the pages of Homer and be clean, and yet he cannot touch the parchment or skin on which the law is written without being defiled?" The answer was, "Because of the peculiar sacredness of the law." Thus extremes meet. It was because the law was so holy, that no man might touch the parchment on which it was written without being pronounced ceremonially defiled. And one commentator tells us that there was something like an ironical and sarcastic joke among the people of the time, who said to those high authorities in the law, "How is it that we can touch the bones of a dead ass without contracting pollution, and yet cannot touch the bones of John Hyrcanus, the most saintly of the High Priests, without being unclean?" And the casuistic answer was, "Because Hyrcanus was a holy man, and his very holiness caused those who touched his bones to be unclean."

It was to this point that religion had been brought by the Scribes and Pharisees, the traditionalists and the literalists of the time before Christ. There were hundreds of refinements, colorings, degrees of violation of the law and breaches of requirements of the letter, and it required a man a lifetime to read all that had been written as to the violation of the law, so that by the time he had become acquainted with all the traditional exaction and requirements of the literalists he was an old man. Can you wonder that when an earnest soul came to take charge of the kingdom of heaven upon earth, he sent a fire on such paper palaces and totally devoured the walls of such sectarian and monstrous restrictions? Jesus Christ came to give *liberty*. "If the Son shall make you free, ye shall be free indeed." With the broom of destruction he swept these things into the sea. He said, "Away with them, the kingdom of heaven is purity, peace, love, charity."

What do you say to following this new Leader? I like his tone, it sounds like the tone of an honest heart. But for him we should have fallen in the wake of these men, in all probability; and our religion would have consisted of innumerable lines of exact requirements, punctual observances, ceremonial cleanness, until our souls would have been vexed within us, and life would have been reduced to one daily chafe and fret. Jesus Christ came and said, "The kingdom of heaven is within you. What doth the Lord thy God require of thee, O man, but to do justly, to love mercy, and to walk humbly with God?" "The sacrifices of God are a broken spirit: a broken and a contrite heart, O God, thou wilt not despise" [Ps. 51:17].

This question arises, and I would put it with the sharpest emphasis of which the human voice is capable, were it in my power to do so— *What is our religion?* I dare not ask what mine is. It is church-going, it is ceremony, it is going to a particular church, it is singing out of a particular hymn-book, it is being set within a certain regular surrounding of circumstances. I am so afraid of my religion—I speak of mine that I may not reproach others—becoming a question of routine and regulation. I now ask a man to put down on paper what he believes, then I take it up and I examine it, and I say, "You are orthodox." To another man I say, "Put down on paper what you believe." The man writes it. I examine it, and say, "Unorthodox." The orthodox man has gone out of the church. I ask him to bring in his week's report of work done, and he says:

> I bound your certificate upon my forehead, I went amongst
> men as orthodox, and I have sent at least two hundred

> people to hell for not believing what I believe. I got them to put down on paper what they believed, and I found they did not know what they did believe, and so I sent them all to perdition, and I have awakened the Church; and I will do the same next week

Unorthodox man, bring in *your* report. How does it read?

> Visited ten poor families, gave each of them five shillings and a word of encouragement, and told them to send for me if I could be of any help to them at any time. Saw a poor woman sitting on a door-step, without a friend or a home in the world—

> "O it was pitiful,
> Near a whole city full,
> Home she had none."

> Made an appointment with her, gave her something to be going on with, and I intend to see this woman as often as possible, until I get her established in life.

Who is the Christian?

What, then, is Christianity? A broken heart on account of sin—going to Jesus Christ, the Lamb of God, the Son of God, the wounded One, the Priest, and saying—

> "Forever here my rest shall be,
>   Close to thy bleeding side,
> This all my hope and all my plea,
>   For me the Savior died."

Then, out of that coming all the beautifulness of life, which grows, and grows only, in the garden of God.

nineteen

DIVINE EDUCATION

Matthew 5:21–32

THIS SHOWS us the principle upon which the education of the world was being conducted by the Divine Teacher. Perhaps the education could not have begun otherwise than very roughly. The mind is not prepared for the higher form of truths, and the more spiritual application of them at the beginning. We all need to be trained. In our higher training we must go, as in our lower tuition, a step at a time. Easy come, easy go, is a proverb which applies in many directions. Always read over again the last lesson before you begin the next, if you wish to be really accurate and profound scholars. You know how you train your child. First you lay down some broad and general commandment. He is not to break things, he is not to endanger himself, he is not to touch the stove, he is to keep away from the water, he is not to use his little fists, and so in some broad and general way you indicate what the child is not to do. If you spoke to the child in any other terms and in any other tone, your education might be of a very superior order, but it would be utterly lost, so far as the child's appreciation and obedience are concerned. You must begin where the child can begin, you must humble yourself and take upon you the form of a servant, and become obedient unto death, the death of your intellectual pride, even the death of the cross, and must break up your words into very little tones and syllables in order to suit your youthful auditor. It would become you, perhaps, by reason of the elevation and range of your own intellectual acquirement, to adopt a very high tone to the child, but you must come down out of your intellectual sky and talk the plain and common language of the earth if you would make any good impression upon the child's mind and heart.

So at the beginning it was, perhaps, enough to say, "Thou shalt not kill." But there came a time in the training and advancement of the world when a keener tone was to enter into the divine teaching. That keener tone we hear in the words that are now before us. Christ has brought us a long way from the broad and rough commandment, Thou shalt not kill. He asks us to pass a line and enter into a kingdom in which we are not to think unkindly or unjustly of one another. He discovers for us that the principle is the same in evil speaking as in murder. With those piercing sharp eyes of his, to which the darkness and the light are both alike, he says that in the unjust thought is the principle of manslaughter. It would, therefore, have been but poor work on his part to come down and repeat the old broad general morality; he must bring in a new standard, he must set up a new kingdom, he must flood the world with a purer light. Herein he sets up his throne of judgment amongst us today, and he calls us up one by one, to be measured and weighed. Let us hasten to obey his call.

What have you to say? He will ply the charge of slaying men—what is your answer? An instantaneous, frank, unreserved denial. So far, so good. Have you ever thought one unjust thought respecting your neighbor? Where is your glibness now? If you have, then you are still in the old school, and you have not entered into the Christian kingdom at all. Where then are the Christians? Judged by that high and pure standard, my mournful answer to the inquiry is, I cannot tell. There are no Christians. Jesus says to us, in effect, "If you come to me, simply saying that your hands are clear of human blood, you belong to the old school, you are faithful scholars of them of old time, but the first condition of entrance into my school, or the first proof of being in that school, is that a man be not angry with his brother without a cause. There must be no evil thinking, evil speaking, evil judgment, uncharitable criticism." Who then can stand the test of that fire? "What do ye more than others? You do not kill, you do not steal, you do not commit adultery, you do not make yourselves amenable to the law of the land—what do ye more than others? Do not even the publicans the same?" So he definitely chides us, and we have no answer.

Still he would lead us on little by little; he would not deny us a place in his kingdom if we can honestly say, "Lord, I believe, help thou mine unbelief. I am still in the body, and I feel all the passion and urgency of my lower nature. So metimes a cruel thought does arise in my heart, and sometimes I give too generous a welcome to uncharitable criticism of my brother, but afterwards I hate myself for having entertained so vile a guest. God be merciful to me a sinner" [see Luke 8:13]. If such be our speech, then it pleases the great Christ, the Man of the shepherdly heart, to give us a position in his school and teaching.

Let us beware of these vain distinctions of ours. A man does not kill, and therefore he claims to be a Christian! Jesus Christ says to him, "That is an insufficient and untenable claim altogether. A thousand men who never go to church can say the same thing. You must adopt a higher tone, or you know nothing of the spirit of the Cross and the love of God." Thus our preachers must urge upon us the ideal side of things, and we must not pardon them if they do otherwise. They must not come down to us and tell us that not killing is equal to loving. Though they condemn themselves with every breath they breathe, and thrust sharp swords into their own hearts with every syllable they utter, yet this must be done, the ideal must be lifted up and magnified that we may see how far short we fall or come of being true Christ-ones. We call ourselves respectable persons; so we are, with the publican's respectability. There is not a man here today, probably, who cannot walk up and down the thoroughfares of the city and defy the magistrate to touch him. That is not Christianity, that is respectable paganism—that is not the religion of the sanctuary of Christ, that is ceremonialism, high paganism, outward cleanliness. Christianity is a condition of the heart.

How is it with us when that question, keen as a sting of fire, is put to us, namely, What about your inner life, your heart? You do not kill, but you think evil of your neighbor; you do not slay a man with the sword, but you whisper unkind words, about your friend. You do not violate the open laws of decency, but yours is an uncharitable judgment; you have not passed a counterfeit coin, but you would take away a reputation and wound a heart. You would not openly tell a lie, you say you scorn to tell a lie; yet if two constructions can be put upon any human action, you elect the worse of the two. If that is true of you or me, by so much we are not in the kingdom of Christ at all. We may be expositors and critics and respectable pagans, but we are not in the Christian kingdom at all.

Terrible is the talk of Christ's as a great burning judgment, and it keeps us at bay like a fire. No wonder if sometimes our hearts are so dejected as to think that no progress is being made with Christian civilization at all. When a man seventy years of age can talk just as he did at thirty, as unlovingly and unfeelingly and hopelessly about his kind; when the very first thought that occurs to his mind is one of ungenerous criticism, how can he have been in the school of Christ? Love thinketh no evil, love suffereth long and is kind, love believeth all things, hopeth all things, endureth all things, love never faileth, and without love no man can be a follower of Christ [see 1 Cor. 13].

Jesus Christ is very urgent about these human relations of ours; therefore he says, "Therefore if thou bring thy gift to the altar, and there rememberest that thy brother hath ought against thee; leave there thy gift before the altar, and go thy way; first be reconciled to thy brother, and then come and offer thy gift." We are not to remember whether we have anything against our brother; that would be easily done, our memory needs no spur on that side, we so soon forget our own delinquencies. Where did my last word of fire drop? What heart did I wound in my last speech? On what right did I trample in my last transaction? Whom did I strike down in order to accomplish my last purpose? Let me examine myself thus, and I shall be a long time in getting to the altar. At the altar, whited, painted hypocrite? Leave the altar and go away to discharge your plain human duties, bind up hearts you have broken, comfort those you have thrown into dejection, and apologize on both knees to the woman, the child, the man, you have injured, and then come and take up your hymn-book and lay your offering on the altar purer than snow.

I do not wonder that Jesus Christ does not make much progress in the world, and I do not wonder that any old trickster in words and conjurer in doctrines can get more followers than Christ. He keeps men away from him by these judgments of fire. His doctrine is a continual rebuke, the very holiness of his speech creates a torment in the heart that is not equal to obedience. But wherein he is severe he makes good work; he builds slowly, but he means that no wind shall ever throw down the towers which he rears. He collects his members very gradually, and by a gate most narrow and straight does he bring men to him, but they never leave him. He is not building a beautiful house of smoke which the wind will blow away; he is building a Church, and he has calculated the strength of the gates of hell, and having built his masonry with a slow hand, he says, "It is finished—the gates of hell shall not prevail against it."

He now passes on to give directions concerning the crucifixion of the flesh and the senses, and he lays down this great principle—and I include the whole teaching under it—that under the stress of fierce temptation either the *body* has to be denied or the *soul* has to be injured. He says in effect, "I put the case before you in this fashion: temptation will come, and one or other must fall, the body or the soul." The body says, "I will have my way, I will enjoy myself, I will throw off restraint, I will do what I please, every appetite shall be gratified." And the soul sits as far back as it can, in the foul house, and mourns like an exile. I see it, I see its drooping countenance, its eyelids heavy and red, I hear its great sob, I see its infinite dejection. The great principle is that denial has to come into your life *somewhere*. You deny the body or you deny the soul. Deny the body and the soul comes to the front and floods your life with sacred light, with heaven's pure splendor. Gratify the body, and the soul retires, and its hot tears fall in the hearing of God. Self-slaughter takes place somewhere; it is for us to say where it shall take place. It can take place in the cutting off of a hand, or in the thrusting of a dagger into the very fountain of life, and it lies within the power of the human will to say where the wound shall be inflicted.

There is a bloated man who never said "No" to an appetite. You see it in his face. That is not the face of his childhood developed into noble age, that is another face: he is made now in the image and likeness of the devil. His very eye has a twist in it, his very speech has lost its music. He does not want to come into a pure home, he does not want to look upon the unsullied flowers, he does not care to listen to the birds singing their sweet song in the spring light. His affections are elsewhere. All the urgency of his life moves amid other directions, he is less a man than he ever was, and very unhappy.

Here is a man who has crucified the flesh, the affections, and the lusts thereof; he has cut off his right hand, plucked out his right eye, struck himself everywhere with heavy blows, but his soul throws over his maimed condition a sacred light, a beautiful expression. The form is rugged, the countenance is marred, but through it there is a soft shining light which tells that the soul is growing angelward and Godward, and everyday sweetens his nature and prepares it for higher society.

In looking at all these injunctions, let me urge you to beware of nibbling criticism and exposition. It would be easily possible for us to spend many mornings over the discussion of the paragraph which is now before us. I question whether it would be profitable to do so. In reading Holy Scripture seize the principle, get hold of the genius, the divine meaning, and in proportion as you are critical about the mere letter, are you in danger of losing the divine inspiration. Suppose, to make the meaning clearer, I should undertake to explain to you the meaning of the word *sky*. I begin by telling you that it is a word of one syllable, I point out that that one syllable consists of three letters, I call your attention to the fact that it opens with the nineteenth letter of the English alphabet, and that it closes with the next-to-the-last letter in the alphabet. What do you know about the meaning of the word *sky?* You know nothing of it. Let me tell you that the word *sky* is not to be looked at or spelled or taken to pieces by rough vivisection of mere letters, but lift up your eyes when the morning is spreading itself above you in all its beauty and freshness, and one look into the great arch will do more for your understanding of the term sky than all the mere conjuring with the three letters that the most skillful literalist could ever do.

So it is possible for you to take to pieces every one of those words in this long paragraph, and yet to know at the end nothing about the meaning of Christ's doctrine. His doctrine is one of inward purity, of spiritual rectitude, of absolute and loving sympathy with God. There be those, no doubt, who are most anxious to know what was meant by "*Raca*," and "*fool*," and "*hellfire*." To take these words to pieces might appear instructive, but so far as the doctrine of Christ is concerned it might easily be destructive. "*Raca*," for example, is a forgotten word. Words come and go. To us it means nothing, but as used by those in the olden time it meant insolence, contempt—the man who called another "Raca," despised him, spat upon him, humbled the manhood made in the image and likeness of God. We have no such word amongst us now, but we have the contemptuous feeling, we have the up-gathering of our conventional respectability and our drawing aside from the unworthy, the poorly dressed, the unfavored, the great unwashed. The great teaching of Christ is that contempt of humanity is punished by being thrown into Gehenna, the valley given up to fire.

In discussing the Temptation of our Lord, we inferred the character of the tempter from the kind of temptations which he urged. We might apply the same principle to the teaching of Christ, and infer the character of Christ from the kind of teaching which he submitted to the world. Mark the undivided responsibility which he assumes—"I say unto you." The personal pronoun is there emphatic, it takes into itself all the meaning. In the first instance you have a plural term, "It hath been said by *them* of old time, but"—now comes the singular term—"I say unto you."

There is no division of responsibility, there is no hiding of himself behind multitudinous precedents, there is no mere focalization of the wisdom of the dead ages. Here is personal responsibility, clear, definite, undivided, incommunicable. It required some courage on the part of a mere peasant to stand up and say to a great multitude of people, "I put myself above all that ever taught you in the ages gone." Yet mark how what he said was in fulfillment of truth and not in destruction of the ancient law. Christ did not say, "You may kill if you please," he accepted the teaching, "Thou shalt not kill," and he carried it one step further. He said, "Out of the heart killing comes; make the tree good and the fruit will be good. It is no use for the hand to be able to uplift itself and show that it is without one drop of blood upon it—the question is, How many murders has the heart committed?" This is the true doctrine of development, this is the true fulfillment of the law.

Mark the intense *spirituality* of all Christ's teaching. He says, "How is it with the heart, how is it with the spirit, what would you do if you could, how far is your respectability a mere deference to the clay god of custom, how far is your outward cleanliness a mere expression of deference to the usages of the time?" A man is what his heart is, "A man is no stronger than his weakest point," says the strategist, and the moralist adds, "A man is no better than in his feeblest morality." We are to be judged by the heart and not by the hand. "Many will say to me in that day, 'Lord, Lord, have we not prophesied in thy name, and in thy name done many wonderful works?' Then will I profess unto them, 'I never knew you; depart from me, ye that work iniquity'" [Matt. 7:22, 23]. If we are humble in heart, contrite, penitential, self-renouncing, always wishing and desiring to be better, Christ will accept this purpose as an accomplished fact, and astound us by the revelation of his rewards.

Understand what kind of Teacher we have now come upon. This is harsh preaching which we read in our text today. It is a judgment upon the Preacher if it be not a vindication. He must keep up to his own standard. Having challenged the righteousness of the Scribes and Pharisees, he must show a better one. Having demanded purity of heart, he must show it, or endeavor to show it. Having scorned as a final consummation all the moralities that everyone before him taught, he must be faithful to the new and larger doctrine. If not, he opens his heart to all the assaults of even the least ingenious of his foes. He did no sin, neither was guile found in his mouth, his robe was seamless, no man could charge him with violating his own doctrine—he was the only preacher that lived his sermons, in him alone was perfect, absolute consistency. What he looks for from us is a humble, daily, loving endeavor to follow him. That is all we can claim, and we claim it with most bated breath.

twenty

THE PRACTICAL
BEATITUDES

Matthew 5:33–48

WE HAD some difficulty in understanding the beatitudes, the music seemed to be too exquisite and refined for the rough instruments at our disposal. We hurried over them, rather than deliberately read them. As your teacher, I had a purpose in this; I knew that the beatitudes would all come up again in practical form. Who can understand abstract and purely spiritual truth? But that which is impossible from one point of view may be rendered comparatively easy from another. Jesus Christ now proceeds to give examples upon what we might call the blackboard. When he said, looking it while he did say it, "Blessed are the pure in heart, for they shall see God" [Matt. 5:8], we did not understand the meaning of the unfathomable doctrine. When he said, "Blessed are the meek, for they shall inherit the earth," we thought he was speaking of himself, or of strangers, for we had never come within the sacred lines described by that simple, yet immeasurable, word, meekness. Now he is proceeding from doctrine to exhortation, and you will find under his exhortations the whole set of the beatitudes: he is giving you now to drink out of the wells he dug when he laid down the doctrine.

I cannot tell what he means by purity of heart, so he approaches my dull understanding with this practical direction—Do not be angry with your brother without a cause, do not call your brother by contemptuous names, do not describe any man willfully and maliciously as a fool. I think these are easy exhortations, and when I begin to give them incarnation in my life I find they are supreme difficulties; I have not motive force in me enough to carry this tremendous engine along. Now I take him aside and say privately in the house, "I know now something of what you meant when you said, 'Blessed are the pure in heart.'" "Yes," he replies, "that was my purpose, and if your heart be not right you will never be able to do the apparently simple duties which I have not indicated. Unless there be pureness of heart there will be pollution of lips, unless there be rightness of heart there will be a hidden and sinister fire in the spirit, and it will express itself in contempt and malice, and harshness and cruelty." So now that he comes into practical particulars, I find that they balance the spiritual doctrine which I could not understand. But I will try to do the duty—I shall be lead back into the doctrine, and be made to feel that I cannot work with the hand except it express the inspiration of a cleansed heart.

So when he says to me, "If a man smite thee on the one cheek, turn to him the other also"; when I ask, "How is this to be done?" he says, "Recall the beatitudes." I then endeavor to remember what he said in the spiritual part of his discourse, and this sweet word returns to my memory—"Blessed are the meek, for they shall inherit the earth." When I heard that sentence the first time I dismissed it as a very beautiful conception, a high and delicate theory, written in clouds and illustrated with sunset colors, but now that it comes down to me in practical form, I find it was no cloudy revelation, no mere touch of intellectual beauty, no flash of the moral imagination, but something sound, honest, vital, divine. So it is no use telling a man to turn the other cheek to the man who has smitten him if he has not first turned his heart towards meekness. You cannot put on meekness except as you put on paint that can be washed off. If you have not the meek heart, you cannot do the meek deed. Do not play at meekness, do not simulate meekness; let us hide ourselves with Christ, who is meek and lowly in heart, then we shall be exactly what he meant when he told us that when we were smitten on one cheek we had to turn the other also. Throughout the whole of these practical exhortations you will find that he is reducing the beatitudes or spiritual doctrines to spiritual form and expression.

Let us now go a little into detail to establish this with some breadth of illustration. "Ye have heard that it hath been said by them of old time, Thou shalt not forswear thyself, but shalt perform unto the Lord thine oaths." That is, you have heard it laid down broadly that you are not to commit perjury; having taken a vow, you must be faithful to it; having uttered your oath, you must carefully and deliberately reduce it to practice. It must not be made a dead letter, it must not be evaded, it must not be inverted, there must be no perjury or false-swearing or foregoing of the most sacred oaths of life: but I say unto you, that that is a very poor advancement in the right direction. So far as it goes it is right enough, but go forward, follow me, so as to relieve yourself from the necessity of ever swearing at all. That is to say, let your heart be so sincere that your speech must be simple; cultivate that state of heart in the sight of God which naturally and necessarily, by virtue of the divine compulsion, expresses itself in simple, transparent, and beauteous sincerity and simplicity.

I do not think the Savior is forbidding what is known as judicial oath-taking or swearing. He always recognized certain necessities of the time, and he adapted his revelation from the beginning to the hardness of the hearts of those whom he had to instruct. But he was bound to point to the ultimate line he set up of ideal conversation. It is his purpose to make us so like himself that we cannot but speak exactly what is true. Consider the monstrousness of any man speaking only what is true because he has *sworn* to do it. That man is a liar. In his very nature and blood he is false, if he will only speak that which is true simply on the ground that he has taken an oath to do it. There can be no formal truthfulness: sincerity is a condition of heart; it is not the result of a mechanical contrivance coming out of the kissing a certain book under a certain adjuration. Jesus Christ therefore educates the race up to the point of not needing to swear or affirm or declare, with unusual emphasis. He would have our very breathing to be the expression of our heart's condition, so that if a man said "yes," he meant that, and that only: if he said "no," there was no mental reservation, no subtle and inexpressed equivocation of meaning, no intention, deep down in the heart, to take advantage of a certain set of terms under a certain set of circumstances—that is the deep and glorious meaning of the Son of God. Be so right within as to be incapable of uttering one word that is not pure as light and as fire. It is to that high result he would bring us. We are dull scholars, and the Teacher has yet an infinite work before him.

Jesus Christ then addressed himself to certain little trickeries that were in custom amongst the people. He told them not to swear by heaven, nor by earth, nor by Jerusalem, nor by the head. Why did he go into this detail? Because such was the corruption of his age, that there were great and learned men who laid it down as right to break any oath in which you could not find, in so many letters, the name Jehovah. There was one great man in history who openly avowed that he felt himself to be at liberty to break any oath in which he did not expressly use the word *God*. If the word *God* had passed his lips he felt himself bound in honor to fulfill his oath, but if he swore by heaven, by the altar, by the queen, by his hair, by his palace, he did but gather so much straw as he could cast into the fire of his passion and burn when he pleased. Jesus Christ, with that marvelous comprehensiveness of teaching which is characteristic of his school, proceeds to show that, though you may not have the name of God in your oath, whatever you touch is sacred and has God in it. "Swear not by heaven, for it is God's throne; nor by the earth, for it is his footstool; nor by Jerusalem, for it is his city; nor by thine head, for he fashioned it and clothed it, and you cannot make one hair white or black." So he delivered the term God from its consisting of so many letters and syllables, and showed that the whole universe was alive with God, and that to swear by a stone was to invoke the Creator that formed it. To be under such a Teacher is an inspiration, to hear such a man is to expose yourself to the mountain breeze or a whiff of ocean air full of life and giving life.

Take the next particular. "Ye have heard that it hath been said, An eye for an eye, and a tooth for a tooth, but I say unto you that ye resist not evil, but whosoever shall smite thee on the one cheek turn to him the other also, and if any man shall sue thee at the law and take away thy coat, let him have thy cloak also. And if any man compel thee to go a mile, go with him twain [two]." We all know to what absurdities and in-iquities a merely literal acceptance of those words would lead. You nibble at the meaning of Christ when you begin to think that you see it all in these bare words, as they would be understood by the unenlightened and unspiritual mind. What is Jesus Christ teaching here? He is teach-ing the great principle of forbearance of long-suffering. He quells all human passion, and sets upon human revenge the seal of his displeasure. Re-venge is not to enter into our thoughts. As to self-protection it is written in our nature; it is not a debased instinct, it was in the original Adam, the divinely-shaped and divinely-inspired man, and the very first word spoken to the man constituted an appeal to this instinct, "Take care; in the day thou eatest thereof thou shalt surely die. Protect thyself." It can-not be taken out of our manhood, this instinct of self-preservation; it can be sanctified, moderated, ennobled, and this is what Christ meant it to be. I may smite in judgment or I may smite in revenge, but the individual man who is injured cannot smite in judgment. I smite in temper—that is the very thing forbidden. We caution a man against taking the law into his own hands—that is exactly what Jesus Christ means in this direction. You ought not to have taken the law into your own hands—Why? Because you were only an individual and the individual is incomplete. What, then, should I have done? You should have referred it to the complete man. What is his name? *Society.* Society will lay its terrific hand upon the man that smote you. You are only a part and not a whole, a fraction and not an integer. The judge, when he sits upon the judicial bench and condemns a fellow-creature to penal servitude for life, is not an individual, he is the embodiment of Society, the representative of the latest civilization of his time and land. If you, being smitten on one cheek, turn round and smite the man who smote you, you may both be taken before the judge. Rather than that, turn to him the other also. Leave your defense and his punishment in the hands of the *social* man, the aggregate humanity, the judge.

This is exactly what Christ did himself. Christ did not personally resist evil. He exemplified the very doctrine now being explained. Personally, when he was reviled, he reviled not again, when he suffered he threatened not; he gave his back to the smiters and his cheeks to them that pluck off the hair. But as Judge, not the Jesus of Nazareth, but the Son of Man, he shall come in his glory and all the holy angels with him, he shall divide the nations and open hell under the feet of those that despised him. We believe that Thou wilt come to be our Judge. Every eye shall see him, they that pierced him shall mourn because of him, those whose hands are the wettest and reddest with human blood shall seek mercy of the rocks and pity of the mountains, for the wrath of his face shall scourge them like the fire that awaits their coming [see Rev. 6:16]. Resist not evil, do not take the law into your own hands; be personally meek, forbearing, long-suffering, show that the spirit of revenge has no place in your life, show that you would rather suffer wrong than do wrong; take the larger view, be gentle,be hopeful, be noble, and as to your sufferings, there is an organized anger that shall destroy the adversary, there is a judicial scourge that shall cut to his bone. "Dearly beloved, avenge not yourselves, but rather give place unto wrath, for it is written, Vengeance is mine, I will repay, saith the Lord" [Rom. 12:19]. and he repays through organized society, through enlightened and established civilization, and by hundreds upon thousand different ministries which we can neither name nor measure.

"And whosoever shall compel thee to go a mile, go with him twain." This refers to the system of forced courierships. In ancient times and oriental lands, messages were delivered by couriers, and persons were required to show the way to strangers. If you were lost upon a mountain or in a valley, it was part of your right to *insist* upon any person who was in the neighborhood to go with you part of the road, to help you out of your difficulty. Persons could be *compelled* to bear messages and letters. One Simon, a Cyrenian, was compelled to bear the cross. Who would not carry that cross every mile he has yet to walk? The Savior said, "If a man compel you to go a mile with him to show him the road, go two miles rather than not go at all. Show a cheerful disposition under the pressure, let your philanthropy absorb your convenience."

"Give to him that asketh of thee, and from him that would borrow of thee, turn not thou away." We all know that society would be wrecked in a very short time if this rule were to be literally applied. In fact it bears upon its face the proof that it does not admit of application in the way which the mere literalist would expect. It is too broad to mean anything as a mere letter, it is, as lawyers say, void by generality. It means so much as to mean nothing. And yet it must have some profound signification? Certainly. Where shall we find that signification? In God's own government, just as we find the explanation of non-resistance in Christ's own conduct. God does not do this himself, as the literalist would interpret it. He does it in the nobler and larger way which is of no use to the mere devotee of the letter. Let me explain. I ask God to give me what I mention to him, yet he turns away. Then he tells me to give to the man that asketh of me. I must find the meaning of these words in the course of his own action. I would borrow of God, and yet he turns away from my cry. He judges what is best for me, what is good for me: he says "No" to many prayers: many a desire of mine that I have sent out towards the heavens has fallen back upon the door-sill like a wounded bird. I know now what Christ means: he teaches me clemency, sympathy, he develops in me an interest in human affairs, he saves me from absurdity and folly and recklessness and from putting myself into the very position in which I should have gone to repeat the doctrine he lays down, and thus keep up a system of absurd borrowing, now one man having it and now another, and so passing it between themselves through every hour of the day.

If you want to find the meaning of these sweet words, you can easily find it. Do not try to discover it in the letter. Whenever you are clement, sympathetic, large-hearted, kind-handed, you are going in the direction of the meaning of this passage. Jesus is not laying down little laws and small maxims, he is developing infinite principles which can be applied in every climate, and which can embody themselves under all the various circumstances which make up all the changefulness of human life.

That I am right in seeking the explanation of the whole doctrine in myself and in God is proved by what Jesus Christ immediately adds, "That ye may be the children of your Father which is in heaven," that you may do in your degree as he does upon an infinite scale. He does not answer every petition, he turns away from some requests, he knows that difficulty has a place in the discipline and sanctification of life, and he uses the rod as sometimes the only admissible lesson. I would be taught by him, I would be like him, I would err, as we sometimes say, on the generous side rather than on the ungenerous. I would rather be taken in than take in any human creature, I would rather try to find the means of healing a man than sourly turn away from his distressed face and his faltering voice. If that be my disposition of heart, I am in the school of Christ.

But take these exhortations as you like, you cannot give their application, unless you have help from heaven. It is not in man that lives to work out this sublime morality, it is not in the human heart as at present existing to find room for these divinities. He who made the heart must disinfect it, cleanse it, enlarge it to give hospitality to such guests.

twenty-one

TRUE ALMSDOING

Matthew 6:1-18

"WHEN THOU doest thine alms do not sound a trumpet before thee, as the hypocrites do in the synagogues and in the streets." The boxes in the temple treasury were shaped like trumpets. Jesus Christ said, "Do not make a trumpet of the box: it looks like one, but do not use it for the purpose of calling attention to what you are about to put into it." It is strange how we may pervert the most exquisite beauty, and turn it to false uses, forms, and colors, which God meant to lead us to higher thought and finer feeling. It is a box for the reception of secret alms, not a trumpet for sounding for the purpose of calling public attention to what is about to be done. Use everything for its right purpose, and beware of perversion; do not say you got the suggestion from the thing itself—it was never meant to convey such a suggestion, it was meant for a totally different purpose. He is the honest man, as well as the wise, who seizes the definite intention of Providence, and works along that line without putting upon it glosses and twists and perversions of his own.

"When thou doest thine alms." Literally, and this may surprise some of you, when thou doest thy righteousness. In the fifth chapter and the twentieth verse, which we have already expounded, we read, "Except your righteousness exceed the righteousness of the Scribes and Pharisees, ye shall in no case enter into the kingdom of heaven." What a different meaning is infused into the sentence now, when we replace the word *alms* with the word *righteousness*. I thought almsgiving was a matter of pity, transient emotion, kindly feeling. It is more than that: under all the flowers of the earth are the great ribs of rocks, without which the earth could not cohere and exist. I understood that when I gave alms

I was displaying pity, kind feeling, nice sentiment, and that I was drawing attention to myself as a man of peculiarly good nature and most amiable sensibility. Nothing was farther from the truth. It is *right* to give:
when the strong man helps the weak, he is not showing the beauties of
amiability, or indulging a merely transient emotion, it is not a specimen
of social chivalry, it comes out of the righteousness of God, the very law
of right. If he had done anything else, he would have been guilty before
God of a violation of the spirit of *righteousness.*

When you took the dear little child off the streets and gave it a chair
at your table, it was not an áction that could be covered with some such
words as pity, kindness, sympathy, gentleness, and amiability. All these
words themselves are used oftentimes with too narrow a meaning. If our
actions do not go back to the rock of righteousness, then they will be,
however beautiful in their immediate manifestation, transient in their
duration. They will be forgotten as dreams are forgotten in the light. On
the other hand, only let us get the notion that to help a man, a child,
a woman, to give alms to poverty, to do any deed of charity, is a right thing,
and then see how our life becomes grand in solemnity, how it grounds
itself on the immutable and the complete, and how we cease to be moved
by caprice and impulse that cannot be calculated and controlled, and
become the servants of a great law, the apostles of an infinite and beneficent righteousness.

This almsgiving is to be done, I observe, in the sight of God. Then is
God always looking? So the great Master teaches us. "Your Father
which is in secret . . . your Father which seeth in secret . . . your Father
who is always looking on." What, am I ever in the great Taskmaster's eye?
Does that eye never close in slumber? Is there not one moment when
it tires of looking? In that moment I might snatch his scepter and dispute his sovereignty. But the Holy One of Israel slumbers not nor
sleeps: the darkness and the light are both alike unto him. That which
is spoken in the ear he hears in thunder in heaven. This gives me a very
solemn and grand view of life.

Why, then, many of our processes in the matter of almsgiving must
be given up. Sometimes men meet and challenge one another to do
good. If it is done with modesty all but infinite, it is permissible. It is a
dangerous trick. "I will give fifty pounds if you will give fifty pounds,"
says a man who imagines he is going to do something great. If it is a mere
matter of taste, so far as any matter can be so limited the challenge is

allowable, but if it relate to the higher charities, to consecration, to the outgoing and uplifting and offering of the heart to God, do not mention what you are going to do, ask not what other people are going to do. Beware of that most mischievous fallacy, which says, "I am only waiting to see what others do." Stand before God, calculate the whole case in his presence, soliloquize in his hearing, have but one auditor, and that your Father which heareth in secret, and then do whatever is right, according to your then sanctified conviction, and God will do the rest.

Compulsion is not to enter into almsgiving, except self-compulsion, the best of all. If you compel me to do an alms or to give a gift, I will undo it if I can, when you are not looking, but if I am compelled by ministries within to do an alms, I do it with my love. I could not withdraw it, it is given to God in holy sacrifice and grateful prayer. In this matter of religion there ought to be no compulsion at all, except the compulsion of love. That love needs continual warming. It is amazing how soon our affections become cooled by the chilling winds of the earth. So we must hurry to the sanctuary, and into the inner spirit of the divine word, we must climb the sacred eminence on which stands the one cross, out of which all other crosses are cut, and so must we renew the fire of our love. For love in the Church is nothing if it be not a constant flame. Let us beware of sudden outbreaks of fire. If they be beside the continual burnt-offering, they are good, but the burnt-offering itself must be steady, continual, daily, and if now and again the flame shoot heaven-high, so be it, but the steady glow must never fail.

We are to see the divine in the human in this giving of alms. When we give something to a little poor child, to whom do we give it, if our motive is right and pure? We give it to Christ. That is his own interpretation of my action, he astounds me by its vastness and brightness. "Inasmuch as ye have done it unto one of the least of these my brethren, ye have done it unto me. I was hungry, and ye gave me meat" [Matt. 25:35]. O hungry one, Christ is suffering the pang that gives thee pain. In all our affliction he is afflicted. Whenever a hand of righteous charity is put out to alleviate our distresses, he feels the tingling of it in his own pierced palm, and writes it, to be spoken of another day.

The hypocrites are not so, the actors are of another temper: their act is the same as the right act, but it is done from the wrong motive, and therefore it has no value in the sight of heaven. It is like a prayer that paints itself on the ceiling, not like a living bird, loosened from the secret heart and sent out to find its invisible nest in heaven.

Jesus Christ, then, is very deep in teaching. He gets down to the fundamental line, and yet in doing so there is a marvelous satire in his tone. Speaking about the actors or hypocrites he says, "Verily I say unto you, they have their reward." They get what they seek; they seek applause, they get it for the moment and it dies away, and they are left with the void air. They get their heaven, an empty place, a silent chamber, a heaven they would gladly part with; when you have received your applause for your almsgiving that is all you will get, if you did it from a wrong motive. You will hear a clapping of hands and a stamping of feet, and an uproarious "Hurrah!" for a second or two, and then, gone; and when it is gone your heaven has vanished. As to the after work, who can tell what that may be when the mask is taken from the hypocrite's face, when the paint is washed from his countenance and he stands out in the ghastliness of his true meaning? My soul, enter not into such a secret.

You will find as you proceed with your lesson that Jesus Christ applies the same principle to everything he now deals with. The fire is the same, he does not change the test, his chemistry is not fickle, throughout the whole he is seeking for purity of heart, and throughout the whole he shows how the trick of the hand may be made momentarily to represent purity of heart and purpose. Thus with regard to prayer. "When thou prayest, thou shalt not be as the actors, for they love to pray standing in the synagogues and in the corners of the streets, that they may be seen of men." Right things may be done in a wrong way, and so may lose their value. It is right to give, right to pray, right to fast, but they may all be done in a wrong way.

We do not understand today what is meant by these words, "long prayers, vain repetitions, and much speaking," though sometimes we say a prayer is long if it went, say, to the length of ten minutes, or fifteen, or twenty; if to half-an-hour, we describe it as very long and tedious, but that was not the measure indicated by the words of Jesus Christ. It had come to be in his time a matter of settled conviction among certain people, to whom he now definitely refers, that if they only prayed long enough, kept on saying the same things over and over again, they would purchase heaven as a matter of right, as you purchase an article by laying down a certain money value for it on the counter. The article is yours, it is not a gift of the original proprietor, it has passed on to you as having value received on the part of the man who first held it. So among the hypocrites and the actors, they thought that if they read a certain document called the *Sch'ma*—if they read that over and over again, and kept at it, and made a question of regular mechanical repetition of it, by a certain turn of the wheel they would be able to claim heaven as men claim a field for which they have paid the price. Jesus Christ, giving reference to this mechanical piety, said, "That is a vital mistake on their part; they think they shall be heard for their abundant speaking. Your Father knoweth what things ye have need of before ye ask him." Beware of vain repetition: in other words, beware of a mechanical piety. No prayer is long that is prayed with the heart: as long as the heart can talk the prayer is very brief—let that be the measure and standard of our long and much praying. Do not measure your prayers by minutes, but by necessities. Sometimes we have no influence with the King. He appears to have deafened himself against us or to have turned into stone at our approach, and our prayers and utterances are lost upon him as rain upon the barren rock. Sometimes we can talk the whole day with him, we cannot tell where the growing numbers of our praises will end, our hearts are enlarged in great and free utterance, and then we enter into the mystery of communion; not asking, begging, soliciting, wanting more and more like a blood-swollen leech but talking out to him as the dews go up to the morning sun. When you have such opportunities, make the most of them, and do not let the words, "vain repetitions and much speaking," come into your minds as temptations. One sentence may be too much speaking, and is so, if it is not from the heart. A day's long talk, a night's long communion, will be but too short, if you see the King as it were face to face.

Thus, again, Jesus Christ brings us to the point—"Blessed are the pure in heart." Jesus Christ came to set purity of heart in opposition to the formalism and corruption of his day. He found that evil hands had written lies and blasphemies upon every beam in the Temple, he found that the windows that ought to have looked heavenward had been cobwebbed with traditions, and curtained and screened so as to conceal the iniquity which was wrought behind them. So, with glowing ardor, burning like an oven, he cleansed the desecrated house, and relighted its shaded chambers with the very glory of heaven, called back the exiled and dishonored angels of purity, mercy, meekness, peace, and he banished the ghouls of selfishness, oppression, cruelty, and strife. He lifted, peasant's son though he was, an arm of thunder and shattered the vile creations that were set up to mock the holiness of God.

"What think ye of Christ?" A grand Teacher. He made no beck and bow to his age, saying, "If you please, will you be good enough to hear me?" He spoke the eternal word, and there was something in the human heart that said, "This is he of whom Moses and the prophets did write" [John 1:45]. You know the true voice when you hear it; there is a spirit in man, and the inspiration of the Almighty gives him understanding.

The Savior then proceeds to apply the same principle to the matter of fasting. He did not find fault with fasting as a religious ordinance, but he said, in effect, "This religious observance has been perverted like prayer and almsgiving; now you must not disfigure your face, and so call attention to the fact that you are fasting; you must fast in your heart, it must be the soul that fasts. Is not this the fast that I have chosen to undo heavy burdens, to let the oppressed go free, to speak for the speechless, and be feet and hands to them that are lame and helpless?" He did not find fault with the words, *almsgiving, prayer, fasting,* but he carried them up to their highest definitions. We have degraded every term we have ever used. In our Savior's time the hypocrites or actors used to spread ashes upon their heads literally, and used to tear their garments and make their faces the very picture and exemplification of hunger and dejection, and they used to walk up and down the streets, saying by these actions, "Look at us, how pious we are, how observant of the law; see to what extreme lengths we carry our devotion." Christ looked at them, and his eyes flashed fire on them, and he said, "Hypocrites, actors, masked men, verily I say unto you, you have your reward. You put out your hand to catch a gilded bubble, you seize it with greedy fingers and it melts and dies."

This matter of fasting was carried so far that one historian tells us it was mimicked and mocked in the Roman theater. At one play, the audience being seated and in expectation of the performance, a camel was led across the stage, and that camel was in such a lean and miserable condition, looking so utterly dejected and forsaken, that voices called out, "What is the matter with the camel?" and the dramatic answer was, "This is fasting-time amongst the Jews, and the camel has been observing the fast." This is what our pharisaical impiety always comes to; it is the tempting, sniveling hypocrite that is put upon the boards of our novels, and not the earnest and loving and true soul. When I come upon any character in a novel or romance that is meant to typify the ministry of the day or the Christian spirit of the day, I give the artist credit for endeavoring to set forth a hypocrisy and not a reality. I do not look even upon those Roman pagans as insulting a grand religious consecration, but as mimicking and mocking and bitterly taunting men who had forsaken the spirit of their religion, and had perverted and prostituted the letter to the most unworthy purposes. If any man shall attempt to insult that which is real, true, pure, divine, the thick end of the beam shall fall upon his own head in due time. As to those who take delight in caricaturing things that are counterfeit and unfit and unworthy—you have a ministry in life, and I wish you success in the discharge of your grave and responsible function.

"What think ye of Christ?" There is a tone of reality about this Man's teaching. Is his ministry vital, is he working in the right direction, is this the reforming ministry which all ages need? Sometimes we say that our ministers preach to the times—in doing so they follow the example of their Lord and Master. If Christ were living now he would speak to the times: he would not speak as if he were speaking to some former generation—he would speak to the men who are living around him, working all kinds of mischief, and having within them counsels and purposes unworthy alike of their manhood and of the divine vocation that is in all human life. I cannot imagine Jesus Christ coming to read something to us of an abstract kind. He would now and again lay down great breadths of noble doctrine, but he would be swiftly out in the age again. You would find him in the marketplace, you would find him in the broad thoroughfares, you would find him where merchants most do congregate, you would find him in all the activities of life, trying everything by the fire of heaven. He lived in a time of corruption, he never shut his mouth concerning it. He saw a kingdom perverted and he lifted up his voice in condemnation of it. He told the painted actors, the dressed coxcombs of his day, that they had not yet crossed the threshold of the kingdom which they pretended to hold in personal custody, and then, having cursed the corruption of his day as no other man had the power to do, he turned around, and with ineffable blessing, and with most tender speech, he spake to the weary and the heavy-laden, and the sad-hearted, to the woman that was a sinner, and to the little child brought for his blessing. And then last of all he poured out his soul unto death. A mistake—does any whisper such a suggestion? Looking at the life that preceded it, at the thunder and lightning of the denunciation of all wrong that went before it, at the beatitudes and the gospels poured out upon those whose hearts were broken and whose lives were weary—that death was the only fit conclusion; it belonged to the antecedent mistake, it set forth in the most vivid and graphic colors what had been indicated in hasty sketches in every day's beneficent ministry.

He died, he rose again, he lives, he expects us, he is preparing a place for us, and when he prepares, what will the result be? I have seen his earth, his flowers, his summers, his mornings—I have seen his sun, I have seen some of his innumerable stars. He will outdo it all, for he will prepare, not to be worthy of me but to be worthy of himself.

twenty-two

SECULAR ANXIETY

Matthew 6:19-34

IN THIS passage there is, first, an *exhortation*, and, secondly, a *reason* for
it. The exhortation is, "Lay not up for yourselves treasures upon earth:
lay up for yourselves treasures in heaven." The reason is, "For where your
treasure is, there will your heart be also." You will never understand the
exhortation till you understand the reason given for it. Vain is all criticism upon the words, "Lay not up for yourselves treasures upon earth."
It is in the treatment of those words that the annotators have failed. A
thousand little and mean questions arise while we confine our attention
to the words, "Lay not up for yourselves treasures upon earth." We are
not in a condition to criticize that language until we complete the
sentence and find at its close the all-convincing reason for giving such
an exhortation.

What is Christ anxious about? What is it that he wishes to take care
of? He himself gives an explicit answer to the inquiry. His one anxiety
is about the condition of the HEART. "'For where your treasure is, there
will your heart be also'; and it is the heart that touches my supreme solicitude. If the *heart* be right, the whole outgoing of the life will be right,
but if the heart be wrong, then all the actions that make up the sum total
of the duties and exercises of life will also be wrong." Now I see the whole
meaning, I understand what my Teacher intends me to receive as his
doctrine. Provided my heart is right, he does not care if my possessions
are heaven-high, if I can rise above them and stand upon them and use
them with mighty strength. He is most anxious that they should not be
bigger than I am, his supreme anxiety is that they should not lure my
confidence and make up the sum total of my hope and expectation. So

long as I can treat them as so many conveniences and use them for the good of my fellow-creatures, he cares not how many, how rich, may be my possessions. He says to me lovingly, with infinite pathos and concern, "Brother, friend, man—keep your heart right, keep your love in its right direction, let your life be a continual sacrifice, burning upwards to the only throne that deserves it. Then, as for your possessions, you will be master, not slave. The more you have, the more the poor will have; you will be treasurer and custodian, you will not be oppressed by the riches, but ennobled to dignity by them." So then there is no exhortation here against accumulating property and wealth. The world must have property, and the more that property is in good hands the better; and, concerning every man who makes a good use of money, I pray the Lord to send him tenfold more. The more he has, the more the poor have; the more money the good man has, the more the whole Church has. It is better that this money should be in the hands of a good treasurer than in the hands of an untrustworthy custodian.

Look at the figures in this exhortation, showing how keen was the observation of Jesus Christ regarding everything going on around him. "Lay not up for yourselves treasures on earth, where moth and rust doth corrupt." The property of the contemporaries of Christ consisted largely of linen and embroidered goods. To have great stores of these was the Jews' great notion of wealth. Jesus Christ, looking at all the piles of linen and embroidery, said, "Take care the moth does not get into them; remember that there is a moth—do not forget the consuming insect." It was a practical and most secular exhortation.

"And rust doth corrupt." The treasures were largely hidden in the earth. Men would dig deep pits in the field and hide their most valuable possessions, and there they would rust. Jesus Christ, looking at the man filling up the earth upon his treasure, says, "Remember the rust: what you have put in the earth there is exposed to danger: you may cover it up very carefully, but the rust will get at it." There is always some danger to be provided against.

"Where thieves break through and steal." The houses were mud houses, the walls were mud walls, and the thief is at the back of the house, breaking through, boring his way through the mud defense that he may get at the treasures hidden inside. Jesus Christ says to the builder of the mud wall, "Be careful—it is only mud, understand that mud is not impervious: always remember that there are weapons of iron that can break through your mud defenses." Again I say unto you, there is always danger to be guarded against, and a man is no stronger than his weakest point. Beware of the moth, beware of the rust, beware of the thief. Life is based upon caution, unless it be founded in God, and then it is lifted up above all danger, or the dangers that affect it themselves fall away before its supreme strength and immovable confidence.

So much for the exhortation, and so much for the reason. Now what is it as an *argument?* I am always struck with the common sense of this divine Talker. Apart from his metaphysics and high imagination and noble courage and heroism, there is an element of marvelous commonsense. He grasps his subject: he lays upon it a grip that means, "You cannot take this easily from me." Let us look at it merely as an argument.

Jesus Christ says, "Riches can be *stolen*, riches can *perish*, riches can *fly away*, therefore look out for treasures that are not subject to these vexatious and harassing contingencies." Is the argument sound? Look at it again. What you have in your hands may be taken out of them, therefore have something in your *heart* that no man can get at and steal. The reasoning is sound and unanswerable. He who has nothing but what he can grasp in his hands, is no stronger in his possessions than his fingers. A man can wrench what he holds out of his possession, and they will be his no longer. Where is your Bible? If it is only in your hands as a book, though you are pressing it to your heart, it can be taken away from you, and you may be without it. But, where is your Bible? "In my head," you say, "in my heart: I know it." Then, though the book be burned with fire, the revelation is untouched.

Jesus Christ says, "Have an inward life, have an interior life, have a soul." The Teacher who teaches in this fashion is a wise man. He warns us against the things that can be destroyed, and points us to the possessions that are indestructible. He tells you in so many words that you are no richer than your heart is; though your books be many enough to make a library of, you are only as rich as you are in your thought, feeling, aspiration, desire after God and all things godly. I feel that such teaching is true: no long and labored argument is needed to make me feel its truthfulness. If I speak right out of my heart and let my better self be heard, I say with the Scribe, "Well, Master, thou hast said the truth" [Mark 12:32].

Take it in another light, that it may be clearly seen by those who can understand better by illustration than by mere argument. You come into the house of your friend, and you are struck with what his books say upon *agriculture*. You look over the volumes and say, "Well, how very many books you have upon agriculture. I am surprised at your collection of works upon this subject." A friend belonging to the house says to you, "If you think the books upon agriculture are many, what will you say when I show you the library upon *astronomy?* If you think these books a good many upon agriculture, when I show you the astronomical works you will be utterly confounded." By the help of that illustration, go a little further and reason thus. If you think this man is rich in shares and stocks and fields and investments of one kind and another, what will you say when you see his thoughts, his feelings, his prayers, his aspirations, his plans for the amelioration of the race? Our inner nature should be so much in excess of our outer nature as to give the impression that we have no outer nature at all. We are to be so much larger in the soul than we are in the hand as to throw the hand into infinite insignificance, though in itself it have a giant's fist and can deliver a herculean blow. Let every man therefore ask himself what he has in the bank of the heart.

"The light of the body is the eye: if therefore thine eye be single, the whole body shall be full of light. But if your eye be evil (double), thy whole body shall be full of darkness. If therefore the light that is in thee be darkness, how great is that darkness!" The heart is the eye of the life: always keep the heart pure and right, sincere and true, and you cannot stumble along. Let your motive be correct, and you will be brought along the right road, even though you may have stumbled into the wrong path for a moment. Let your heart be right, and I care not in what thicket you be tangled, you will see a clear, broad road out of it, and you shall yet rejoin the main path that lies right up towards the light and the heaven that is at the end of it.

How is it then with the heart which is the eye of the life? What is your *motive*, what is your purpose? Dare you throw back the screen and show the motive to heaven's light? If so, you cannot be weak; you cannot be the subjects of long-continued depression and fear. O youth— my child, my son—give God thine heart; and as for thy mistakes, they prove thee only to be mortal. But for once let your motives become mixed, allow them to double themselves back into reservations and ambiguities and uncertainties, let the inner life become a hesitation and a compromise and a trick in expediency, and you are blinded in your very center and fount of light. And if the light that is in thee be darkness, how great is that darkness! If your supreme manhood be debased, how utter is the degradation. If you have gone down in your motive, you have gone altogether. So let a man examine himself as to his motive and purposes, and keeping these right, so as to bear the very test of fire and to stand the examination of light, he may maintain his life in the quietness of religious confidence. If you have got wrong in your motives stop. Do not be lured away by inventiveness in making excuses and palliations. Fall on your knees, and become strong by first becoming weak. No coverings up, no clever juggleries, no assumptions of appearance, but complete, unreserved, emphatic, contrite confession, and then begin again. Remember that your eye is the center of light, and if the eye be put out or injured, no other part of you can receive that great gift. The eye once blinded, your finger tips cannot be flamed up into illumination, your whole body is darkness. With the eye, the light is gone forever, and wisdom at one entrance quite shut out.

How marvelous it is that a single organ should hold so much, that there should be no alternative arrangement in this matter of light, looking at which we can say, "Well, it matters little if the light goes out at one point, it can come in at another." Such is not the arrangement of divine providence: you have the one inlet of light, lose that, and your whole body, though it be great and strong and healthy, and apparently beyond the touch of death, will be full of darkness. See how much depends upon one faculty, one organ. Let the ear be deafened and all music is lost; let the eye be blinded, and the whole firmament, with all its sun and stars, is but a covering of darkness. There is only a step between you and death: you have but one right hand, take care lest it be paralyzed and fall uselessly by your side forever. These are the cautions of no alarmist; they are the strong, grand, pure teachings of a Man who breathed the mountain air, and had the sea's freshness ever breathing through his magnificent, caring heart.

"No man can serve two masters, for either he will hate the one and love the other, or he will hold to the one and despise the other. Ye cannot serve God and mammon." We do not understand this in English. Men run away with very shallow notions of what is here said; these English words do not express the Savior's meaning, except with indefiniteness and a great distance of appreciation. No man—literally, no slave, and we do not know, thank God, what a slave is. The slave had no will of his own; every pulse of his body belonged to his master; he dare only look as the master approved; there must be no protest even in his eye, or he lost his life. He must stand, sit, come, go, at the will that was iron and that could not be broken. No man, says Christ, can sustain that relation to two masters; he cannot belong, absolutely, body, soul, spirit, will, imagination, energy, feeling, to two different masters. Masters — we do not understand this in English. We never can enter into the tragic pathos of that awful word; never to be able to call an hour my own; never to be at liberty to utter the voice of complaint; never to be permitted to look my true self, but to wear a mask to please another's eye: to be at the beck and call of a man who can take my life from me with impunity — that is what it means to be under a master.

How many persons there are who have read this text so as to sever the spiritual and the secular. It is in this way the Bible has been mistreated by some of its friends: it is in this way that great excisions have been made, so that religion has been left in the Church as an all but impalpable shadow. That is the meaning of this great Teacher — we must use the spiritual and secular, for all things are sacred according to the hand that touches them. What God has cleansed do not call common or unclean [see Acts 10:15]. You miss the grandest side of life when you separate it into spiritual and secular. There are some persons who talk about the temporalities of the Church — there are no temporalities in the Church. There are those who speak of the business side of the Church — there is no business side of the Church in any degrading sense of the term: it is all business. "Wist ye not that I must be about my Father's business?" [Luke 2:49]. He who lights a lamp in the Church is as he who preaches a sermon; he who opens a door or keeps a gate, as he who breathes a gospel and unfolds a revelation. The difference is in the degree, not in the quality; "he who sweeps a floor for thy sake, makes that and the action fine." We must be lifted up in our whole conception of life and labor, industry and reward, if we would enter into the spirit of Christ in his interpretation of our life and its duties.

Now comes the grand wondrous discourse concerning *secular anxiety and worldly fear*, the beautiful sermon wherein you find the reference to the lilies and the birds and the grass of the field. Let us look at that wonderful sermon a moment. We are treating this Gospel by Matthew in its *wholeness* and not going into the mere detail of the occasion — as a painter paints a landscape with a church upon it. He does not take you into the church, he simply throws the church upon the landscape as part of something else, and you must catch it in its proper outline and relationship. In the same way I am treating this Gospel. By-and-bye we shall go to the church and spend a day there; by-and-bye we shall come into the detail and study each particular delicate line; meantime we have to treat the gospel in its totality, and under the direction of this feeling look at this most marvelous discourse.

"Take no thought for your life." We do not come close to the Savior's meaning in this English word "thought." We do not, indeed, get into the right meaning of the word *thought* some three hundred years after the use which it first assumed. When this translation [King James Version] was made, the word *thought* meant something different from what it means today—it meant anxiety, restless, carking care; it meant that penetration of fear which upsets the balance of life and turns the whole soul into moods of dejection and wearing anxiety. The word *thought* meant this in the time when the English Bible was translated—hence one of the historians says, "Queen Catharine died of *thought*." Hence Cleopatra said to Enobarbus, "What shall we do, Enobarbus?" And the answer was, "*Think*, and die." In other words, "Fear, fret, pine away, succumb to depression, anxiety, and all the influences that can vex and tear the balance of the heart." It is against such thought that Jesus Christ warns his disciples.

Is it possible that any man here can be encouraging himself in languor and indifference and idleness by saying that he is considering the lilies and beholding the fowls, and yielding himself to the genius of this Sermon on the Mount? I must rudely disturb his foolish and atheistic lassitude. Let us behold the fowls of the air for a moment, and see how far their course justifies the man who is simply folding his arms and sitting still and letting God take care of him. First, the birds get up very early in the morning—where are you early in the morning? There goes one of your props! In the next place the birds are most industrious: it is one of my little pleasures to watch the industry of the birds, and, indeed, they seem to have no hours. I trust nobody will ever form them into a union for the purpose of shortening the hours of labor: that would be a great mishap in the air, to cut short their song exactly as the clock struck five! O, the building that is going on now! The straw-carrying and the feather-catching and the leaf-binding—what industry! Up with the sun, working all the hours of the light, and twittering and trilling and singing all the time. There is another of your props gone, you lazy man.

I find, too, that the birds are *self-supporting*: they would never take anything out of your hand if they could help it. A bird is sadly driven when it comes to any man and says, "Let me peck out of your hand, if you please." The birds support themselves—who supports you? You would borrow a shilling of your poor old mother if you could, and you talk about beholding the fowls of the air. You have borrowed of every friend you ever had—be just in your exegesis of the divine word, and add not the blasphemy of a fool's criticism to the behavior of a cowardly spirit.

And the lilies—is it a happy-go-lucky life with them? Far from it. The word *lilies* here is a word that may be so interpreted as to include *all* flowers, and the flowers are found in their *proper places*, they are where they were meant to be, if they are growing properly; not only so, the flowers are working in harmony with great *laws*. Every flower draws its beauty from the sun: the flower roots itself in dark places, and yearns with open face for the great light, and holds itself out with gracious willingness to catch every drop of dew that it can hold. So we must be in our proper spheres, in our right relations: we must keep the economy of life and nature as God has established it, then we shall truly, with a wide and healthy wisdom, behold the fowls and consider the lilies.

Jesus Christ gives a reason for this exhortation again. He says, "Which of you by taking thought [being anxious, or worrying] can add one cubit unto his stature?" He thus shows the *uselessness* of anxiety. Suppose now you sit up all night with your hands folded or twisted, in expression of keen unappeasable solicitude and yearning—what good does it come to in the morning? None! Suppose you should belabor yourself all day long, what does it come to tomorrow? To weariness, dejection, sadness, and to all the results of misdirected energy and irreligious folly. A great teacher now living has well said that if any friend of ours had told us one hundredth part of the lies our fears have told us, we never would have allowed him to speak to us again. We would have said, "Get thee behind me, thou lying man." But our fears come every day and tell us exactly the same lies, and we give them exactly the same confidence. Is that religion? It is, but only the religion of paganism. The religion of trust, love, faith, rests in the Lord and waits patiently for him; forms a grand and loving expectation, directs it often in speechless prayer to the generous and over-arching heavens, and calmly awaits the revelation and the whole answer of God.

This is how I want to live: I want to subordinate every desire to the one aim of seeking the kingdom of God and his righteousness; I want to interpret that kingdom as meaning and including all other kingdoms; and I would calmly await the leading of divine providence. Why fidget yourself, why fret and annoy yourself, why go out and throw yourself into a bed of stinging nettles merely for the sake of doing something? I would not anticipate tomorrow anymore than I would anticipate death. Death is abolished; there is no dying for the man who is in Christ. Let the child close his eyelids; he will open them in heaven. Let a pagan call that death if he likes; the Christian calls it *eternal life*. Nothing wrong can happen to me if I am really rooted in God, and if my eye be set towards him with the one anxiety of receiving his light.

Given that I have to take care of myself, and make all my arrangements, and go up and down life as if everything depended on me, and my life becomes a cloud, a fear, a sting, a great distress, but given that I am creature, not creator, child of the one ever-living, ever-loving Father, the very hairs of my head are all numbered, my name is written in heaven, and the whole plan of my destiny is mapped out in the skies—that I am, consciously or unconsciously, so long as my desire is as a pure flame, working out the divine intention. Let me feel that to be the case; then, come wound, come woe, high hill or cold river, or bleak wilderness or beauteous garden—come what may, God will come with it, and my life shall be a great, sweet peace.

twenty-three

TWO MASTERS

Matthew 6:24-34

"NO MAN can serve two masters, for either he will hate the one and love the other, or else he will hold to the one and despise the other. Ye cannot serve God and mammon." I venture to say that the true meaning of this passage has not been always represented. The common notion is that a man may *try* to serve God and mammon. Jesus Christ does not ask you for one moment to believe so flagrant an absurdity. The experiment cannot even be tried. What, then, becomes of your interpretation of your neighbor about whom you have said, many a time, "That man is trying to serve God and mammon"? The experiment does not admit of trial. You must get into the profound meaning of this word *cannot*. It indicates an impossibility even so far as the matter of trial or experiment is concerned. So the passage is a consolatory one: it is not a warning against any kind of practical hypocrisy and double-handedness—Jesus is not lifting up his voice against the ambidexters who are trying to do the same thing with both hands—he lays down, as he always does, a universal and everlasting law; ye cannot serve God and mammon, equal to—ye cannot go east and west at the same time. Have you ever tried to do that, have you ever made such a fool of yourself as to endeavor to cross the Atlantic by staying on shore? The meaning is, if a man's supreme purpose in life is to seek God and to glorify him, whatever his business upon earth may be, he elevates that business up to the level of his supreme purpose.

Where, then, is the value of your criticism upon the rich Christian man? You have said, mockingly, "That man has served God and mammon to some purpose, for he has accumulated immense wealth." Your

176

reasoning I would call childish but for my fear of degrading the sweet name of child. Where a man's heart burns with the love of God, if he be the owner of the Bank of England, he lifts up all his property to the high level of the purpose which inspires him.

I now see a new and gracious light upon the Savior's words. I have cudgeled myself mercilessly in many a piece of self-discipline, by imagining with the foolish that I could be serving God with one hand and serving mammon with the other. I thought the Savior was teaching that narrow lesson. Today he says to me, "I lay it down as a law that the supreme purpose of a man's life gives character to all he does."

Now let us look at the subject from the other end, and thus get double light upon it. Ye cannot serve mammon and God. The meaning is— if your one object in life is to accumulate property, power, renown, anything that is earthly, ye cannot serve God, though you may sing hymns all the day long, though you may attend church whenever the gates are open, though you may give your body to be burned and your goods to feed the poor.

All these are but so many mammon arrangements, without religious value. The supreme purpose of your life is to be satisfied with the things at hand, within the circumference of this world, and therefore you cannot be religious, you cannot serve God. God can only be served by the supreme purpose, the dominating and all-inspiring impulse that moves the heart and controls the behavior.

Poor soul, you thought when you asked for an increase of income that the people would suspect you of being something of a mammon-worshiper. Never mind: they were cruel and foolish, and they did not know Christ's wonderful gospel. You were no money-lover, no money-grubber, you only wanted to work your way honestly in the world, and to eat the bread earned by the honest labor. And you, when you told that huge lie, so black that there is no paint in the darkness grim and gloomy enough to give it right character, when you said that if you had a thousand pounds more you would feed the poor and support the Church and did not mean a bit of it, it was a lie you told—you were serving mammon. As the poet says of you, anticipating your coming into the world, "You stole the livery of the court of heaven to serve the devil in."

The passage no longer frightens me, I understand its glorious meaning now. It is impossible to go east and west at the same time: the whole law of gravitation says "No," in an instant. It cannot be done. And so if I want to be heavenly and worldly at the same time it is impossible; if I am heavenly I sanctify the world, if I am worldly I debase the heaven. You are therefore one of two things, and there is no mixture in your character. Judge what I say.

Now we come again to the long and yet pithy lecture on earthliness, and its degrading and fruitless anxieties. I have gone at length into that subject, yet I have something more to add. You tell me, when the Savior warns you against worry—understanding by that word, as explained in the last lecture, cankering anxiety, killing fretfulness—that man is an anxious being; you say that no allowance is made for that great constitutional fact that man must forecast and provide and previse and meddle with things contingent and uncertain. You say the gospel arbitrarily forbids that which is instinctive. Let me once more correct your mistake. Jesus Christ does provide for this very instinct of anxiety; in effect he says, "You say you must be anxious: very good, by all means be anxious; be true to your nature, obey the law of your constitution—only this is what I have to say to you, be sure you direct your anxiety along the right lines, do not waste your anxiety, do not make your anxiety a leak in your nature through which all that is sweetest and best may ooze." Anxious? Certainly, be anxious, but fix your anxiety upon the right object. Thus: here is a friend who is planning to take a railway journey. We will, in imagination, accompany him up to the point of starting. He has everything with him that he thinks he requires. He drives to the station, he rushes to the newsstand, he is most anxious to get the last and best news. He buys papers representing every section of religious and political thought, he fills up his compartment with that varied literature. He has been most anxious about it, most fussy, almost turbulent; he has pushed other people aside in order that he might get his favorite paper and the principal antagonist to the doctrines which he believes in. And now there he is, with his compartment almost snowed up with the literature of the morning. The train will start in a minute. "Tickets, please." He has not got his ticket. Then he cannot go—too late; the law says that if you have not got your ticket there is no time to get it, and you must wait for the next train. Has the man been anxious? Most anxious—about nothing, about the wrong thing. Of course I say to him, "Be anxious, be vigilant, be on the alert, do not close your eyes and fall into a slumber; be anxious, but be anxious about the right thing, sir." What does it matter that he has stuffed his carriage with the literature of the morning and has forgotten the one thing without which he cannot go? How would you accost him, if he explained his case to you on the platform? You might audibly accost him in the language of sympathy—I fancy you would mentally accost him in a more appropriate tone.

That is precisely what many of us are doing, and Jesus Christ says: "Be anxious, most certainly, but do not waste your anxiety; fix it on the right objects, direct it to the proper quarter and the right end; seek, seek, seek"—and that word seek, as he spoke it, has in it agony, paroxysm, passion, importunity—"seek." O, how you did misunderstand him when you thought he forbade anxiety, and had omitted a constituent element of your nature, and had made no provision for the outgoing and expression of an almost necessary anxiety. He hits the case very graphically, with a sharpness the dullest eye must see; for he says, "Which of you by taking thought, by doing all this kind of thing, of the nature of fretfulness and peevishness, which of you by indulging in that expensive luxury, can add one cubit to his stature?" What does it all come to in practical effect? What is the meaning of Christ's doctrine. Which of you by fretting about tomorrow, by planning for it and scheming about it, and worrying out your very souls concerning its various fortunes and destinies, can make one hair white or black? There are rocks which your anxiety cannot melt into water; there are great rolling seas which it is not in the power of your anxiety to divide. Spend your solicitude upon the right objects; be careful about the supreme purpose of your existence: in that direction there cannot be too much solicitude. Give your eyes no rest nor close your eyelids in slumber until you have acquainted yourselves with God and become at peace with him. And remember that anxiety, improperly used, wastes your nature, dissipates your energy, incapacitates you for the discharge of the noblest duties of life.

Let us put the thing again before us illustratively. Here is a man whose son is very delicate. He has not known what it was to enjoy a day's real health since he was born. He appears to be declining day by day in strength. The father comes to us, and we ask questions concerning the child; and in reply to our inquiries the father says, "I am always most anxious that he should dress well, that his gloves should fit him like his skin, that his boots should be of the best possible quality, and that he should never go out without being so dressed as to attract the admiring attention of those who may pass him on the road." What would you think of a man who could talk so under such circumstances? Do not be hard upon him, because your admission I will take and apply to you as a whip. Do you acquit him? Remember that the judge is condemned when the guilty are acquitted.

This is the very thing we are doing, and Jesus Christ comes to us and says, "Is not the body more than raiment?" So you have said to the man described thus imaginatively, "Sir, what about your boy's health? Is he getting stronger? Is he more robust? What can be done to establish his health? And as for his dress and his gloves and his attire altogether—all these things may be left to settle themselves. Seek first the establishment of the child's health."

Well, then, this Christian doctrine is not so impracticable and other-worldly. This Christian doctrine is not a metaphysical quibble in the clouds; there is downright common sense—strong, robust, graphic common sense about this Christian preaching. I should not wonder if this carpenter's Son seated upon the mountain talking to his disciples should turn out, in the long run, to be the world's greatest preacher. Let us not, however, anticipate, but attend him, and listen with the understanding to the gracious words which proceed out of his mouth.

It is not enough to speak against anxiety or to direct it into proper quarters. Jesus Christ, recognizing this fact, proceeds to mitigate the anxiety which eats up the life like a canker. What do you think he does in the way of mitigation? Something most beautiful. He takes us all out for a day into the open fields. It is only recently that some doctors have apparently learned from the great Physician to get their patients out of town as soon as they could. I speak now to many doctors: stand by that rule, get your patients away out of their old associations, out of their old chambers, where they know every pattern upon the paper, and get them away to the sea, and into the country, and up the mountains and by the riverside as soon as you possibly can, and take your own course as to whether you throw physic to the dogs. This was Jesus Christ's plan: he said, "Take a walk, change your circumstances, get rid of these narrow brick walls, get into the wide fields, read the flowers, listen to the music of the birds." Was this a novel suggestion on the part of Jesus Christ? Not at all. Did he borrow from any man? No, other men borrowed from him, only he was not always the revealed and incarnate Teacher; he was the invisible and incomprehensible Inspirer of all who went before him in the kingdom of truth and light. Where do we find this recipe before? A thousand years prior to the incarnation of the peasant Teacher, and a thousand years more than that. Once Zion was ill; she was bowed down to the dust; there was no more hope in her fainting heart, and Jacob was slain with an intolerable thirst. What was the recipe of the divine Physician? Nature. How did it run in English? Thus: "Lift up your eyes and behold who hath created all this." First he points to the stars, then to the lilies, then to the birds— to all nature! Its infinite light, its minute flushes and blushings of color, and its little trills of song from tiny and tremulous throats. Are you in great trouble and care and anxiety? Go away as soon as you can. First of all get a right theological conception of your circumstances, and understand that anxiety is wasted energy, if it be directed to such things as lie beyond your control. And then, having taken a right theological view of the case, go away, go into the fields—there is healing in nature; she is a kind and noble mother, always ready to nurse and carry us in her generous heart. The soft wind cools our fever, the infinite light charms our despair, the great space offers us new liberties; the all-filling music, subtle as an odor wafted from distant paradises, stirs the heart to better hope. You have no money to go far away, do you say? Then go as far as you can walk. You cannot tell how medicating this is. Kind Nature, Loving Mother, she spreads her bounties with infinite hospitality, and by every open way to our nature she sends her healing ministries.

You now tell me that while you have no doubt about the doctrine, you are confronted by certain facts which astound and distress you, facts, for example, of this kind, that good men of your own acquaintance are often in great trouble, that praying men who really and truly love God and wait upon him are sometimes in great straits, and you are puzzled to harmonize the doctrine and the fact. There I think you occupy solid ground, and deserve a respectful answer. My reply is threefold. Trials are useful, trials often develop the best faculties of our nature, qualities that stir us sometimes into our healthiest energy. I would never have known how rich and good some friends were but for the afflictions that fall upon them. I have often seen what I thought were pampered children, spoiled boys and girls; I have sometimes ventured to reason with the parents as to their method of bringing up their children; I have ventured perhaps to say, "Now, what can become of them in the event of any misfortune falling upon you?" I have seen that misfortune come, and I have seen the children of such parents turned out to make their bread, and they have done it with such noble temper, such a high quality of heroism, as to affect me deeply with a consciousness of my entire ignorance of what lay hidden in their character. Those children themselves have come to bless the misfortune that battered in the roof of the old house they called their home, those children have, in some cases, traced the beginning of their best and healthiest developments to afflictions which, for the time being, distressed them with intolerable agony. I call you to witness whether you would have been the man you are today in wisdom, in range of experience, in mellowness, if your one ewe lamb had not been taken from you, if your fig-tree had not been barked, if your little heritage had not been shaken by the rude winds. You are the sweeter for every loss you have sustained. You are the kinder and nobler for every affliction you have rightly received, your weakness has, in effect, become your strength.

Then I would remember in the second place that prosperity has its pains and trials. Do not imagine that prosperity of a worldly kind is another word for heaven. You think what you would have done if your circumstances of an outward kind had been very different. You are mistaken. Let us go into this rich man's fine house and sit in the sumptuously garnished room until he comes in. What a room it is; I see the artist's hand everywhere. What a beautiful outlook, what noble grounds, what ancient trees, what singing birds! The man who lives here cannot be unhappy; surely this is the very vicinity of some better land. So you soliloquize, and when you get into confidential conversation with the occupant of that noble mansion you may find that there is a thorn under every rose, a worm at every root, bitterness in every cup, and that the house is but a garnished sepulcher. It may be so, it may not be so — still the solemn fact remains that prosperity itself is a continual temptation, a subtle and persistent trial of every virtue of the heart.

To this double reply I add another answer, namely, that God knows exactly with how much we can be trusted. If he knows what temptations we can bear, understanding that word in its strictest sense as including only diabolic assaults on the heart, he knows also what prosperity we can bear. He gives me exactly what I can deal with; he that gathers much has nothing over, he that gathers little has no want. A contented spirit is a continual feast; when the heart has rest in God there is always enough bread on the table. We think we can deal with more, but God knows what we can deal with, and he will see that we shall have it. Your heavenly Father knows what you have need of, and his knowledge is the measure of his service. I rest in that doctrine, and no fool can throw a troubling stone into the peaceful lake of my most profound confidence.

twenty-four

MUTUAL CRITICISMS

Matthew 7:1–6

"JUDGE NOT, that ye be not judged." Do not criticize with a censorious and unkindly spirit, do not be bitter, do not be moved by the spirit of animosity and illiberality and uncharitableness. We must judge, in the sense of forming opinions and estimates of one another—that is not the kind of judgment which is forbidden in this exhortation by Jesus Christ. We may get the true meaning of the word by another use which is made of it elsewhere in the Scriptures. Thus, in John, third chapter and seventeenth verse we read: "For God sent not his Son into the world to condemn the world"; the same word is translated *judged* in our text that is translated *condemn* in this verse. And in the twelfth chapter of John: "I came not to *judge* the world" [John 12:47], to take a bitter and unkind and hostile view of it. And again we read: "Of the hope of the resurrection of the dead am I"—the same word—"*called in question*" [Acts 23:6]. And once more we read: "One man *esteemeth*"—the same word—"one day above another: another man *esteemeth*"—the same word—"every day alike" [Rom. 14:5]. When we are called upon to judge, we are warned against that self-righteousness which condemns everybody who does not do exactly as we think they ought to do. The spirit that is condemned here is one of infallibility. Find a man who makes himself the standard of everybody's conduct, who judges everybody by himself, by what he would have done under such and such circumstances, and who gives large license to his tongue in forming and giving opinions upon such persons, and you find the very man referred to in this exhortation. Insofar as you are self-contented, self-pleased, self-righteous, insofar as you think it to be your duty to sit down upon the throne of judgment and to judge all your neigh-

184

bors and the whole human race, insofar are you guilty of the spirit of judgment which Jesus Christ condemns in this text.

Jesus Christ tells you that such judgment does not fall to the ground: you are doing more than merely uttering words when you pass such judgment upon your fellow-creatures. You are not whiling away an hour, you are sowing seed which you will one day have to reap in the form of fruit, for, "with what judgment ye judge, ye shall be judged: and with what measure ye mete, it shall be measured to you again." Do not suppose that you are merely passing an opinion upon your fellow-men, do not fall back upon your supposed innocence, and say that you merely observed or remarked so and so. You shall give an account for every idle word; you shall be made to feel the bitterness of your own speech, the cruelty of your own judgment shall come back upon you like a devouring flame. Jesus Christ undertakes to warn men as to the consequence and issue of certain conditions of spirit, so that no man goes forward in these matters in ignorance of what the result will be.

Let us understand what he meant by this. Did he mean, literally, "with what judgment ye judge, ye shall be judged"?—that is to say, that some other man would pass exactly the same opinion upon us that we passed upon others. Not at all in that little narrow sense of the word. That was not the punishment according to the law which he laid down: therein he would have but repeated the old law of a tooth for a tooth and an eye for an eye, whereas he came to lay down a broader judgment. What, then, did the words mean? Not that we should have snarl for snarl, hostile criticism for hostile criticism, one for one and two for two, according to the number and measure thereof. He meant that somehow or other all society, the aggregated man, the all-but-God, would encounter us in our own spirit; people who never heard of us would somehow rise up to condemn us and reward us according to our own spirit. By some mysterious action of divine providence, society would condemn us with the condemnation we had accorded to others.

You have often been puzzled to know how it was that such and such consequences arose from such and such acts. You have wondered at the unkindness of men, at the bitterness of their judgment. Has it ever occurred to you that the reason may, possibly, have been in yourself— a reason that has been sleeping twenty full years, and is now only bearing fruit? You remember your unkindness to your father and your mother; how you sat on the throne of criticism at the fireside and condemned the whole household in a spirit of self-righteous pride? You remember what an intolerable nuisance you were in the Church twenty years ago, snarling at everyone, snubbing everybody, setting up your great righteousness as a rebuke of their feeble morality—how the unkind word was always upon your tongue, and how men might feel perfectly sure that you would go along any censorious line along which they might lead. All that is now coming back to you. You have been smitten first on the one cheek, then on the other. You have been smitten on the head; society scorns you, repudiates you, views you with judgmental suspicion, unkindness and distrust. You sowed the wind, you are reaping the whirlwind; you have eaten forbidden fruit, and you are now undergoing its most painful consequences.

Find a kind man, one of noble and liberal spirit, whose thought is always of the charitable type, who cannot be gotten to say a harsh or unfeeling word about anybody—the time will come when society will throw its arms around him and take care of him and nourish and defend him. He shall reap the bountiful harvest of his own beneficence. Such a man will not be allowed to be friendless in the time of his old age: he took no pains to defend or befriend himself, he had a kind word for everybody, he had a crust of bread for the poor and a cup of cold water for the thirsty—he could always be looked to for the glowing and kind word, nothing mean, bitter, selfish, hostile, unamiable, ever fell from his ruddy lips—and now in the time of his old age and decrepitude, or when any evil report maliciously arises against him, society will close around him and protect the grand old tree from the knife and the ax and the sword of those who would cleave it down.

And what is true of the kind man is true also of the bitter man. There are some persons who cannot speak sweetly. I do not altogether blame them, for their life seems to be one of the mysteries of Providence, inscrutable, wholly beyond our explanation, here and now: we can only say it were better for such that they had not been born—but they cannot speak the noble word, they cannot give you a grand beneficent judgment of any human creature or any human deed, their criticism is bitter, highly acidic—something even worse, highly vitriolic, most pungent, and every word has in it an intent of cruel death. What will be the judgment society will pass upon such persons by-and-bye? They will get what they have given, they will reap as they have sown—let that word never be forgotten. "God is not mocked: whatsoever a man soweth, that shall he also reap" [Gal. 6:7]. Not in some little literal way of a man dealing with him as he dealt with others, but with that marvelous social influence which gets around a man to help him up or to smite and blast him. Thank God for these great promises and laws that make society secure! They give solidity to the whole constitution of humanity. We cannot play at criticism and be harmless, we cannot be censorious and then retire upon our respectability. Every bitter word you have spoken about man, woman, or child has gone out to come back again, and will smite you someday. With what judgment you judge you shall be judged, and with what measure ye distribute, it shall be measured to you again. This is a great law, and all human history is its exposition and justification.

Jesus Christ now proceeds to give a vivid application of these words, and to accent them as with the point of a sword. "And why beholdest thou the mote that is in thy brother's eye, but considerest not the beam that is in thine own eye?" Are we sure that we have laid hold of the right exposition of these words in our other lessons received upon them from various teachers? What is the beam in the eye of the judge? Does it mean that though I condemn some little fault in you I have a greater fault of my own which has not yet been discovered? I do not interpret it in that light. Here is a man about whom no fault can ever be found of the usual kind, and yet he is continually judging other men, sentencing some to darkness and others to oblivion, and passing various sentences upon those who are around him, and yet he is sober, chaste, good in all we can say about him, punctual in his church attendance, exact in his payments, of good standing in the marketplace—what beam is there in the eye of such a man? Now we come to the right meaning. He is censorious: that is the beam referred to by the great Teacher. The very fact that he judges another man in an uncharitable spirit is the beam, compared with which any other fault is a mere mote or speck, a mere splinter of wood compared to a great beam of timber.

That is how Jesus Christ estimates the censorious spirit. He says it is to other faults as a beam is to a little splinter. The man is a model man in everything else so far as society knows him, exact, punctual, critical in all his relations, a more honorable man is not to be found in the marketplace, all his payments are promptly and completely made, and there is nothing at all about him except this miserable spirit of criticism upon other people, always finding fault with somebody else. Now Jesus Christ says that although he be faultless in all the ordinary senses of that term, the very spirit of censoriousness that is in him is a great beam across his eyes. Let us, then, take great care lest the very thing that we had imagined to be no fault at all is the supreme fault.

Let us illustrate this: here is a man who will slander his neighbor by the hour, and calls himself a Christian, never doubts his own Christianity; he sends unorthodox thinkers to hell by the thousand, he whips the Unitarians into the very hottest perdition—all that he himself does is to slander his neighbor, and then engage in prayer. It never occurs to him that slander is a deadlier sin than mere intellectual error. Jesus calls the slanderous spirit a beam compared with which any other mistake is a little thin splinter. Here is a man who condemns every poor creature that is overtaken in a fault. He has no sympathy with such. A man has a little too much to drink, loses his equilibrium, is seen in a reeling state—that circumstance is reported to the man who only indulges in slanderous criticism, and the man instantly calls for the excommunication of the erring brother from the Church, not knowing that he himself is drunk, not with wine, but drunk with a hostile spirit, drunk with uncharitableness, drunk with the feeling that rejoices in the slips and falls of others. O you hypocrite, actor, masked and visored man! Pluck the beam from your own eye—then shall you see more clearly the mote, the splinter, that is in your brother's eye.

I would preach to myself as loudly and keenly as to any other man, herein, if so be I have been guilty of this ineffable meanness, and this most detestable of all tricks of the devil, to speak an unkind word about any human creature, or suspect the honesty of any man. If ever I have said about a brother minister, "He is a fine man in many respects, a noble creature, grand, chivalrous kind of soul—*but*—" if ever I have said that *but*, God will punish me for it. I shall suffer loss therein. If my brother has fallen, and I have said, so low down in my consciousness that I could hardly hear it myself, "I am rather glad of it," God will chastise me for that! "It is a fearful thing to fall into the hands of the living God" [Heb. 10:39]. Have I ever said one unkind or thoughtless word about any human creature? It has been as a beam in my eye, while your faults, even if you have been intemperate, are virtues, compared with my huge overshadowing sin.

We do not lay hold of this great truth sufficiently. We think that a little slander is of no consequence. To be called up before the church and condemned for *slander*? Condemn the drunkard, turn out the man who by infinite pressure has committed some sin—turn *him* out—certainly, and never go after him and never care what becomes of him, let a wolf gnaw him at the core—only get rid of him—if we go home and speak unkindly of man, woman, or child, who is the great sinner, the drunkard we have just expelled, or the closely-shaven, highly-polished Christian who does nothing but filch his neighbor's good name? "It shall be more tolerable for Tyre and Sidon in the day of judgment than for you" [Matt. 11:22; Luke 10:14]. You do not know the meaning of Christ's gospel, you are not in the kingdom at all; you have learned a few words which you chatter with parrot-like accuracy, but the gospel, the all-redeeming, all-hoping, all-saving gospel, you know nothing about.

So then do not imagine that this is the case of a great drunkard speaking against some person with a much smaller fault. It is the case of censoriousness against any other fault, the slander-spirit against the whole catalogue of devilisms. Wherein then shall we wash our hearts and cleanse our souls? Perhaps I may have spoken against some men—if I have, I shall yet feel the rod of the divine vengeance upon my life. "Thou art inexcusable, O man, whosoever thou art that judgest: for wherein thou judgest another, thou condemnest thyself; for thou that judgest doest the same things" [Rom. 2:1]. That is the meaning of the Savior's teaching. Wherein you judge you condemn yourself. To judge is to condemn. Cleanse the Church of this spirit of bitterness and its orthodoxy will take care of itself. O I cry before Christ sometimes, when I see him very clearly— I just fall right down at his feet and cry, and tell him that the people are most anxious about their intellectual views, and would curse any number of people who did not subscribe their catechism, and take a keen delight in damning and ramming them down in the deepest and hottest hell—but, O Thou wounded One—when they get together they have not a kind, noble, hopeful word to speak of any creature that differs from them! "Then," said he, "they have a beam in their eye, compared with which, the faults of others may be but splinters." "Why dost thou judge thy brother, why dost thou set at naught thy brother, for we shall all stand before the judgment seat of Christ?" [Rom. 14:10].

Now let us come to verse 6. "Give not that which is holy unto the dogs, neither cast your pearls before swine, lest they trample them under their feet, and turn again and rend you." Now here is the spirit of judgment: how am I to know which is the dog, how am I to know how to classify those who are no better than swine—is not this the very spirit that has been condemned? No, we are not now talking about men who belong to the same universe. We have been speaking, or hearing Christ speak, rather, about brother's treatment of brother; we are now hearing him speak about the treatment of those who neither understand nor appreciate our heart's best life. The word *brother* now drops out of the criticism and other words are imported into the consideration of the case. Jesus Christ when he went before Herod would not give that which was holy unto the dogs, neither would he cast his pearls before swine. You must speak your deepest thoughts to the ear of sympathy, you must find out who has the spirit of communion with your spirit, when you come to utter the most profound feelings and highest aspirations of your heart. Speak not in the ears of a fool; for he will despise the wisdom of your words. Reprove not a scorner or else he will hate you, rebuke a wise man and he will love you.

You know what it is to be in urgent need of sympathy. You have a great grief, and you say, "To whom can I tell this?" If I tell it to one, I get it all back again, as if I had spoken to a rock; if I tell it to another kind of heart, why the very telling of it seems to be a kind of evaporation by which my oppressed spirit is relieved. Do not speak the deepest secrets of your soul to those who have never been in the same mental or spiritual condition: they will think you erratic, romantic, eccentric — they will pity you: when they go away from hearing your tale they will intimate that your mind is a little unsettled, and that they have their fears about you. They do not understand the graphic language of your tragic experience, they have never been in the same darkness, never fought the same battle, never drunk of the same bitter cup; therefore, when you come near them, speak not: silence is better than speech in such society — "give not that which is holy unto the dogs, neither cast ye your pearls before swine, lest they trample them under their feet, and turn again and rend you," and you hear that your most sacred feelings have been travestied and your most solemn words have been mocked.

We have all had experience of this kind, it may be, in some degree: we have told what we thought was a friendly heart some bitter thing that was troubling us very much, and it has turned again and rent us. Do you have a friend? Treat him as such, invite him to your heart with hooks of steel, tell him everything: he will divide your burdens, he will double thy joys. Beware of the unsympathetic ear, beware of the unsympathetic heart: you will get nothing from those but trampling and rending.

Now some may say, having heard this preaching of Jesus Christ, "Where is the gospel? There is not a word of gospel in all the sermon which Jesus Christ has preached to us this morning. There is nothing evangelic, there is nothing doctrinally savory, there is no old wine of blood. Seneca might have said this, it might have been written in old Latin." You think so? You try to carry out the injunction of the text, and before you have gone two steps in the direction of its accomplishment you will want Christ and the cross, and the blood and the Holy Spirit, for this is the last and chiefest of the divine directions.

This teaching, some may say, is purely negative; it is telling us what not to do. You try to realize the doctrine and you will see how far it is merely negative. If you sit within the narrowness of the letter you may call it a negative kind of teaching, but if you try to carry it out in your life, if you never more have to slander a man, think or speak unkindly about any human creature you will soon know whether the doctrine is negative or positive. It is courageous, for the Scribes and the Pharisees were the princes of slander, and of malicious hostile criticism; it is spiritual, for it searches the heart, and lays down a principle which cannot be carried out by mere mechanism. This is not a trick in handicraft, this is an outgoing and blossom of the renewed heart; it is practical, there is nothing sentimental in this, this is the eloquence of action.

If you, from this time forth, could show the spirit of charity you would strike the mocker dumb. He has his best hold upon us when he hears us criticizing one another. He says, "See how these Christians love one another." When he hears ministers undervaluing one another, running down each other's preaching and methods of work, he says, "See how these Christians love one another." When he hears various communions of Christians insulting one another, proving one another wrong, and excommunicating one another, he says, "See how these Christians love one another." When he comes to the cemetery and sees a chapel on one side on consecrated ground and a chapel on the other on unconsecrated ground, he laughs a laugh, he has a right to laugh, and says, "See how these Christians love one another."

My friends, it has too long been the case of orthodoxy *versus* unorthodoxy, Trinitarian *versus* Unitarian, and A against B. "Thou hypocrite," says the great Teacher, "thou hypocrite, first cast out the beam of hostile judgment and uncharitable criticism out of thine own eye; then shalt thou see more clearly to cast out the little splinter that is in thy brother's eye."

twenty-five

CHRISTIAN CRITICISM

Matthew 7:7-12

SO, THEN, the commerce between earth and heaven is perfectly honest and straightforward. There is nothing of moral jugglery about it. The wayfaring man, though a fool, may read these plain words and understand them. Do not attempt to steal anything from heaven; ask for it. Do not try any illegitimate methods of getting, finding, or anything else. The plan is simple, honest, perfectly intelligible and available to every sincere and simple-minded heart. Did you suppose that any man got something from heaven by a sleight of hand technique? Has it ever entered into your heart that some man was richer in spiritual graces than you are because he deluded God? Such is an infinite mistake on your part: the human side of this transaction is beautiful in its simplicity—ask, seek, knock. You thought religion was an affair of mystery—deep and dark clouding, and full of impenetrable haze. It is the commerce between a child and his father. There is no mystery whatever about it, it is honest commerce. The bread we get from heaven we get honestly: you are not ill-used if you have not got that bread: you have not, because you ask not, or because you ask amiss.

It is something to know that the human side of this transaction is perfectly intelligible and simple, and it is something to know that the human side of this transaction is that which applies to all our progress in life, whatever it be, insofar as it is honest, substantial, and really good and durable. There is no particular masonic word to get hold of, nor is there any Eleusinian grip of the hand to learn. This is not a trick in the black art; it is asking, receiving—seeking, finding—knocking and having the door opened in reply to the appeal. All religion will be found at last, insofar as it is true, to be equally simple, equally to illustrate the law of cause and effect. The mystery that we find in the Christian religion we too often bring to it: it is but a gilding of the cloud of our own ignorance. The way of the Lord is equal, and his path among men is often such as can be apprehended by sanctified intelligence.

"Ask, and it shall be given you; seek, and ye shall find; knock, and it shall be opened unto you. For everyone that asketh receiveth, and he that seeketh findeth, and to him that knocketh it shall be opened." If you want your income increased, ask for it; if you want your health reestablished, seek the Physician—God, the one Healer, in whose heart grow all plants with healing juice flowing in their salubrious veins. If you want to advance in life knock at the door, and while you are knocking it shall be thrown open to you. There is no condition specified, there is no particular class of persons identified as the favored sect or denomination—for everyone that asks receives. There is no condition of title, character, claim: words cannot be more simple and more inclusive. If you want increase, health, joy, satisfaction, advancement, riches, honor—ask, and ye shall receive, for everyone that asks receives. Why sit we here, therefore, poor dwarfs, empty of pocket, feeble of hand, blind of intellect, failing in health, crushed before the moth and the worm, and courting with cowardly spirit our own grave, that we may be hidden from the light of the day? Nothing lies between me and what I want but honest supplication. "Be careful for nothing, but in everything by prayer and supplication make your requests known unto God" [Phil. 4:6]. Never mind how bad you are—you need simply to ask what you like and you shall have it.

There is not one word of truth in that statement, and yet who would wonder if some persons who read the Bible in fragments and morsels should openly and emphatically declare that to be the divine revelation? Learn to trust not only in the text but in the context. What I have now laid down to you would seem to be the very first meaning of the words I have read. That meaning seems to be written upon the very face of the text, and yet every sentence I have uttered in the latter part of the exposition is utterly false. How can that be proved to be so? By Christ's own words. But is there any condition signified in the text? Most undoubtedly there is a vital condition, not only signified but explicitly laid down in so many words. You must not break in on the Savior while he is preaching and teaching: you must hear his whole statement and compare part with part, and by comparing one part with another you must establish the truth which he came to reveal and enforce. Let us, therefore, look at the illustration which he himself gives of the doctrine which he has laid down.

"Or what man is there of you, whom if his son ask bread will he give him a stone, or if he ask a fish will he give him a serpent? Then there is a certain class specified in the text? Undoubtedly. What is that class? "What man is there of you whom if *his son* ask bread." It is not an alien, a stranger, a rebel, it is a child's heart praying a child's prayer. What further condition is there specified in the text? The next condition laid down in the text is that what we ask for is good. Read again. "What man is there of you whom if his son ask *bread*, or *fish*, or *egg*." Why, these are necessary to life. You talked just now about asking for a double income, and a larger house, and fifty more fields added to your small estate. No, no— the doctrine relates to bread, fish, egg—food—necessaries of life, and it is the son that prays. So, then, the foolish man who first ran away with the idea that we only had to go and ask and have, is altogether disqualified for the exposition of this portion of Scripture. He talks a foreign tongue, he utters the fool's swift language that has no faith or sense in it. The strong limitation, the definition of boundary that is not to be trespassed is—Son, as the suppliant; Bread, Fish, Egg as the subjects of petition. Bodily nutriment, intellectual nutriment, spiritual nutriment, the bread, the fish, the egg applied to all the necessities of our multifold hunger and thirst that evermore besiege and urge and distress our nature. Give not that which is holy unto the dogs. Dog, you cannot pray! This is a portion of meat for the king's children; it is a special household that sits down at this table, and eats and drinks abundantly of this divine hospitality.

"What man is there of you, whom if his son ask bread will he give him a stone, or if he ask a fish will he give him a serpent?" and elsewhere, "if he ask an egg will he give him a scorpion? What is the great deduction of the divine Teacher? "If ye then, being evil, short-sighted, mean-hearted, children of miscalculation, know how to give good gifts unto your children, how much more shall your Father which is in heaven give good things to them that ask him?" This is the true method of teaching, climbing up step by step from the human to the divine. Said I not unto you that you are gods [see Ps. 82:6]? Learn from the little divinity that is in yourself, the infinite divinity that is in God. When you are at your very best, in love, pity, sacrifice, care for others, multiply that condition of heart by infinity, and the result will be your Father which is in heaven. Let common-sense assist you in all these expositions, and you will have no difficulty in getting down to the root.

Look at the case of your own family today, and your child shall come and say to you, "Give me your most precious possession." What would be your reply to the little child? Would it be an instant imparting of the gift? Nothing of the kind. Your child shall come to you and say, "Let me go out all today and all tomorrow, and never you ask where I am or what I am doing. Now I have asked you, you give." What would you say to your seven-year-old little boy who came with that prayer? If you then, being evil, children of the night, and of the bewildering shadows, unable to see straight and clear, know how to say "No" under the inspiration of love, how much more shall your Father which is in heaven say "No" to your poor prayers, your mean and ignorant supplications, your asking for scorpions under the supposition that they are eggs? For the naturalist tells us that the scorpion coils itself up so as to look very like an egg; hard-hearted would be our Father in heaven, having heard our prayer when we have mistaken a coiled scorpion for an egg, if his answer would be the reply of death.

How do I stand then towards this Giver? Just as a child stands towards a wise father. Sometimes a father says to a child, when the child asks for more bread, "You have had enough, child." The father does not begrudge the bread, he delights in the child's healthy appetite for food, but having some regard to the child's capacity and health, he may, even in that direction, interpose the suggestion that the boundary has been reached. Is he therefore cruel? Is he therefore unkind? He may simply be wise and thoughtful, a prudent father whose love asserts itself even in the form of prohibition. Is he a wise father who lets his child do exactly what the child wants to do, who gives a hearty "Yes" to every appeal of the child, who has no will of his own, no love, no firmness? What can become of a child brought up under such loose government, if the word government in that connection be not wholly a misapplication of the word? The child will come to ruin. It is not love that suspends discipline, it is love that adjusts it, measures it, lifts it into a sacrament, making it holy, often straining the sensibilities of him who enforces or inflicts it, but under the sweet and bright hope that its infliction will terminate in health and blessing. We have had fathers of our flesh who corrected us, and we gave them reverence; shall we not much more be subject unto the Father of spirits and live?

So we find the element of character and discipline and prohibitive wisdom even in this domain of supplication and desire. Be sure you ask for good things and your answer shall be plentiful, and thank God that he says "No" to some prayers. I have gone, as no doubt you have, with prayers to God to be sent, or to be spared, or to be directed thus and so, and if the answer had been "Yes" we should not have been living men today. Let us, therefore, learn to put our prayers into the court of heaven, and having delivered them word by word, it may be sometimes with strong crying and tears, as if our life depended upon an instant reply, let us learn to say, "Nevertheless, not my will, but thine be done."

Read again. "Ask, seek, knock." That might be the development of one action; these may not be three distinct services on our part, but this line may mark the growing intensity of our religious application. Ask—the easiest and simplest of exercises: seek—implying more industry and anxiety: knock—suggestive of vehement desire and perhaps impatience of spirit and eagerness of will and resoluteness. Our prayer has passed through all these transitions. Hear the good man's wise, rich prayer, how he asks in quiet, deep, fluent speech, how he passes on into seeking, stooping, lighting a candle and sweeping the house diligently, as if in search of that which is more precious than gold. See how he engages himself to one supreme effort, laying down torch and broom, and going with both hands to the door of heaven, and knocking as if God had hardly time to open the door, because the wolf was so near. It is one grand prayer, beginning with the ease of a child's communion, ending with the resoluteness and the violence of a man who feels that time is dying and opportunity closing swiftly.

Do you know all the manners of prayer? Is your prayer quite an easy exercise, or does it strain the soul and awaken the highest efforts? Look how much we have that we do not ask for, and that does not come as the result of our seeking, knocking, or any variety of our supplication and appeal to heaven. And yet they must have come in answer to some word that is equivalent to prayer. For example—all the light of day: the sun does not come out of his eastern chamber because some suppliant begged that he might return. And all the beauty of the spring, the luxuriance of the summer, the infinite largess of the autumn—these are not God's "Amens" to our small petitions, they are divine anticipations of human necessity, they are answers before the prayer is spoken—he *prevents* us with his goodness, and his goodness should lead us to repentance. And we learn from the infinitude of his gifts, laid upon our life without our asking, how to utter big prayers, vast petitions, petitions worthy of himself.

Have we not measured our prayers by ourselves, and only stretched our supplications over the lowly breadth of our own conception of life? When shall we learn to fill our mouths with great words and to utter prayers meant for heaven? "Ye have not, because ye ask not." God says, "Bring your vessels, and the oil shall flow." More vessels, more oil; more still, and still more oil. Who gives up? Man. He says, "I have no more vessels"—and God causes the oil to cease its flow. Never did God say, "There is no more *oil*"; it is always man that says, "There is no more *room*."

I have spoken of the gift of the light of the day, and of the beauty and richness of the succeeding seasons, but these are relatively ordinary gifts compared to God's greatest gift to us—Jesus Christ! "He that spared not his own Son, but delivered him up for us all, how shall he not with him also freely give us all things?" [Rom. 8:32]. Christ did not come in answer to prayer, the cross was not set up because some ardent heart desired its elevation; Jesus Christ is the Lamb slain from before the foundation of the world, God's answer to God's own prayer. So also is the gift of our life and all its responsibilities; we did not ask to live, we did not ask for one talent, or two, or five: I did not ask to be preacher or teacher, you did not ask to be merchantman or writer or thinker, or leader of human opinion—we are what we are in all these matters of capacity and appointment by the grace or wisdom of God.

So then there is a region in which prayer seems to be uncalled for, or to be utterly without opportunity and avail. The gifts of God in nature, in redemption, in life, in responsibility, these are determined by his own will and not by our prayers. Yet there are, in relation to our life, many cracks which are to be filled by our own supplications and prayers. A man comes to feel somewhat of the range of his own capacity, then he besieges the throne of grace for direction, sanctification, and for the upholding and comforting of holy grace that he may not waste his life pouring it out like a plentiful rain upon the unanswering sand. The man comes to find that he was born into the world with feeble constitution, with an irritable temperament, with physical defects or excesses that require the continual vigilance of his heart and the continual sanctification of God. Then he begins to pray, God having in all things left an opening for prayer. There be those who pray for fine days: I do not now—all days are fine. There be those who pray for health: I would like to live to be able to pray for health with this supplement to my prayer: Nevertheless, if sickness be better for me, the Lord make me sick everyday.

Now the Savior comes to his last word. Let me ask you to read it. "Therefore, all things whatsoever ye would that men should do to you, do ye even so to them, for this is the law and the prophets." Who has an eye acute enough in vision to see the connection between this *therefore* and the argument that has gone before? It startled me: I did not know that the argument stretched itself beyond the eleventh verse—"If ye then, being evil, know how to give good gifts to your children, how much more—" Said I, "The argument ends with that inquiry," and, behold, in the twelfth verse I was challenged with a great *therefore*, as if the syllogism did not complete itself until we came to this conclusion—"All things whatsoever ye would that men should do to you, do ye even so to them." What has that to do with the subject? "Evidently nothing," say you. "Evidently much," says Christ. This is no incoherence on the part of the divine Teacher. He does sometimes startle by taking what are called new departures, but in this *Ergo* he stands steadily by the argument he has been establishing. Let us read it with the intent of discovering his meaning.

"If ye then, being evil, know how to give good gifts to your children (the good gifts being indicated in the ninth and tenth verses), what man is there of you whom if his son ask bread will he give him a stone? None. Therefore, whatsoever ye would that men should do to you, giving you bread when you ask bread, and not a stone. Or if he ask a fish, will he give him a serpent? No. Therefore all things whatsoever ye would that men should do to you, in answer to your prayers, never giving a serpent for a fish, a stone for bread, a scorpion for an egg, do ye even so to them. How would you feel, if asking your father for an egg, he gave you a scorpion? Would he not disqualify himself for the paternal relation? Therefore go by your own judgment, follow out your own reasoning—if you would not receive a scorpion for an egg, as an act of love and of honor, never perpetrate that bitter and disastrous irony in your own dealings with mankind, for this is the law and the prophets—this is the blossoming into love and fructifying into noble charity and honor."

Does not this seem a small result for so great a prophecy? Did it require thousands of years to grow this tree and to mold and mellow, in complete sweetness, this fruit? What is the fruit? Love. All the law is fulfilled in one word—Love. "Thou shalt love thy neighbor as thyself" [Lev. 19:18; Matt. 19:19; and other verses]. For this the ages have travailed in birth, and this the child—Love. This is the law and the prophets.

Where are you? Still in the region of opinions—still discussing tiny metaphysics, still asking one another about your little narrow hazy theological views? I despise you, if you mean to rest there, chaffering and chattering about your denominational peculiarities and your meta-physical and theological distinctions, your orthodoxy and your un-orthodoxy, your "*isms*" and your "*ations.*" If you are there and still mean to stop there, I want to go on. What to? Love. Again and again remember that love is the fulfilling of the law. "He that loveth not knoweth not God, for God is love" [1 John 4:8]. "If a man say, I love God, and hateth his brother, he is a liar: for he that loveth not his brother whom he hath seen, how can he love God whom he hath not seen?" [1 John 4:20]. I am more anxious to cure the disease of your affections than to correct your purely intellectual mistakes. Believe what you may intellectually, if your spirit be not bathed in the very love of God you have not entered into the inner places of the holy kingdom. This blessed love is often the best guide of the intellect. It makes men modest, it prostrates them in the lowliness which is acceptable to God, and it expels from the heart every passion that would contest the supremacy of Christ. I do not call you to brilliance or grandeur of intellect, but I do most strenuously exhort you to follow in the upward direction that is ever taken by the spirit of heavenly love.

twenty-six

THE STRAIGHT GATE

Matthew 7:13, 14

THIS IS rather a mournful view, not only of human life, but of the kingdom of heaven itself; as if it would be thinly populated, and give us at last rather a representation of infinite failure on the one side than of real success and completeness on the other. That, however, would not be a correct exposition of the text. There is more light in it than seems to flash upon the eye at the first look. There is really nothing novel or unintelligible in the principle which is here laid down, namely, that, because straight is the gate and narrow is the way, few there be that find it. We know that to be a true principle in the common walks and ranges of life. It is the principle which applies at home, in the school, in the marketplace, everywhere in fact; the principle, that is, that according to the value of any kingdom is the straightness of the gate which opens upon it. If you will accustom the mind to that thought for a moment or two, you will not be struck by any novelty, certainly, by any harshness in the conditions which are attached to entrance into the kingdom of heaven.

Into what kingdom is it that you are anxious now to enter? Above all things you wish to enter into the kingdom of music. Very well. This is the New Testament doctrine concerning the kingdom of music. "Straight is the gate and narrow is the way which leadeth unto excellence in music, and few there be that find it." You have to study night and day, you have no time for yourself, you are at it, always at it, or getting ready for it, criticizing or being criticized, repeating, rehearsing, going over it again and again, still higher and higher. If that is the law of your little kingdom of music, why should it not be the law of the larger kingdom of life, which includes all beauty, and learning, and music, and power? Show me any musician that is ever really and completely satisfied with his own attainment; in that proportion will he be no musician at all—an amateur, easily satisfied with himself. When Handel composed his "Messiah," and sat a long way off to hear it, he came again and again to some of the players upon the wind instruments, and said, "Loudaire"; and again he came and said, "Loudaire," and away he went, and came again and said, "Loudaire," and at last they said, "Where is the wind to come from?" He wanted all the winds of heaven, and all the thunders that slumbered in the clouds, and all creation to take up his Amen and sing it, till the universe vibrated with its infinite life.

What is the kingdom that you are most anxious to enter into? "I am," you say, "most anxious to enter into the kingdom of painting pictures, the mystery of color, the language, subtle and infinite, that expresses itself through the medium of color." Is it easy? You shake your head in despondent reply, and say that you seem to get worse rather than better. At first you were rather pleased, and now you could tear up the canvas—it vexes you by the vulgarity you write upon it with your clumsy fingers. Straight is the gate and narrow is the way which leads unto art, and few there be that find it. My young friend, do not imagine that you can jump into eminence: if you can jump into it, you may easily jump out of it. Character must be a growth, long-continued and patiently cultivated. Somebody took me into his study the other day, and said, "I want you to look at this sketch."

Said I, "This lies a long way from your range of studies."

"Yes," was the reply—"my temptation is towards impatience; I get tired of things, and I at the last lump them and hurry them through, becoming utterly careless towards the close. I undertook this work to teach me patience, slowness, and completeness of toil. How long do you think I was over that?"

"I cannot tell how long."

"I spent two hours upon that, everyday, except Sundays, for two months."

A little thing about the size of the palm of your hand: he could have done it in half the time, but then he would have missed the direct purpose of his attempting to do it. He must straighten the gate and narrow the road, because he wants to go into a kingdom that is worth going into, and there is no kingdom worth having that you can snatch and pocket, and keep without equivalent toil or thought.

Do you want to enter into the kingdom of influence, do you want to be a man that shall be consulted in difficulties, to whom people shall come in hours of perplexed thought, to whom they shall state their cases, and for whose opinion they shall anxiously wait? Influence comes out of time, care, experience, and these things are not to be hurried. A man, well-known to most of us, is lying sick today, and a physician of renown was called in to see him not long ago; and the doctors, having heard the opinion of this eminent physician, declined, one and all, to give his own conception of the case. Why is it so amongst you that if a great physician gives his opinion, you will not give yours? "Yes—there is no opinion after his." The man grows to that—do not suppose that you can dream yourselves to that. Inspiration there is in it, no doubt, but a man has to work for it, and pay for it, and climb his way to it, one step of the ladder at a time. Straight is the gate and narrow is the way which leads unto supreme influence, and few there be that find it.

I have troubled you with these illustrations, just to show that really there is nothing novel, extraordinary, or harsh in the principle that, according to the value of any kingdom that you aim to reach, is the straightness of the gate and is the narrowness of the road leading unto it. It is my wish—bear me witness if you please—always to speak a word for the weak man. Have I ever put out a finger and laid it upon any soul as a burden that was trying to be better? Cheer me by telling, what is only the truth, that I may have erred in excess of charity, never in excess of severity. Comfort me with these words, tell me you have so understood me, and I shall preach to you with a broader and warmer love. I want to do so with peculiar tenderness just now.

Enter ye in at the straight gate—or, as we read elsewhere, strive to enter in at the straight gate, seek to enter in, labor to enter in, agonize to enter in. The fear is that some of you may imagine that striving is conquest, and you may visit upon a man who is merely, though with all his heart, striving to enter in, the judgment that you would accord to him after he had passed the gate, and had walked long miles up the heavenly steep. You have been cruel to some of your friends, you have taunted them with bitter mockery when they have been striving to enter in; you thought they had already professed to have entered, and you have mocked them with bitterness; you have asked them if that was their goodness, you have taken up little specks of their life, and said, "Aha, is this a sample of your piety?" It is only a sample of their agony, it was only a pattern of their striving. It was not to be picked up as a trophy of conquest, but to be referred to as an incident in the great agony of striving to enter in.

When the young Christian slips and falls, don't mock him; when a man is laboring, even in agonistic earnestness, to be better, and when in the midst of it all he gets tripped up, and somehow or other falls down as he were dead drunk at your feet, he may be a better man than you are: you never went wrong socially—you may be the worst man alive for anything I know to the contrary, you proud Pharisee, you whitewashed sepulcher, you trick undiscovered—be careful, or else you will be wounding good men who have the true seed in them, but who, peculiarly constituted, fall twenty times a day, and have the devil's iron teeth crushed, crushed— through them, all over. I do not defend their vices, I sympathize with their weakness; I have known the prayers of such men, and to no other prayers have I ever added so cordial an Amen—prayers that had blood in them, and music subtle and far-brought and far-sounding, prayers of the very inmost soul; and I did not judge them harshly, I saw they were striving to enter in, seeking to enter in, agonizing to enter in, and the measure of their earnestness was the measure of the diabolic assault upon them. If I speak to such hearts now, when possibly I may do so, let my word be one of the broadest cheer, a great sun-like word, brightening upon their lives with infinite hope. Still strive to enter in, and God will be pitiful to you.

But we read that some will seek to enter in and shall not be able. That we read in another Gospel [Luke] than the one we are now expounding. How singular it is then that some shall seek to enter in and shall not be able. Is not this a mockery of human effort? How many persons have been puzzled by that expression, and have gone to their pastors and teachers with it, as men would go with a great pain, and said, "Can you heal this mortal agony? I am discouraged because it says some will seek, yea, many will seek to enter in and shall not be able. I may be one of the many—God help me. Tell me if it is so: I feel this thought darkening upon me like a cloud of thunder." O distressed one, shall I call you Fool and slow of heart to believe all that the Speaker spake when he uttered these words that give you trouble [Luke 24:25]? The answer is in the very next verse—"When once the master of the house is risen up, and hath shut to the door, and ye begin to stand without, and to knock at the door, saying, 'Lord, Lord, open unto us'; and he shall answer and say unto you, 'I know you not whence ye are'" [Luke 13:27].

The seeking and the knocking referred to, take place when the day of mercy is no more. When the master of the house has risen up and gone to rest, when Christ is risen from the mediatorial seat and has delivered up the kingdom unto God and his Father, then the shout of agony shall die in space, and the cry of despair shall be the awful music of hell.

The words, therefore, do not apply to you at all. The master of the house has not risen and shut the door, the Son of God has not completed his priestly ministry, Jesus Christ is still able to save to the uttermost all that come unto God by him, God still waits to be gracious, the door is set wide open, and therefore, the verse which before was a burden to you and a great darkness may now be lifted off your shoulder and chased away, to the last shadow of it, from your life path, for it never referred to any man who earnestly sought the Lord while he might be found, and called upon him while he was near. What say you to seeking now, and striving? What if we make this day the most memorable day in our life by sending the heart out like a living bird to such a rest in God? Let your heart fly God-ward, poor soul; gather yourself up into one flaming prayer, and say, "God be merciful unto me a sinner," and your joy shall be too great for words, your rapture shall leave even music behind it, as the lark leaves under his wings the clouds of the smoking city. "Now is the accepted time, now is the day of salvation" [2 Cor. 6:2].

"Few there be that find it." Do not judge success by numbers. It is always pleasant to see great numbers gathering around the standard you set up, but always remember that quality is better than quantity, the audience may be fit though few. They are strong men who gather themselves around Christ, for they have nothing to rest upon but inspiration; no property, no ancestry, no fine clothing, no parchments, nothing but the grace of God. Jesus Christ never sought to make his kingdom popular in the sense of bringing into it one and everybody that casually applied for admission. A young man once came to him and said, "I would like to enter in at the gate"; and Jesus Christ said, "Why not? This gate is a straight one, and thou knowest the commandments." Said the young man, "All these have I kept from my youth up." A commandment that can be kept is by necessity a very narrow one; a commandment must always overflow its own letter, if it is really a revelation of the highest morality. The young man measured off the commandments, ten in number, and he said that he had kept them, letter by letter, every one, from his youth up. Jesus Christ, closing his eyes that he might see better, said,

"There is an eleventh commandment: sell all thou hast and give it unto the poor, and come and follow me"; and the young man went away sorrowful, for he had great possessions [see Luke 18:22]. He thought the gate was broad enough surely to admit him and all his wealth-burden; and Christ said, "You cannot all get through: there is room only for the soul, and not for these poor perishable holdings that are of no use on the other side of the gate." So Jesus did not add to his numbers rashly.

Another man said to him, "Lord, I will follow thee, but—" Christ said, "No, that word *but* must be dropped, there must be no qualifications; let the dead bury their dead, come thou and follow me" [see Matt. 8:22; Luke 9:60]. On another occasion he said, "If any man will follow me, let him take up his cross and come after me. Let a man deny himself and follow me; except a man deny himself he cannot be my disciple" [see Matt. 16:24; Mark 8:34; Luke 9:23; cf. Luke 14:23]. You do not wonder therefore that very few people attach themselves livingly and lovingly to a man whose conditions were so precise and severe. His conditions ought to make us all tremble. Have I denied myself? Where? Have I taken up my cross? What weight is it? Can men see it? Do I feel it? Why, Christianity has been my maker: by the grace of God I am what I am. Christianity, every one of us may say, has made me respectable; I owe all I have to Christianity: I have been a receiver—what have I given? I have held out both hands, what have I returned? Do I not encourage every whim, do I not cultivate every prejudice, do I not give scope to every antipathy, am I not harsh in judgment, uncharitable in feeling, pharisaical in self-sufficiency, scribe-like in my obedience to the mere letter of the law, while I neglect its infinite spirit? Such questions as these I could inflict upon myself until I destroyed every whit of comfort and solace that I now enjoy. There is no cross-bearing in being a Christian of the nominal sort: what cross-bearing there would be in being a Christian of the real sort, who can tell? If any man will live godly in Jesus Christ he shall suffer persecution [2 Tim. 3:12].

When I go into trade and arrange all my business, I say I have arranged this business on the principle that I must live. Then it is a false principle, for there is no need for you to live. Did that thought ever strike you? There is great need that every man should be honest, but not the slightest necessity in the word that any man, either in the pulpit or out of it, should live an hour. "In making my arrangements and dispositions of energy, and talent, and time, I have always had in full view the fact that

I must have subsistence." There is your error: that is the fallacy in your practical logic. What is your subsistence? Who wants that mechanism of bones you call yourself to stand upright for five minutes longer? What do you mean by subsistence? You must have infinite capacity of eating and drinking. Subsistence for how many years? On what scale? Do not even the publicans the same—is not that pagan talk—do not the heathen write such maxims upon their papers and hang them up in their business places as their only Bible? "Labor not for the meat which perisheth, but for that meat which endureth unto everlasting life" [John 6:27].

This is the high gospel of Christ. Who can live it? I cannot, I do not. How then can we classify ourselves? We are as those who are *striving* to enter in. Sometimes I have tried for a day or two, but with such ample reservation that it destroyed my action so far as I claimed it to be one of faith. Sometimes I have said, "Now I will try the sea." I have gone down to it, and waited till it was very quiet, and then have touched it with one timid foot, and called that trusting the sea—with a friend holding my hand and my other foot well on shore. I have gone down to touch with reluctance that little foaming wavelet that broke on the golden sand. That is not sea-faring, that is not sea-going—but that is my religion in Christ, too much. I speak of myself, lest I should offend any by unnecessary harshness—for if any man has gone a mile out into the water, thank God for him, and let him go a mile further still. Yet I feel as if going down to the water was moving in the right direction, and perhaps someday—who can tell?—I may boldly throw myself on the great wave and be caught by Christ's hand and led to the better land.

Do not let us give up our striving and our seeking, and our persevering—"in due season we shall reap if we faint not" [Gal. 6:9]. Try once more, go again—what do you see? Nothing. Go a third time—what do you see? Nothing. A fourth time, and a fifth, and a sixth—what do you see? A cloud about the size of a man's hand. Hurry! That cloud will spread faster than you can run, and presently there will be a splash of descending rain, and the earth shall rejoice in the baptism of the divine blessing.

This is the great lesson of striving, and seeking, and trying, and persevering. "Though faint, yet pursuing" [see Judg. 8:4]—be that thy motto, my poor soul. The discouragements are innumerable, but the promises are many and large. "He giveth more grace" [James 4:6]. Try again! Let me summon your utmost hopefulness into exercise, for when we fear we do down in the volume and quality of our being. Hope is power. Hope is inspiration. Hope is one of the guarantees of its own fulfillment. The great and loving One is watching you from his bright heaven, nor will he spare his angels, even should twelve legions be needed, to give you victory and rest. My soul, put your hope in God, and wait for him until his brightness drives the gloom away forever!

twenty-seven

THE FINAL TEST

Matthew 7:15–29

"BEWARE of false prophets, which come to you in sheep's clothing, but inwardly they are ravening wolves." Beware of the false in everything: encourage the instinct and spirit of truth—then you will have no need to be instructed as to particulars and details. Be as true as fire, a perpetual disinfectant, a test that can never be deceived. Have in you, ever dwelling in the temple of your heart, the spirit of truth, then you will know the false man the moment you look at him: the detection of falsehood will not be an act of skill or cleverness, but you will shudder when the false man is within a mile of you, as the wind in some parts of the sea has a sudden chill in it because of the far-off icebergs. Beware of the false in everything—false promises, false directions, false appearances. Then add the word *prophets*, for there is more in the word *false* than there is in the word *prophets*. A man is not a good man simply because he is a prophet: do not trust to the goodness or the nobleness of your office for your personal vindication: you should be bigger than your office—no pulpit on earth should be as grand as you are, no prophet's robe that ever covered human shoulders should be worth your majesty.

"False prophets." What ironies there are in speech. To think the word "false" should ever have been married to the word "prophets." Surely that sacred word *prophet* might have escaped this foul contamination. Let the word *false* go wooing elsewhere, let it marry the marketplace, but let it keep a thousand miles away from the snow-like purity of Christ's Church. "False prophets." What an oxymoron! Who can imagine two words more positively contradictory? Who can imagine a union so palpably and grossly absurd? Who can effect a junction between two words that shall mean so much that is mischievous, disastrous, ruinous? It required Jesus Christ surely to say the word *false* before the word *prophets.* Surely that word *false* was written in faint ink, and required his eyes of fire to see it. In other cases, it was written large enough: it seemed to boast of its haziness, and to make its very largeness a kind of satirical virtue, but in connection with the word *prophets,* who ever found it before? False professor, false prophet, false teacher, false thinker—it is in that line that lying does its worst mischief.

There is arising amongst us a class of men who are exceedingly anxious not to tell lies in art. It is provocative of secret laughter, and much of it. Solemn persons, who will not allow a painter to tell lies in oil. Yet it is not ugly, and not wholly unsuggestive of things heavenly. Mr. Ruskin would never allow you to paint a piece of wood as if it were oak: such an action would send him half-wild. Paint it as black as soot if you like; paint it a glaring, fiery red; steep it in amber—but do not imitate oak. To such an art-critic it is a lie, it is a piece of hypocrisy in art, it is not true, and therefore it ought to be frowned out of your houses. You, skillful amateur, have painted a piece of common slate so skillfully that your neighbors suppose it to be marble. Your mother insists that it is marble; or, at all events, that she never could have told the difference between it and marble. Your neighbors almost go to the length of applauding you as an artist. If one of the class to which I have referred could come into your house and see that painted slate, veined and shaded like a cutting from the rock, he would call it a lie, and your cleverness would be so much set down to your discredit.

Now, while I am not able to say much either for or against these purists in art, I have sometimes wondered if it could be possible for a man who would go into a rage about seeing a piece of common deal painted like oak to tell a lie. The swallowing powers of man are painful mysteries to his Creator. I will tell you what a man can do: he can strain at a gnat and swallow a camel. Yet he will not believe in miracles. Who can believe anything with so roomy a throat? It would seem to swallow up the whole man that he should seem to be nothing but throat. Have you never met in life persons who would almost go into a fit if you were to suggest to them any falsehood in certain directions, who yet could turn right around in pious rage from that suggestion and tell falsehoods of another kind the clock round? So curious a creature and irregular and unmanageable is man.

In all ages the false has followed the true. I do not wonder: it is an excellent speculation. In all ages the false has brought the true into trouble. "Of your own selves shall men arise, speaking perverse things, to draw away disciples after them. They that are such," says the apostle, "serve not the Lord Jesus Christ but their own belly, and by good words and fair speeches deceive the hearts of the simple" [Acts 20:30; Rom. 16:18]. The nearer the false approaches the true, the more dangerous is it. What do you think they are doing now? Making stones which they call *genuine faux* diamonds. Be careful! People are now making stones very much like diamonds as to deceive the unwary. My wonder is that people who are so anxious along that line of life should exhibit anything but the slightest anxiety in matters of doctrine touching correct thinking and the like. Present them with a false diamond as a true one, and let them find out the mistake, and then—you know the rest. But suggest to them a false idea, a crude and self-contradictory philosophy of the universe, any mad theory of creation you like, and they will call it ingenious, skillful—what a young man once called to me "a clever doubt." Where will be their intense rage, where their sublime madness, where their fiery and honest indignation?

The fear is that we become technical purists and moral liars. Your life cannot be good if your teaching is bad. Doctrine lies at the basis of life. There may be those who refine upon doctrine and turn it into useless distinction and vexatious definition, but doctrine, teaching, a correct idea, lies at the root and core of our life. You are what you believe. You may profess to believe a good many things which you do not turn into life, but in reality what you believe is the very substance and inspiration of your character. How needful, therefore, that we should be rooted and grounded in it, and saved from perversion and folly, and hold the truth of God with a grip not to be relaxed by the most importunate fingers that try to tear us from our attachment to divine verities.

How are we to know the false from the true? Jesus Christ tells us. "By their fruits ye shall know them." The purist I have been speaking about would be horrified with this kind of preaching; if it were done so by any living man, he would write a paragraph in the newspaper about it; he would say, "The preacher in such and such a church is the most remarkable character for mixed metaphor that probably ever lived. That we may not be apparently speaking to his disadvantage without reason, let us cite the following example." Then in small type would come, "Beware of false prophets which come to you in sheep's clothing, but inwardly they are ravening wolves. Ye shall know them by their fruits. Do men gather grapes of thorns or figs of thistles?" He was talking about a wolf, and now he is talking about grapes and figs and thistles. The teaching of the great teacher whoever he is, is full of ellipses. He thinks more rapidly than he can speak: words cannot keep pace with his intellectual velocity. This is preeminently the case with all the teaching of the New Testament. The gaps, and breaks, are innumerable, and only the man who wants to find the truth can find it amid many of the statements which are of the figurative or metaphorical kind. If you really want to know what Christ means in this case, do not trouble yourselves with the rapidity with which he changes the metaphor, but, with an honest and sober heart, look at the case, when he says, "By their results shall ye know them." So then a false teacher may require a little time for self-revelation. The nearer he approaches the truth the longer time may he require fully to disclose his doctrine and his purpose. The hand may be the hand of Esau, the voice may be the voice of Jacob: it is difficult for the false hand to get a false voice, and for the false voice to get a false hand: nature is set against such conjunctions, and will not afford facilities for the completion of lies.

Jesus Christ submitted to his own test. His words are, "Many good works have I showed you from my Father; for which of these works do you stone me?" [John 10:32]. And, again, "If I do not the works of my Father, believe me not, but if I do, though ye believe not me, believe the works, that ye may know and believe that the Father is in me and I in him" [John 10:37, 38]. Judge all preaching by its results, judge all doctrine by its effects. My young friend, let me speak soberly and with great breadth of persuasiveness and sympathy to you upon this subject. The doctrine to which you have been listening recently in various places seems to you to be brilliant—you are enamored, you are under a spell, you say the doctrine seems to refute all other doctrine, and to be bright with new hopes. You are now in the intellectual period. How does the doctrine come down into life? What does it make of its believer? Is it a painted cloud to be gazed at and wondered about like an apocalypse in the air, or is it an inspiration that expresses itself in charity, love, patience, forbearance, sympathy, and that compels to honorableness of conduct? My first question about any doctrine is—how does it come downstairs out of its dreamer's intellect and behave itself in the kitchen? How does it put on its apron and tuck up its sleeves and go to life's daily work? How does it go into the chamber and hush itself into gentleness and quietness, and what does it say to the pained heart, and what to the ebbing life? By its fruits let it be known: What it can do in the plain, everyday circles of life shall be its proofs to me of its heavenly origin. It requires God to make himself of no reputation [Phil. 2:7], and do earth's lowest, humblest work. I ask you not, therefore, how much your doctrine titillates your intellect, inflames and pleases your fancy; I ask you how it comes down to the counter and pays its bills?— How it stands by a man when all hell seems to be against him in huge and terrible assault on his integrity and his peace? The rainbow is to me most beautiful, but I cannot live upon it.

Now we come to a remarkable passage, in which the tone of the great Preacher changes with some suddenness—the twenty-first verse to the twenty-third inclusive. "Not everyone that saith unto me, Lord, Lord, shall enter into the kingdom of heaven, but he that doeth the will of my Father which is in heaven." That is a new tone in the sermon—Lord, Lord. Why, whoever thought of saying "Lord, Lord" to the carpenter's son? Inflamed by the passion of his own rhetoric he has started up into lordship. We never thought of calling you Lord, poor Peasant. It is a matter of consideration amongst some of us why certain men should be called "Mr." at all. Think of that, that we solid-headed Englishmen make a matter of inquiry as to whether certain persons should be called "Mr." And then a very acute subject, rising into a kind of social agony, is as to whether certain persons can properly be called "Esquire." These are the mighty problems that tear and vex our nineteenth century utterly now and then. Here is a man who began life in a manger, and whose parents absconded suddenly into Egypt and wandered about homelessly from some time, who says that at a certain time people will be calling him "Lord, Lord," and he will not know them. It is in these subtle touches that I find the true quality of my Teacher's character.

"Many will say to me in that day." What, and is he to be Judge as well as Lord? Is he to be the Arbitrator as well as the Teacher? What a forecast, what an assumption, how high the ground on which he stands. If it be not a rock, he will fall off, and we shall hear no more of him.

"But he that doeth the will of my Father which is in heaven." Is he not *our* Father which is in heaven? Yes, mediately, not immediately. Through a priestly intercession, not by right of filial obedience and uncorrupted and incorruptible love.

"Many will say unto me, have we not prophesied in thy name?" There he feels the throbbing of his own almightiness: he feels already that his name is to be a charm in the world: thus early he forecasts the marvels that will be wrought in his name. Men will wear it as an amulet, speak of it as a charm, offer it as a certificate, wear it as a seal and an endorsement. This he said not after ten centuries' experience, but at the very beginning of the beginning. Let time testify how true this is.

"Then will I say unto them, Depart from me." What, then, does he make heaven, and does he make hell; and is everything to be determined by his will, and have we all to be subjected to his criticism and to undergo his judgment? All this is most fully involved in the statement we are now perusing.

Now I see what it meant when he went up into a mountain. He speaks as if he were on a mountain. I wondered why he withdrew to that height; he explains it in the conclusion of his sermon. Why the sermon itself is a mountain, in shape, in bulk, in dignity; beginning with the gently flowing slopes of the beatitudes, easy, vernal slopes, green with spring's own loveliness, he passes on to rugged places, modified Sinais, stony, rough, rugged places that would frighten us but for the light of his smile which falls upon them—and on he goes, higher and higher in his doctrine, he rises to high challenges and new proclamations, and now the sermon culminates in lordships and supremacies which overlook and dominate the whole earth. We saw him by the quiet river, we watched him driven into the bleak wilderness, we saw him walking by the seaside; now we behold him seated upon a mountain—a culmination in very deed, an upgathering of all that went before, and a place from where he projected himself across the whole abyss of time. Henceforward Jesus takes the name of Lord; henceforward "these sayings of mine" are to be the root and core of the only durable philosophy, and henceforward men are wise or foolish according as they build or build not on Christ.

Now we see why he chose the mountain; no other pulpit would have been worthy of such a discourse, no scaffold of man's making could have borne that infinite weight, no platform of human construction could have supplied a strong enough foundation for the projection of such teaching. Great Husbandman, on the top of the mountain, Thou dost scatter a handful of corn; the fruit thereof shall shake like Lebanon and the cities of the plain shall rejoice in its abundance [see Ps. 72:16].

twenty-eight

CHARACTERISTICS
OF THE SERMON

Matthew 7:24–29

WE HAVE, as you are aware, gone verse by verse through all the preceding chapters in the Gospel by Matthew. We began with the words, "The book of the generation of Jesus Christ, the Son of David, the Son of Abraham," and from time to time we have pursued a consecutive study of the Gospel by Matthew, and we have come to the close of the Sermon upon the Mount. My object now is to review the Sermon upon the Mount as a whole, having already perused it sentence by sentence and commented thereupon.

It is a very common question which men ask of one another, "What did you think of the sermon today?" It is that question which I intend to answer, the sermon being the Sermon upon the Mount and the Preacher being the Son of God.

Looking at the sermon as a whole, I will take it for granted that you ask me what I, having heard the sermon, thought of it. Let me tell you first of all, how much I was struck with the omissions of the sermon. I am told that a sermon is right in proportion as it begins with the creation of man and steadily pursues its heavy way through all human history, and sums itself up by the events of the day of judgment. If that is a correct interpretation of a sound and good sermon, then the sermon delivered upon the mount must be regarded as being most remarkable for its serious omissions. I am not aware that the Preacher has ever referred to the existence of Adam. To the best of my recollection, there is not one solitary word in the sermon about what took place in Eden, and the terms "original sin" are not to be found in the discourse from beginning to end. Nowhere did the Preacher say, to the best of my recollection, "You are wounds and bruises and putrefying sores, and there is no health in you" [see Is. 1:6]; never once did he say, "All we like sheep have gone astray, we have turned every one to his own way" [Is. 53:6]; in no instance did he say, "There is none righteous, no not one" [Rom. 3:10]; "The LORD looked down from heaven upon the children of men, to see if there were any that did understand, and seek God. They are all gone aside, they are all together become filthy: there is none that doeth good, no, not one" [Ps. 14:2, 3; Ps. 53:2, 3]. How then?

In the next place I am struck by the utter absence of what we call now-a-days Evangelical Doctrine. There is nothing here about the blood of Christ, there is nothing here about the Cross of Calvary, there is nothing here about believing on the Lord Jesus Christ and thou shalt be saved, as that word is evangelically interpreted and applied. There is nothing here of the doctrine of grace, nothing of the doctrine of justification by faith, nothing of the grand savory doctrine of the assurance of adoption into the family of God. The Preacher himself calls his discourse a set of sayings. Where is orthodoxy? Where is grace? Where is faith? Where is election? Where is assurance? Where is a single element that is denoted amongst us today as evangelical? Where is unction? So far, I think, I could justify myself in every sentence I have uttered by the letter that is now spread open before me in the sacred volume. And yet it would be only a justification in the letter, for every one of the grand doctrines I have now referred to, though not specifically named in the discourse, is absolutely and profoundly assumed as the basis of the entire utterance. So mistaken may we be when we hear preachers: we bind them too severely to the mere letter: if we do not hear our favorite set of terms and tones exactly as we have always heard them, the temptation is to feel and to suggest that the preacher is not preaching the grand old doctrine by which we obtained our personal salvation.

Now the reality of the case is that this Sermon upon the Mount could not have been preached if man had not fallen from his first estate. The language would have been an unknown tongue, the doctrine would have been without application and point to any living creature. Jesus Christ takes human history as he finds it: he addresses the human nature that is before him, and I ask you to lay your finger upon a single point in his discourse that would have been appropriate if there had not taken place, some time in human history, a total collapse of human integrity. We must allow our preachers therefore some latitude of expression, we must allow that some things are to be taken for granted; we really must not insist on having in every discourse a correct and formal statement of all our theological beliefs and doctrines; we must seize human history as it actually is, we must modernize some antique expressions, and must mint again some grand old words and turn them into the coinage of our present phraseology. Be careful how you take away the reputation or character of any man for not being evangelical. Such persons as I now refer to might have taken away the reputation of the Son of God himself by confining their attention strictly to the narrow letter. Rely upon it that the evangelical doctrine is to be found sometimes under apparently uncouth forms of expression. Now and again the rocks of our thinking may be reddened with unseen blood, the blood of Jesus Christ himself, while we who only see imperfectly what is taking place, may blame the preacher for lack of evangelical grace and unction and pathos.

Suppose a man should say to a student, "In order to be a sea captain, you must be able to take the latitude and the longitude of a ship at sea. That is one thing which you must be able to do." What would you think of that young student turning around and saying to his father, "This teacher ignores great fundamental truths: he never said a word to me about the first four rules in arithmetic—do you call that orthodox direction and calculation? He uses long, fine words: he says I must be able to take the latitude and the longitude of a ship at sea—is that fundamental teaching? The man ignores the very root and base of arithmetical reckoning." How would you esteem such a criticism? Surely as a piece of blatant folly: for how can any man take the latitude and longitude of a ship at sea if he is ignorant of the first four rules of arithmetic? To be able to do it assumes all previous knowledge and training. The teacher states results rather than processes, and this form of teaching must sometimes be allowed to the pulpit. Jesus Christ speaks to human nature as he finds it; he takes human history for granted, and he lets his gracious words fall upon the hearing of mankind to be received, adopted, and applied according to the personal conditions and requirements.

If you ask me again what I thought of the Sermon on the Mount when I heard it, I should say how much struck I was by the infinite wisdom and tact of the preacher, in beginning just where his audience was prepared to begin. Instead of coming with some high-flown morality, of which the world had never heard before, he said, "What are your maxims? How far have you gone in the Book already?" And when they said to him, "We have come up to this point, namely, Thou shalt not kill," he said in effect "Very well; so far so good. But that is a rough and vulgar morality that hardly begins to be morality at all; it is a very little way beyond the merest barbarism. It is a little from it, and so far it is upon a right line—but I say unto you, Ye shall not be angry with your brother without a cause. How far have you got upon the line of civilization?" The answer is, "Thus far, namely, Thou shalt love thy neighbor and hate thine enemy." Jesus Christ says, "You must alter your doctrine upon the latter point: I say unto you, Love your enemies" [see Matt. 5:43, 44].

Still the point to be noted is this, that Jesus Christ took morality as he found it, began where the people were prepared to begin. He took upon him the form of a servant and became such to their ignorance: he made himself of no reputation—instead of talking in a high-flown language which the people could not understand, he took their germs and elements of morality and civilization, and carried them onward to their proper development and culmination.

This is the right method of teaching, this is the philosopher's plan. If I want to teach a child, I must ask the child where he can begin—I must not play the great scholar with my little pupil, I must lay aside my intellectual divinity, and be born in the child's place. I must make myself of no reputation, and find little words for my little hearer, and begin the race where his little feet can begin to run. The child looks at his alphabet, and his face, his eyes, his mouth, round into a great wonder, not unmarked by a peculiar trace of distress, for he thinks it impossible that he can ever make friends with such monstrous-looking figures. What have I to do? To sympathize with his distress, to tell him that once upon a time I was quite frightened, and that little by little I got to know them, and that now we are the best friends in the world. Then I say to my little hearer, "You have not got to tackle the whole twenty-six at once, you have got to take them one by one. Now we will drop the other twenty-five and see what we can do with the first one." Is that the man I have heard talk in polysyllables and in long and well-connected sentences, and who has endeavored to work his way up into high climax and ringing appeal in the hearing of the great congregation? Yet he is talking so to that little child—why? Simply because he is a little child. If I were to talk so to a man, I would talk below the occasion, I would not rise to the height of my responsibility. Jesus Christ therefore says in effect, "Where can you begin? You begin at, 'Thou shalt not kill, Thou shalt not commit adultery, Thou shalt hate thine enemy, an eye for an eye, and a tooth for a tooth—now hear me.'" And then he proceeds to unwind and disclose the superior revelation, and to lead his disciples onward, little by little, from height to height, until they are all on the mountain with him together, a happy, thankful, well-instructed band.

And yet there are dangers about that method of teaching. It is God's method in the Bible, and he has gotten himself well-affronted for it; every pygmy who could double up his fist has smitten God in the face for adopting that kind of teaching. Persons have written books which disregard Mosaic history, Mosaic science, Mosaic archaeology, geology, and many other "*ologies*" with awkward names. Well, now, how does all this intellectual opposition arise? Here are men with sharp eyes and pointed fingers gathered around the first chapter of the book of Genesis, and they are saying, "How can this be?" not knowing that God spake to men as children, and as they were able to hear it. He, in effect, said, what Christ said upon the mount, "How far have you come?" Men talked about the sun rising and the sun setting—it seemed as if it did. A man said, "I saw the sun in the East, and I watched and waited, and I saw him sink in the West; so the sun rises and the sun sets." And the Lord said, "So be it; that is your conception of the astronomy of the universe; then let us begin there and say the sun rises and the sun sets, and let us talk as if that were really so."

And again, they say, "How can all this take place in a day?" The Lord spoke to those to whom he was speaking in the only language they could understand. What is a day? Twelve hours? Nothing of the kind. Twenty-four hours? Nothing of the sort. That is only one kind of day. *Day* is a long word, a broad word, a strange word, spreading itself out over great spaces. Why, you say, "Every dog has its day"; you say, "I must preach to the day"—what do you mean? That I must preach to every twelve hours the clock ticks off? You know that you have no such meaning, and yet now that God gave us these infantile lessons because we were in an infantile state of mind, we go up to him and say, "What did you mean by talking to us about the sun rising and the sun setting, when the sun never does anything of the sort? And what did you mean by saying this and that were done in one day when there are only twenty-four hours in the day, and part of that must be spent in sleeping?"

Why it is just like this: you gave your little boy at four or five years of age a rocking-horse, and when he is twenty-four he comes to you and says, "What did you mean by so insulting me—giving me a rocking-horse—

what did you mean by giving a man a thing like that, a dead piece of wood, a painted horse—what did you mean by giving a man such a gift?" Suppose you had such an idiot son, what would you say to him? You would say, "My boy, it was not given to the man, it was given to the child; it was not given to one twenty-five years of age, it was given to a five-year-old infant: it was not intended that you should always be on the rocking-horse, it was a hint, a suggestion, something to be going on with—the only thing you could then use. It was adapted to the then state of your mind, and all this abuse you are now pouring upon me is utterly undeserved and beside the mark."

So there are persons who still regard the Bible in its letter only; they have not seen into the inner meaning, their religious imagination has never been inflamed, they know nothing of the holy passion, the secret heart-unction which breaks a loaf into a feast for thousands, and which finds in one cup of water wine enough for a life's long drinking. O, my friend, you are a personal letter, locked up in the little jail of some literal verse. I heard of a person the other day who thinks that she ought not to pray unless her head is covered. To think of the eternal Father of us all looking down to see if you, dear old mother, or young sister, have got your head covered before you say, "Our Father which art in heaven." So, to meet the circumstances of the case, not always having an umbrella at her disposal, she puts a pocket-handkerchief on her head in order to accommodate the infinite Jehovah. Would you believe that such absurdity were possible in the nineteenth century?

This is the difficulty of the preacher: he cannot get his hearer or student away from the letter. The student will not sow the seed of the letter and let it grow into the fruit of the spirit. "No, no" says he, "I have got this seed: I am not going to part with it," and he is thought to be very tenacious of the truth, he is reported to be exceedingly attached to the old truth. The man who takes his handful of corn called the biblical letter and sows it in his consciousness, sows it in his imagination, sows it in his heart, sows it in every part of his nature, and lets it grow in the sunshiny blessing and the dewy baptism of heaven until it blooms into verdure and blossom and beauty and culminates in fruitfulness, is the man who uses the Bible in the right way. The Son of God used it this way: he met us where we could be met, he took us by the hand as little children, and he left us under the ministry of God and the Holy Ghost to grow in grace, to grow in the knowledge of the Lord Jesus Christ, to grow in that subtle, loving sympathy which sees God and touches him and holds him with a heart grip for which there are no words. Have you attained that height in the divine life? Then truly you are born-again, and truly are your ears circumcised to hear the inner music of the celestial word.

You have asked me what I thought of the sermon as a whole: now I should like to know what Jesus Christ himself thought of it. The preacher has an estimate or an opinion of every sermon which he is permitted to proclaim. I cannot but wonder therefore what Christ's own opinion of his discourse was, and happily we have a reply to that inquiry. He treated his sayings as fundamental: he said, in effect, "These are foundation stones, these are not fine things to put on the top of the capitol, these are great rough, unhewn rocks to build on." We like polish in our modern preachers; in fact we have gone so far as to say of certain preachers, that they are extremely finished—which is painfully true. Jesus Christ laid foundations: he himself is revealed to us as a rock, and we may say of those who do not follow us, "Their rock is not as our rock, our enemies themselves being judges. He is a stone, a tried stone, a precious cornerstone, elect, tested by every means at the divine disposal." That is the kind of preacher we ought to hear every now and then, and though we do, now and again, hear a man who is in every sense of the term most finished, we should again and again for our soul's bettering and arousing hear a kind of preacher that is fundamental, that brings us back to the rock, that puts a test into the base we are building upon, and that says, "Either this is rock or this is mud—sand. Beware."

He also regarded his sayings as supplying an indestructible basis of life. The rain descended, and the winds blew, and beat upon the rock-founded house, and it fell not. Like foundation, like building, Jesus Christ thus gave his hearers assurance of durability, strength, protection, indestructibleness, immortality. I cannot see the foundation of this building; it looks well as an edifice, its proportions, its decorations, its defenses are excellent, so far as my eye can judge, but what the foundation is I cannot tell. So it is with many a human life. Many a man talks to me of whom I form an excellent opinion. He looks well, he speaks well, his appearance is all that can be desired, but what his foundation is I do not know. Do not be content with appearances, nor satisfied with mere external decoration. If you are going to build me a house, I say, "Be sure first of all about the foundation: never mind about the decoration, let me know that the house is well founded, do not tell me that the drawing-room is well-papered. Mere decoration I can take in hand little by little, as I may be disposed to expend money upon it, but the foundation once laid, who can get at it again?"

Both the houses had trial. The rain descended and the floods came, and the winds blew and beat upon both houses. So I have heard men say, "Well, it seems to me as if you Christian people had quite as many trials as other folks." So they have. I have heard you say, "It seems to me as if being religious did not save you from trouble, for really you seem to have just as much to contend with as I have, and I make no profession of religion." So it is. What is the result? Everything depends upon the foundation: if your foundation is not right, I do not care how high your building is, or how it is decorated, or how it is put together. I do not care if it is pinnacled all over with gold, all but piercing the clouds—it will come down, and great will be the fall of it. I have seen the wicked in great power and spreading himself like a green bay tree, yet he passed away, and behold, he was not—I looked for him but he could not be found.

What is your foundation? Are you resting upon the eternal Son of God; are you resting upon Christ? You shall be saved, for the foundation is safe. Your house is a very odd one, my friend; I never look at it with any pleasure; you are peculiar, crotchety, odd-minded, eccentric, extremely impracticable, and very few people care to visit you or sympathize with you—but you shall be saved, for the foundation is elect, precious, tried, laid in Zion by hands divine.

On the contrary, here is a man that I like very much; I like his look, his voice, his culture, I go with all his aspirations and sympathies of a social, civilizing, and literary and elevating kind. So far as this world is concerned, he is a beautiful and noble soul to all outward seeming, but he has no foundation except a foundation of sand. Then your rejoicing is but for a time: so long as health continues and business is prosperous and all around you is sunny, men will praise you and believe in you—but there is a *trying* time coming. I know it will come upon you: you are broad-chested, heavy-boned, full-blooded, nobly built from a physical point of view, and it would seem as if death could never strike such a target. But he will—that great thunder voice shall be contracted into a whining whisper, that great strong frame shall be bent down like a broken bulrush, the time will come when you will be thankful for the most trivial service which your most menial servant can render you. The time will come when the window that used to be a blaze of light will be darkened and there will be a shadow upon it, grim as a skeleton. Then the quality of the man will be discovered: in that hour it will be well to know the Son of God, the sweet Jesus, the infinite Savior the bleeding Lamb.

Having thus come to the close of the great Sermon it may be proper to look with some carefulness at the whole subject of *Christ as a Preacher.* Men preach well only in proportion as they preach like Christ. Speaking generally of the preaching of the present time, I may venture to record my opinion that there is decidedly too much preaching in this country, and that infinitely unreasonable demands are made on the preacher. He must unstop deaf ears, open darkened eyes, and awaken the dead, three times every week. He must incessantly cudgel his brains for something new; not to be new is fatal; not to be startling is to be flat and unprofitable. Hence the itch for originality is the curse of our time. Steady, quiet, earnest exposition, goes down before anecdotes, tragedies, and rockets. Of course the exceptions are neither few nor inconsiderable, and are to be recognized with grateful honor; still, there is the unhappy and mischievous fact that our congregations can do with any number of small rhetorical miracles, and are prepared to regard them as signs from heaven. The preaching of the day, therefore, is in great danger of becoming a series of surprises, or a succession of very clever and exciting feats. Another thing that has struck me in close connection with this fact is, that the preaching that is often most popular is least scriptural. The question is now not so much *what* is preached, as *how* it is preached. Sermons must above all things be short. Brevity is fame. A noted French preacher said that if any man would have the courage to preach just five minutes and no more, the whole city would go out after him. I have no wish whatever to preach a body of divinity in every sermon; on the contrary, I have a strong opinion that bodies of divinity when unworthily and clumsily handled have done infinitely more harm than good; at the same time it is of the greatest importance that congregations should be well instructed in the divine word and should have the word of Christ dwelling richly in them. Above all things let the ministry be scriptural. To be scriptural is to be powerful. To be scriptural, it is neither necessary to be dryly critical nor tediously doctrinal. Am I far wrong when I hint that the text itself is often the only piece of Scripture that is in the sermon? Plenty of shallow philosophy, plenty of questionable anecdote, plenty of unfelt appeal, would not these go a long way towards the making of a popular sermon in the nineteenth century? *Expository* preaching is of necessity scriptural, and should therefore be largely adopted by ministers who are deeply concerned for the edification of their hearers. It is not likely to be what is called popular preaching. The mob likes anecdotes. The sweltering throng cheers the climax which then loses itself in the midnight clouds. Or where the climax, gleaming with artificial Cherubim and Seraphim, fails, there must be that rough power which takes no note of varying mental tone, but rushes through the commonplaces of salvation and damnation with a kind of violent jollity which regards the gospel as a species of cheap insurance. Against all this mischievous blasphemy let us lift up the standard of expository preaching. Let the word of God be heard in its own grandeur and beneficence, assured that it cannot return void to the Fount whence it flowed, and the preacher may lift up his head with all the joy and confidence of intelligent hope.

Is there not a somewhat dreary similarity in the construction of modern sermons? Having heard one sermon we may in reality have heard a thousand, not as to its doctrine only, but also as to its form. Many preachers speak in fear, largely unconfessed, of an imaginary hearer who is supposed to be the guardian genius of orthodoxy and pulpit propriety. Much as I dislike any attempt to sensationalize the pulpit, I also dislike quite as strongly the insipid propriety which turns the pulpit into a place for the exhibition of ministerial deportment. Where every attitude is studied, where the voice is held in check lest it should startle some timid hearer, where passion is subdued lest it should be regarded as exaggeration, and where old phrases are retained out of deference to their mere antiquity, it seems to me that not only is the genius of great preaching dishonored, but the Holy Spirit is limited and distrusted. To many preachers might Christ address the rebuking inquiry, "Why are ye so fearful, O ye of little faith?" [Matt. 8:26]. Fearful of conventionality, fearful of rich hearers, fearful of pedantic criticism, fearful of failing in mere literature, fearful of not being pretty or pleasant in delivery—such is the temptation of many who have assayed to represent and reveal the kingdom of heaven! What wonder if they are beaten out of the field by a rivalry which laughs them to scorn, and are left in the desolation of empty pews, the victims of their unworthy fear, men who have extinguished divine fire lest they should irritate human indifference!